T0302145

Enterprise Risk Management

Enterprise Risk Management: Advances on its Foundation and Practice relates the fundamental enterprise risk management (ERM) concepts and current generic risk assessment and management principles that have been influential in redefining the risk field over the last decade. It defines ERM with a particular focus on understanding the nexus between risk, uncertainty, knowledge and performance.

The book argues that there is critical need for ERM concepts, principles and methods to adapt to the latest and most influential risk management developments, as there are several issues with outdated ERM theories and practices; problems include the inability to effectively and systematically balance both opportunity and downside performance, or relying too much on narrow probability-based perspectives for risk assessment and decision-making. It expands traditional loss-based risk principles into new and innovative performance-risk frameworks, and presents fundamental risk principles that have recently been developed by the Society for Risk Analysis (SRA). All relevant statistical and risk concepts are clearly explained and interpreted using minimal mathematical notation. The focus of the book is centered around ideas and principles, more than technicalities.

The book is primarily intended for risk professionals, researchers and graduate students in the fields of engineering and business, and should also be of interest to executive managers and policy makers with some background in quantitative methods such as statistics.

Terje Aven is Professor of Risk Analysis and Risk Management at the University of Stavanger, Norway. He has recently served as Chair of the European Safety and Reliability Association (ESRA) and as the President of Society for Risk Analysis (SRA) worldwide. He is Editor-in-Chief of the *Journal of Risk and Reliability*, and Associate Editor for *Risk Analysis*.

Shital Thekdi is Associate Professor of Management at the University of Richmond, USA.

Enterprise Risk Management
Advances on its Foundation and Practice

Terje Aven and Shital Thekdi

Routledge
Taylor & Francis Group
LONDON AND NEW YORK

First published 2020
by Routledge
2 Park Square, Milton Park, Abingdon, Oxon OX14 4RN

and by Routledge
52 Vanderbilt Avenue, New York, NY 10017

Routledge is an imprint of the Taylor & Francis Group, an informa business

First issued in paperback 2021

British Library Cataloguing-in-Publication Data
A catalogue record for this book is available from the British Library

Library of Congress Cataloging-in-Publication Data
Names: Aven, Terje, author.
Title: Enterprise risk management : advances on its foundation and
    practice / Terje Aven and Shital Thekdi.
Description: Abingdon, Oxon ; New York, NY : Routledge, 2020. |
    Includes bibliographical references and index.
Identifiers: LCCN 2019043725 (print) | LCCN 2019043726 (ebook) |
    ISBN 9781138386235 (hbk) | ISBN 9780429425028 (ebk)
Subjects: LCSH: Risk management. | Uncertainty.
Classification: LCC HD61 .A936 2020 (print) | LCC HD61 (ebook) |
    DDC 658.15/5—dc23
LC record available at https://lccn.loc.gov/2019043725
LC ebook record available at https://lccn.loc.gov/2019043726

ISBN: 978-1-138-38623-5 (hbk)
ISBN: 978-1-03-208269-1 (pbk)
ISBN: 978-0-429-42502-8 (ebk)

Typeset in Bemo
by Apex CoVantage, LLC.

Contents

Preface

In recent years, ERM has elevated into a common and critical tool for modern organizations, including commerce, engineering, public sector, policy and healthcare. ERM provides the concepts, frameworks, principles, methods and models for how to conceptualize, understand, assess and manage all relevant risks in a holistic way. Considerable literature has been developed – including standards like the Committee of Sponsoring Organizations of the Treadway Commission (COSO) framework (COSO 2018) – to guide organizations on how to best implement this tool in practice. This literature is influenced by risk management knowledge in general, but it is also to a large extent tailor-made for the enterprise and business context.

The present book is based on the conviction that there is a potential for significant improvements in ERM foundation and practice by using recent advances in the risk field and science. These advances relate to conceptualization and characterization of risk, as well as fundamental principles for assessment and management of risk.

Specifically, this book focuses on improving the understanding of the nexus between risk, uncertainty, knowledge and performance. It expands traditional loss-based risk perspectives to new and innovative performance-risk frameworks. The current distinction between risk related to events having negative or undesirable impacts on the one hand and opportunities related to events with positive impacts on the other, is considered inadequate and is replaced by broader risk concepts in line with current ideas and principles of generic risk analysis and management. These concepts are supported by fundamental risk theory research and are endorsed and further developed by the SRA in a series of publications (SRA 2015a, 2015 b, 2017a, 2017 b). The SRA work has been conducted by a broad group of senior risk scientists, and is informed by and relevant for a wide variety of applications and disciplines, including business, engineering, public health, policy, safety and communication.

The book also aims at providing new insights in other ways. Four areas are considered of special importance:

Firstly, the book clarifies and reflects on the difference between overall enterprise risks and more specific task or project risks, as introduced and discussed by Aven and Aven (2015). The ERM literature has a strong focus on meeting objectives, but risk exists also when objectives are not defined, as long as the activity considered involves something that humans value. Failing to meet the objectives of a project can to varying degree affect overall enterprise risk. ERM needs to distinguish clearly between the different types of risk, as project or task risk control could easily be misinterpreted as a goal in itself, independently of the overall enterprise performance and risks.

Secondly, traditional ERM relies too much on narrow probability-based perspectives for risk assessment and risk management, using for example standard risk matrices to guide the decision-making. Generic risk science has proven that these approaches are inadequate as risk management tools and hence also ERM tools, as important aspects of risk are not properly reflected. A main problem is that the probabilities assigned are conditional on some knowledge and this knowledge could be more or less strong, and even erroneous. Approaches and methods exist for characterizing the strength of the knowledge, but current ERM standards are not updated on this important point. A special challenge is related to potential surprises relative to the knowledge (black swans). These potential surprises represent risk but are not normally incorporated in the risk management and ERM procedures, at least not systematically. But they should be, as this type of risk is of utmost importance for avoiding disasters.

The third point relates to the integration of complementary concepts like reliability, robustness, resilience and vulnerability. Current ERM theories and practices do not provide coherent frames for the understanding and use of all these concepts. The book aims at presenting such frames using the broad risk conceptualizations referred to above. In this way a unified and general set-up is defined which, for example, clarifies how ERM builds on resilience analysis and management. Resilience is often considered a tool supplementing risk management, but in this book, resilience management is an integrated part of ERM.

The fourth and final aspect relates to cost-benefit analysis and related analyses that are commonly used in ERM-related decision-making. The risk science has shown that these types of analysis can seriously misguide decision-makers, yet they represent a backbone in ERM theories and practices. The book provides guidance on how to improve these theories and practices, to properly balance different concerns and use the analytical tools available to support the decision-making.

The new theoretical insights of this book strengthen the foundation of ERM, which in turn can strongly improve ERM practice. For example, there is need to assess and characterize enterprise risk in new ways, and this has implications for the management and decision-making processes. The book highlights the practical aspects of ERM, in order to serve as a tool that is applicable to any organization or role. Several case studies are used to illustrate concepts and ideas using the context of business, engineering and information-technology.

The book enables risk managers to adapt to key challenges in the age of data, artificial intelligence, cybersecurity, globalization and new technologies.

This book is organized as follows:

Chapter 1 introduces some cases from public and private sectors, based on actual events and thought-constructed scenarios. The idea is to motivate the ERM concepts, principles and methods, and point to challenges concerning both theoretical and practical ERM aspects. In Chapter 9 we return to these cases, and we discuss how to use methods and principles from this book to address the key issues presented.

Chapter 2 introduces the concepts of risk and enterprise risk. ERM is about management of enterprise risk, and understanding the key concepts are important as we need to know what we are going to manage. The discussion is based on current ideas of risk as discussed above.

Chapter 3 presents the guiding principles for ERM that this book and the coming chapters are based on. The chapter will also introduce the taxonomy of ERM maturity, with distinction of *Beginner, Intermediate*, and *Advanced* maturity of an organizational ability to manage risk. On an overall level, the ERM principles are the same for all three maturity levels, but there are differences with respect to degree of detail and sophistication of approaches and methods used.

Chapters 4–7 discuss and provide guidance on the key principles of ERM highlighted in Chapter 3, reflecting the new insights provided by this book as summarized above. Chapter 4 addresses the need for distinguishing between ERM and Task (project) Risk Management (TRM). Chapter 5 looks into potential surprises (black swans), whereas Chapter 6 discusses the integration of performance, risk and resilience-based thinking and methods. Chapter 7 considers the challenge of balancing different concerns, seeing beyond traditional cost-benefit types of analysis using expected values.

Chapter 8 discusses practical challenges and solutions for improving ERM practice. The discussion specifically addresses how to systematically implement ERM in various decision-making situations. This includes discussions of how to obtain and coordinate risk resources, and maintain and grow risk expertise and a risk culture. The chapter also discusses troubleshooting and diagnosis of common issues and challenges that exist in forming, maintaining and improving ERM practices in an organization.

In addition, the book includes four appendices. Appendix A provides a list of terminology used in the book. Appendix B summarizes key knowledge about probability and probability models, as well as expected values. Appendix C provides an overview of basic ERM theory as presented in textbooks and standards. Finally, Appendix D provides some student cases studies.

The book is primarily intended for risk professionals, researchers and graduate students in the fields of engineering and business. The book should also be of interest to executive managers and policy makers with some background in quantitative methods such as statistics. The book is considered conceptually rich, but easy to read. All relevant statistical and risk concepts will be clearly explained and interpreted using minimal mathematical notation. The focus of the book is centered around ideas and principles, more than technicalities.

Acknowledgements

We would like to acknowledge Eirik B. Abrahamsen, Eyvind Aven, Roger Flage, Seth Guikema, Jahon Khorsandi, Vidar Kristensen, Ortwin Renn and Enrico Zio for their valuable input to this book through their collaboration on relevant projects and papers. Their work and inspiration have strongly contributed to innovate the risk field, allowing for this book and others to be a reality. In particular we are grateful to Eyvind Aven and Roger Flage for the time and effort they spent on reading and commenting on an earlier version of the book. Many other scholars have also contributed to the book by contributing to active discussions about the foundation of risk analysis, including Tony Cox, Sven-Ove Hansson, Michael Greenberg, Wolfgang Kröger and Katherine McComas. All of the enthusiastic researchers mentioned here are much appreciated, while also bearing no responsibility for the book content, views and possible shortcomings.

Terje Aven and Shital Thekdi
August 1, 2019

1 Some illustrating examples

This chapter presents some cases that will be used to illustrate the coming discussions about enterprise risk and ERM. The first example relates to product liability risk – the General Motors (GM) ignition switch case. It shows how ERM needs to carefully balance safety aspects and costs. The second example relates to environmental risk and sustainability – the Volkswagen emissions case. It demonstrates the need to consider aspects of risk that cannot always be meaningfully quantified, such as sustainability and reputation. The third and final example relates to cybersecurity – the Equifax data breach. The case explores the role of ERM in the rapidly changing and uncertain cyber-technology environment.

1.1 The GM ignition switch scandal

The automobile manufacturing industry is highly competitive, and firms achieve competitive advantage in aspects of cost, quality, service, brand, innovation and convenience. One major factor in the assessment of vehicle quality is safety. The United States Code for Motor Vehicle Safety defines motor vehicle safety as "the performance of a motor vehicle or motor vehicle equipment in a way that protects the public against unreasonable risk of accidents occurring because of the design, construction, or performance of a motor vehicle, and against unreasonable risk of death or injury in an accident, and includes non-operational safety of a motor vehicle" (US Department of Transportation 2019). When vehicle manufacturers knowingly mislead customers about safety, there is potential for severe consequences, as described in this case study.

In 2001, GM detected an ignition switch defect during pre-production testing of the Saturn Ion vehicle. In 2005, GM detected an ignition switch defect for the Saturn Ion vehicle, then again in the Chevrolet Cobalt (Valukas 2014). The ignition switch in these vehicles could unintentionally be moved out of the "run" position and into "accessory", and disable airbags, engine, power assists and other safety features. In 2005, GM sent a bulletin to dealers indicating that drivers of vehicles should remove unessential items from their key chains, to avoid the weight of these unessential items causing the initiation switch to be moved (GM 2005).

In February 2014, GM announced that a safety defect existed in several 2005–2007 model year vehicles, totaling over two million vehicles (NHTSA 2014). The consequences were severe, with allegedly 124 deaths and nearly 300 injuries resulting from the faulty ignition switches (Read 2015). In May 2014, GM agreed to pay a $35 million civil penalty due to their failure to report the safety defect to the federal government in a timely manner (NHTSA 2015). GM also faced hundreds of lawsuits alleging injury or death related to the recall (Stempel 2017), hundreds of class action lawsuits alleging economic harm from the recalls, investigations by state attorneys general and a criminal probe by the Department of Justice. Eventually, GM paid a $900 million penalty to settle a US Department of Justice criminal case (Department of Justice 2015), about $600 million in compensation to victims of accidents caused by the faulty switches (Shepardson 2015), and also paid $120 million to settle claims from dozens of states (Lawrence 2017).

It was found that this ignition switch issue resulted from an engineering decision to continue using this switch, despite knowing the switch was defective. For example, a 2002 email was signed "Ray (tired of the switch from hell)" (Valukas 2014). The supplier, Delphi, claimed the automaker approved the switch while knowing it did not meet GM's performance specifications (Staff 2014). Despite the evidence of severe safety concerns, GM continued to use the faulty switch, knowing that a fix would cost less than one dollar per vehicle, in addition to $400,000 in tooling costs (Lienert and Thompson 2014). It was later found that in 2006, GM had redesigned the switch without changing the part number, severely complicating the ongoing investigation (Valukas 2014).

During the time when engineers were considering whether to change the ignition switch, GM and other automakers were facing fierce competition, eventually leading to bankruptcy in 2009. This led to a culture that prioritized cost savings, in order to provide competitive pricing and promote profits. GM was forced to consider risk in their balancing of cost and customer safety, knowing they operated in a highly regulated industry (Jennings and Trautman 2016; Valukas 2014).

We ask the reader to consider the following questions:

- What risks and uncertainties were relevant to the various stakeholders?
- How can and should a company in a similar position measure and describe performance, risk and uncertainties?
- How should the risks have been handled? What risk strategies and policies are relevant to a company in a similar position? Which should be adopted?

In Section 9.1 we will return to these topics.

1.2 The Volkswagen emission case

Over the last decade, there has been growing interest for companies to develop and impose policies for environmental sustainability. The rise of the sustainability movement follows major legislations, including the United States Clean Air Act (CAA) that aims to reduce emissions from both stationary and mobile sources of air pollution (EPA 2019b). These regulations include tailpipe emissions standards for pollutants, such as NOx. Similarly, the European Union has enacted the Ambient Air Quality Directive, which includes the control of emissions from mobile sources (EU 2019).

The CAA regulation requires that new vehicle manufacturers submit an application for a Certificate of Conformity (CoC), demonstrating that test vehicles meet emissions standards (EPA 2019a). While this CoC is used as evidence for CAA compliance, there is potential for manufacturers to mislead regulators about vehicle emissions. This was the case of Volkswagen as they installed cheating software, also described as a "defeat device" on their vehicles. While 2009–2015 model year diesel vehicles were being tested, the vehicles switched to a mode that was specifically designed to pass the test, then immediately switched back to normal driving mode. It is estimated that the normal driving mode NOx emissions were 10 to 40 times the federal limits (House Committee 2015). This affected 482,000 Volkswagen and Audi vehicles in the United States, and a total of about 11 million vehicles globally (House Committee 2015). In May 2014, West Virginia University published a study suggesting that on-road emissions for Volkswagen sample vehicles were far above the Environmental Protection Agency (EPA) standards (Clemons 1995). While executive testimony claims that a key executive was not aware of this defeat device until after the West Virginia University publication, testimony quotes the following (House Committee 2015):

> "Mr. Murphy. Thank you, Mr. Horn. I now recognize myself for five minutes of questioning. On September 3rd, 2015, VW admitted to CARB and EPA that it had installed defeat devices in certain model year 2009 and model year 2015 vehicles. To the best of your knowledge, did VW install this software for the express purpose of defeating emissions controls?"
>
> "Mr. Horn. To our understanding – and this is also part of the investigation – it was installed to this purpose, yes, for this purpose".

As part of the settlement, Volkswagen was required to remove or perform an approved emissions modification on at least 85% of the affected 2.0-liter engine vehicles or else pay an amount equal to $85 million for each percentage point by which it fell short of the recall target, and $13.5 million for each percentage point for which it fell short of the California recall target (EPA 2019a). Similarly, Volkswagen was required to remove from commerce or perform an emissions modification to affected 3.0-liter engine vehicles. These were in addition to a $1.45 billion civil penalty for civil violations of the CAA (EPA 2019a). As for the environmental mitigation, the CAA settlement required Volkswagen to fund a $2.7 billion trust to pay for projects that reduce NOx mitigation actions including reducing NOx from heavy duty diesel sources near population centers, such as large trucks, school buses and freight switching railroad locomotives

(EPA 2019a). Also as part of the agreement, Volkswagen was required to establish a whistleblower system and establish a survey to gauge environmental compliance (EPA 2019a). Volkswagen implemented the "Trust Building Measure" in European countries, intended for:

> informing its customers that it would consider any complaints that are established to have arisen as a result of the implementation of the technical measure on vehicles with EA189 type diesel engines and that relate to certain parts of the engine and exhaust treatment system.
>
> (Volkswagen 2018)

While Volkswagen is one example of a company using a defeat device, they are not the first (Myers 1995), and other car manufacturers also continue to face similar allegations (Staff 2018).

We ask the reader to consider the following questions:

- What risks and uncertainties were relevant to the various stakeholders, in particular the corporation?
- How can and should performance, risk and uncertainties be characterized in a situation like this?
- How should the risk have been handled? What risk strategies and policies would have been relevant to a company in a similar position? Which should be adopted?

1.3 Risk in information technology – Equifax data breach

Cybersecurity continues to be a critical issue for businesses, societies and nations. Cybersecurity threats are described as: "Sophisticated cyber actors and nation-states exploit vulnerabilities to steal information and money and are developing capabilities to disrupt, destroy, or threaten the delivery of essential services" (DHS 2019), making cybersecurity and resilience an important mission. This need for effective cybersecurity is echoed in a recent CEO survey, stating that 53% of CEOs in North America are 'extremely concerned' about cyber threats (PWC 2018). At a global level, the United Nations Global Cybersecurity Index states that only 38% of countries have a published cybersecurity strategy (ITU 2017). While cybersecurity frameworks exist (NIST 2013), and continue to adapt, it is important for these cybersecurity frameworks to be integrated within ERM processes.

While there are many recent examples of cybersecurity incidents, this case discusses a data breach at Equifax in 2017. On March 8, 2017, the US Department of Homeland Security Computer Emergency Readiness Team notified Equifax of the need to patch the "Apache Struts" software system vulnerability. On March 9, Equifax disseminated the patch notification by email to request a software upgrade. Equifax's internal policy required patching to occur within 48 hours of notification. However, this software was not patched in response to this notification. On March 15, Equifax security scans also should have identified the Apache Struts vulnerability, however the vulnerability was not identified (Smith Testimony 2017). The software system was attacked from May 13, 2017 through July 30, while Equifax's security tools did not detect this attack. On July 29, the attack was detected and the attack was immediately blocked (Smith Testimony 2017).

Over 143 million people were impacted by a data breach resulting from the attack, which is about 44% of the total U.S. population. The illegally accessed information includes names, birthdates, addresses and drivers' license information. A total of 200,000 people had their credit card information stolen and 180,000 had credit dispute documentation stolen (House of Representatives 2017).

Other Equifax security measures have been questioned, such as the revelation that the breached data was not encrypted (House of Representatives 2017). Additionally, there were issues with the dedicated website www.equifaxsecurity2017.com where consumers could learn whether their personal information was included in the data breach. This dedicated website address was easily confused with similar-looking fake phishing websites. Even the official Equifax Twitter account posted a link to a fake website. Additional delay was caused when a massive hurricane disrupted the already understaffed call centers for days following the breach. (House of Representatives 2017).

While class action and individual lawsuits have been filed, the true financial consequences of this data breach are still unclear (Henning 2017).

We ask the reader to consider the following questions:

- What risks and uncertainties were relevant to the various stakeholders, in particular Equifax?
- What ERM processes/procedures could avoid this type of event?

2   What is risk and enterprise risk?

This chapter first reflects on the meaning of the risk and enterprise risk concepts. Then, we discuss how to measure, describe and characterize risk and enterprise risk. We address a common risk management issue: How should we express the magnitude of risks, recognizing that some risks are big while others are not? The chapter is partly based on SRA (2015a) and Aven (2017b).

2.1 The risk and enterprise risk concepts

The concept of risk is intuitively clear. Think about the activity driving a car from point a to b. Some values are at stake, such as the lives and health of the people in the car. The activity may result in an accident with loss of lives or injuries. Looking into the future we do not know what will happen or what will be the consequences of the activity. There are uncertainties. The persons in the car face risk.

As another example, think about a company that runs a project. The focus is the project costs. A cost budget of c is specified. The company faces risk when looking into the future. The real or actual costs could be higher than c. They could also be lower. In advance, we do not know, there are uncertainties. The company faces risk.

As a third and last example, consider a global risk issue, for example climate change. What will be the consequences for the planet and human beings of climate change? Will it have severe effects on the world economy? Looking into the future we do not know, there are uncertainties. We face risk.

If we look at these three examples, we see that there are some common features (see Figure 2.1). There is a context, an activity, which has some consequences with respect to something that humans value (life and health, environment, economic assets). The activity in the first example is "driving the car from a to b", whereas in the second example, the activity is "execution of the project". In the last example, we can consider the activity as "life on the earth". The consequences in the car example relate to life and health, whereas they are linked to money in the second. In the third example, all types of consequences are addressed, including environmental ones. In all examples, the consequences could be negative or undesirable: loss of lives, economical loss, or environmental

The risk concept

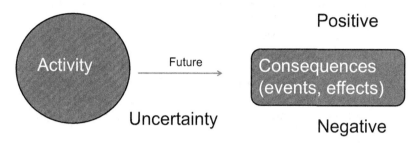

Figure 2.1 The basic features of the risk concept

damage. However, the consequences could also be "neutral" or positive, for example, that the car trip gets the people successfully from a to b, the budget of c is met, and the effects of climate change are not becoming as bad as predicted. The consequences can be viewed as comprising events (for example an accident in the first example) and the effects of these events (the effects on life and health given the accident).

In addition, there are uncertainties about what these consequences will be. That is the second feature of the risk concept, which together with the consequences give the basic ideas of what risk is.

There are different ways of formalizing these ideas. The SRA refers to seven definitions in its glossary (SRA 2015a) in line with this type of reasoning:

a) Risk is the possibility of an unfortunate occurrence.
b) Risk is the potential for realization of unwanted, negative consequences of an event.
c) Risk is exposure to a proposition (e.g., the occurrence of a loss) of which one is uncertain.
d) Risk is the consequences of the activity and associated uncertainties.
e) Risk is uncertainty about and severity of the consequences of an activity with respect to something that humans value.
f) Risk is the occurrences of some specified consequences of the activity and associated uncertainties.
g) Risk is the deviation from a reference value and associated uncertainties.

In this book we will use definitions g) and d). We can interpret "deviation from a reference value" as an example of the consequences of the activity; hence g) is a special case of d). The reference value in the car example is the "current health state of the people in the car", whereas it is the budget cost c in the second example. For the third example it could be linked to pre-industrial global temperature levels (see e.g. IPCC 2014).

The International Organization for Standardization (ISO 2018) defines risk as "the effect of uncertainty on objectives". This definition is unclear, has a lack of scientific basis, and it is not used in this book. See discussion of this definition in Aven and Ylönen (2019). It is possible to interpret the ISO definition in different ways; one as a special case of those considered above (e.g., d) or g)), with the consequences seen in relation to objectives.

The ISO definition of risk ties the risk concept up to formulations of objectives. We can question: Does not risk exist if objectives are not defined? Following Aven (2017e) and Aven and Ylonen (2019), think of some researchers who are to explore an unknown substance. Would it then not be reasonable to say that they face risk? For sure, despite the fact that no investigation objective has been formulated. As another example, consider a situation with many stakeholders having diverse interests and objectives. Some of them may be reluctant to state their preferences and goals. Nonetheless it should be possible to conceptualize and express risk. However, using the ISO definition, this is difficult. In practice, risk assessment is commonly used as an instrument for developing formulations of objectives, by for example identifying aspects contributing strongly to risk. The ISO conceptualization, however, makes this impossible as the objectives are included in the risk term.

Goals may be used as a reference value as indicated in our definition of risk, but normally more information is reflected by looking into deviations, "Consequences – Reference values" (the differences between the Consequences and the References values), rather than deciding whether the goal is met or not.

Definition of risk:

We consider a future activity (interpreted in a wide sense to also cover, for example, natural phenomena), such as the operation of a system, and define risk in relation to the consequences C (effects, implications) of this activity with respect to something that humans value. The consequences are often seen in relation to some reference values (planned values, objectives, etc.), and the focus is often on negative, undesirable consequences. There is always at least one outcome that is considered as negative or undesirable.

Overall qualitative definitions:

- Risk is the consequences of the activity and associated uncertainties
- Risk is the deviation from a reference value and associated uncertainties

If U denotes the uncertainties (we do not know what C will be), we can formally write

Risk = (C,U).

The consequences C can have many dimensions (it can be viewed as a vector). Alternatively, we can write

Risk = (A,C,U),

where A are events (hazards, threats, opportunities), C the effects given the events A, and U the uncertainties.

Now we are ready to define enterprise risk. The set-up is the same as above, and we need just to clarify the context. The activities are the businesses of the enterprise. Different types of consequences can be defined, but they should be related to the principal objectives or overall performance judged important for the organization (Aven and Aven 2015). A common principal objective for an (profit maximizing) organization is to maximize the value but at the same time to avoid Health, Safety and Environment (HSE) and integrity incidents. The consequences can thus be formulated as deviations in relation to change in monetary value and occurrences of incidents.

Enterprise risk:

Risk of an enterprise where the consequences are related to the principal objectives or overall performance judged important for the organization.

Risk referred to in the second example involving project management can be labelled project or task risk. It is not enterprise risk because the consequences are not linked to the overall objectives or performance of the organization. We will discuss the link between enterprise risk and task risk in more detail in Section 2.2, and also Chapter 4.

In an enterprise context it is common to distinguish between strategic risk, financial risk and operational risk, where:

• strategic risk is risk where the consequences for the enterprise are influenced by mergers and acquisitions, technology, competition, political conditions, laws and regulations, labor market, etc.;

- financial risk is risk where the consequences for the enterprise are influenced by the market (associated with changes in the value of an investment due to movements in market factors: the stock prices, interest rates, foreign exchange rates and commodity prices), credit issues (associated with a debtor's failure to meet its obligations in accordance with agreed terms) and liquidity issues, reflecting lack of access to cash; the difficulty of selling an asset in a timely manner, i.e. quickly enough to prevent a loss (or make the required profit); and
- operational risk is risk where the consequences for the enterprise are a result of safety or security related issues (accidental events, intentional acts), as well as supply chain disruptions.

In addition, we often refer to social risk, which is risk where the consequences for the enterprise relate to, for example, customer satisfaction and reputation.

2.2 Measuring or describing risk. How big is the risk?

The above discussion showed that risk has two main features, consequences of the activity considered, and associated uncertainties. We note that risk exists without using probabilities to measure the magnitude of the risk. In line with the ideas of the SRA glossary and measurement theory, we distinguish between overall qualitative definitions of the concept and how it is measured or described. This is an important distinction. Broad consensus on how to define and understand risk is not possible if one seeks to define risk as a generic concept using some metric, for example, the probability of an undesirable event. Clearly, different metrics can be defined, and which to choose depends on the situation considered. However, broad agreement can be achieved if we define risk qualitatively and focus on the key features that this concept is to reflect, as shown above.

To measure or describe the risk, we need to measure or describe the two features of risk, the consequences C and the uncertainties U. Let us first look at the consequences.

2.2.1 Describing the consequences C of the activity considered

When describing the consequences, we need to clarify which aspects of the consequences we would like to address. Are we to focus on the number of fatalities, the enterprise value, or the project cost, or are we to consider the whole scenario covering risk sources, events, barrier performance, and outcomes? In an enterprise, these four elements could be security culture, occurrence of an incident (e.g. fraud), the performance of a security barrier (e.g. automated electronic security system), and the enterprise value, respectively. When using the pair (A,C), we have simplified the description by including A for a risk source/event (hazard/threat), and C as the resulting effect given A.

Let C' denote the consequences specified in the risk description, capturing the quantities of interest. Similar to C, some components of the specified consequences C' can express deviations relative to some reference values (e.g. specified goals or targets). Note the difference between C and C': The consequences C are the actual consequences of the activity considered, whereas C' are specified consequences when aiming at describing risk using a risk assessment. In some cases, these are the same, C = C', for example if we restrict attention to the cost of a project. But in other cases, C is not the same as C'. Think of a study where we aim at assessing different types of threats A that the organization can face. The assessment specifies a set of A' events, but it turns out that an event A occurred, which was not included in the assessment. It was not known to the assessors (an "unknown known" if others had the knowledge about this event, or "unknown unknown" if the event was not known to anybody). By distinguishing between C and C' we highlight that the consequences C' is based on a selection, and this selection may not cover the actual C. To reflect a potential for surprise is one reason for the distinction between C and C', another is to clarify the analysts' deliberative choice of addressing some aspects of the actual consequences and leave others out. An assessment could for example address the costs for some stakeholders, but not others.

2.2.2 Describing the uncertainties U

The quantities C' introduced in the previous section are unknown and thus subject to uncertainties. The challenge is to represent or express these uncertainties. Basically, for doing this, there are two lines of thinking:

a)   Seek to obtain a characterization of the uncertainties that to the extent possible is objective or intersubjective, reflecting the evidence available.
b)   Provide a subjective characterization of the uncertainties by the risk analysts, reflecting their knowledge and judgements, often on the basis of input from other experts.

A simple example will illustrate the differences between these two perspectives. A person refers to a special coin, with unknown frequentist probabilities for head and tail. A frequentist probability of an event A is interpreted as the fraction of times A occurs if we could infinitely repeat the situation considered under similar conditions. This person does not see the coin. Let r be the frequentist probability of head. The assessor has no knowledge about r, and the question is how to represent or express the uncertainties about r. The reader may alternatively think about a continuous production system where r represents the fraction of units produced with a failure.

A common approach is to assume a uniform or rectangular distribution over r. However, by introducing such a distribution, the assessor states for example that the probability of r being in the interval [0, 0.1] is the same as r being in the interval [0.9, 1]. It seems that the approach is of type b. But where did the probability judgements come from? These judgments are to reflect the knowledge of the analyst, but, for the problem we defined, we excluded these types of insights. Hence, something has been added which was not originally there. The use of a probability distribution forces the analyst to state his/her degree of belief for different values of r. The information value of this distribution may not be strong in case the basis for the probability distribution is weak. Thus, using such probabilities alone to describe or measure the uncertainties is problematic, if not also reflecting in some way the knowledge on which the probabilities are founded. See related discussion by Aven (2010) and Dubois (2010).

The alternative is to apply a), which forces the analyst to simply state that r is in the interval [0,1]. Based on the available knowledge, he/she cannot be more precise. We see that such an approach is rather extreme compared to b); we are led to a very wide interval saying nothing. The presentation is objective, but the information value for the decision-maker is reduced. More information is obviously needed to make this approach useful. Now, suppose that the experts express that ½ is the most likely value of the quantity r. Then we are led to imprecise probabilities, stating, for example, that $0 \leq P(r \leq 0.25) \leq 0.5, 0 \leq P(r \leq 1/2) \leq 1.0$ and $0.5 \leq P(r \leq 0.75) \leq 1.0$ (see Aven et al. 2014, p. 47). The analyst is not willing to be more precise than this, given the available information and knowledge. However, in this case we also need to include the knowledge and strength of knowledge supporting these imprecise probabilities. The basis for the expert judgement when expressing that r = ½ could be poor or strong, but this is not reflected in the specified probabilities. The transformation process from the evidence to the probabilities is here "objective", but of course, the knowledge as such is not.

A recommended approach for the uncertainty descriptions is provided in the following.

2.2.3 Recommended approach

To characterize the uncertainties about the unknown quantities C', three elements are needed:

1   Knowledge-based (also referred to as a subjective, judgmental) probabilities P, or related interval (imprecision) probabilities
2   A judgement of the strength of the knowledge K (SoK) supporting these probabilities
3   The knowledge K that P and SoK is based on

In addition, processes are required to scrutinize the knowledge K to reveal potential surprises. Thus for measuring or describing the uncertainties, it is recommended to use the combination of probability P and a strength of knowledge judgment, (P,SoK). Using Q as a general term to denote the tool used to measure or describe uncertainty, we have Q=(P,SoK). Adding K, which supports the judgment Q, we are led to an uncertainty characterization with elements (P,SoK,K). A knowledge-based probability P of an event A is interpreted with reference to a standard: If a probability of say 0.15 is assigned, the assessor has the same uncertainty or degree of belief that the event A will occur as drawing at random a red ball out of an urn comprising 100 balls where 15 are red (Lindley 2006). We often write P(A|K) to indicate that the probability is conditional on the knowledge K. The knowledge reflects justified beliefs (SRA 2015a) founded on data, information, modeling, tests and argumentation, and is often expressed through assumptions. If the assessor assigns a knowledge-based imprecise probability, for example [0.1, 0.2], this means that the assessor is not willing to be more precise than the interval expresses, given the available knowledge K. Hence the assigned probability is judged higher than randomly drawing a specific ball out of an urn comprising 10 balls and less than randomly drawing a specific ball out of an urn comprising five balls. Alternatively, the probability is considered similar to drawing a red ball out of an urn having 100 balls where 10 to 20 are red, but the exact number is not specified.

To evaluate the strength of knowledge, we need to address issues such as:

- The reasonability of the assumptions made
- The amount and relevancy of data/information
- The degree of agreement among experts
- The degree to which the phenomena involved are understood and accurate models exist
- The degree to which the knowledge K has been thoroughly examined (for example with respect to unknown knowns; i.e. others have the knowledge, but not the analysis group)

For some concrete examples of scoring systems based on such issues, see the Appendix B.

An alternative approach to the use of such SoK judgements is to perform judgements of the importance or criticality of the justified beliefs that form the knowledge basis K, a type of judgment of the assumption deviation risk. As knowledge is justified beliefs (often formulated as assumptions), such judgements would be useful supplements to the probabilistic metrics. The idea is to consider possible deviations from the assumptions made, assess the effects on the high-level quantities analyzed and make crude qualitative judgments of likelihood with related strength of knowledge judgments (Aven 2013a).

In practice, a combination of a) and b) is often preferred (see Section 2.2.2). The latter method ensures that the experts' and analysts' judgements are reported and communicated, whereas the former method restricts its results to a representation of documented knowledge.

The risk characterization (C', Q, K)

Combining C', Q and K gives a risk description or characterization. The format of this characterization has to be adapted to the concrete case considered and the need for decision support. Often metrics are introduced linking consequences and probabilities, for example using some expected values, or F-C curves showing the probability (frequency) of an accident with consequence of at least C. The suitability of these metrics is always an issue, especially when it comes to the use of expected values, see Appendix B. In any case, the knowledge dimension needs to be reflected and in particular the strength of this knowledge, as highlighted above.

Risk metrics/descriptions (examples) (SRA 2015a Glossary):

1   The combination of probability and magnitude/severity of consequences
2   The combination of the probability of a hazard occurring and a vulnerability metric given the occurrence of the hazard
3   The triplet (s_i, p_i, c_i), where s_i is the ith scenario, p_i is the probability of that scenario, and c_i is the consequence of the ith scenario i = 1, 2, ..., N.
4   The triplet (C', Q, K), where C' is some specified consequences, Q a measure of uncertainty associated with C' (typically probability) and K the background knowledge that supports C' and Q (which includes a judgment of the strength of this knowledge)
5   Expected consequences (damage, loss). For example, computed by:

    i   Expected number of fatalities in a period of one year (Potential Loss of Life, PLL) or the expected number of fatalities per 100 million hours of exposure (Fatal Accident Rate, FAR)
    ii   *P(hazard occurring)*
        xP(exposure of object | hazard occurring)
        xE[damage | hazard and exposure]
        i.e. the product of the probability of the hazard occurring and the probability that the relevant object is exposed given the hazard, and the expected damage given that the hazard occurs, and the object is exposed (the last term is a vulnerability metric)
    iii   Expected disutility

The suitability of these metrics/descriptions depends on the situation. None of these examples can be viewed as risk itself, and the appropriateness of the metric/description can always be questioned. For example, the expected consequences can be informative for large populations and individual risk, but not otherwise.

2.2.4 Example

The Board of an enterprise has challenged the enterprise risk manager to present an overview of the risks that the enterprises faces. Focus should be on hazards and threats which have a potential for extreme outcomes. The enterprise risk manager considers first to use an extended risk matrix. This matrix has the following elements:

1　Events A' with consequences exceeding some specified levels
2　Probabilities of these events
3　Judgments of the strength of knowledge SoK supporting these probabilities

See Figure 2.2 for an extended matrix based on three events.

The common approach where risk is described by the probability P of an event A, and the expected value of the consequence given the event A, i.e. $E[C|A]$, is rejected. In this case the risk description covers the pair $(P(A), E[C|A])$. The problem with this approach is that we are ignoring two main aspects of risk:

1　The fact that $E[C|A]$ could be a poor prediction of the actual consequences C given that the event A occurs
2　The fact that the knowledge K supporting the probabilities could be more or less strong and even wrong (for example erroneous assumptions)

Using unconditional expected values as in $E[C]$, by basically multiplying $P(A)$ and $E[C|A]$, a third aspect is being ignored, namely variations in $P(A)$ relative to $E[C|A]$. We can have two completely different situations, one with low $P(A)$ but high $E[C|A]$, and one with high $P(A)$ but low $E[C|A]$, giving the same expected values. Clearly, to be adequately informed about risk, these situations

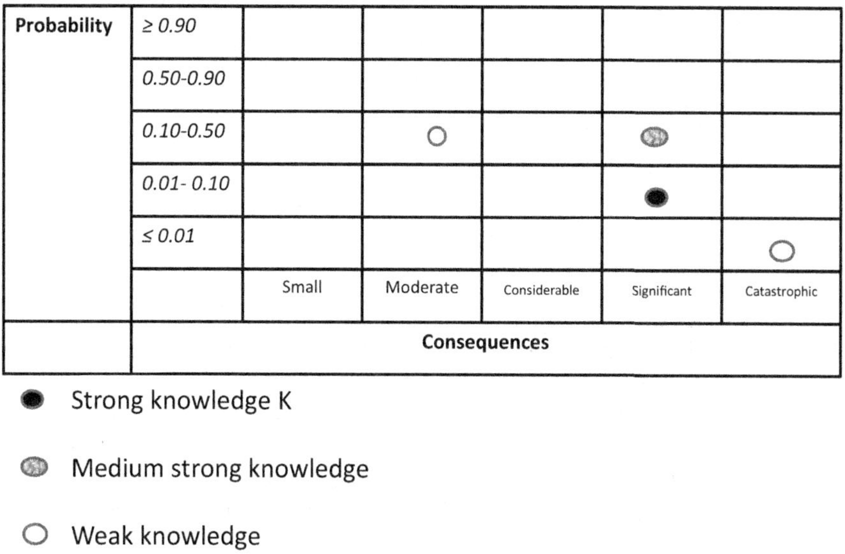

Probability	≥ 0.90					
	0.50-0.90					
	0.10-0.50			○		◑	
	0.01- 0.10					●	
	≤ 0.01						○
		Small	Moderate	Considerable	Significant	Catastrophic
				Consequences			

● 　Strong knowledge K

◑ 　Medium strong knowledge

○ 　Weak knowledge

Figure 2.2 Example of extended risk matrix

should not in general be seen as identical (Haimes 2015; Paté-Cornell 1999; Aven 2012a), see also Appendix B.

The extended risk matrix provides some information about risks. The matrix does not provide clear answers as to what are the biggest risks. The following approach has been suggested (Aven and Flage 2018):

1   Very high risk: Potential for extreme consequences, relatively large associated probability of such consequences and/or significant uncertainty (i.e., relatively weak background knowledge)
2   High risk: The potential for extreme consequences, relatively small associated probability of such consequences and moderate or weak background knowledge
3   Moderate risk: Between low and high risk. For example, the potential for moderate consequences, and weak background knowledge
4   Low risk: No potential for serious consequences

For the risk management, however, such a ranking is not essential. What is most urgent cannot be based on whether the event is categorized as, for example, very high risk or high risk. What matters is that key features of the risks are highlighted, and this can be done without transforming the information to a one-dimensional scale.

When presenting the extended risk matrix to the Board, it is observed that the matrix is rather static. The interesting discussion is related to the knowledge K, and underlying influencing factors. A table is added to the risk matrix with information of the following form:

- Risk source, hazard, threat
- Effect (using intervals, indicating potential)
- Probability (imprecision interval)
- Knowledge that this is based on (data, information, justified beliefs, models, assumptions)
- Strength of knowledge
- Potental for surprises relative to the analysts' knowledge (so-called black swans):
  - The possibility of unknown knowns (i.e. others have the knowledge, but not the analysis group). Have special measures been implemented to check for this type of event (for example, the use of an independent review of the analysis)?
  - The possibility that events are disregarded because of very low probabilities, although these probabilities are based on critical assumptions. Have special measures been implemented to check for this type of event (for example, signals and warnings influencing the existing knowledge basis)?
  - Risk related to deviations from assumptions made
  - Changes of knowledge over time

- Risk influencing factors (sources) are listed and evaluated in terms of risk importance, for example using a scale of high, medium, and low. Only the most important factors are mentioned.

  The idea is this: Make a thought-construction; if this risk factor (source) is removed or reduced, how does the risk change (sensitivity)? To what degree is the risk factor present (degree of exposure, probability)? In addition, we need to reflect on the strength of the knowledge on which these assessments are based.

Focusing on these objects ensures a more dynamic understanding of risk. It also contributes to bridging the gap between the risk characterization and the risk management. We will provide further details and examples illustrating these aspects in the coming chapters of the book.

3 Basic principles of ERM

This chapter presents the main principles of ERM as recommended in this book. First, we highlight general risk management principles, then we look more specifically at the ERM setting. We look briefly into risk programs which summarize the activities for proper implementation of ERM. The last section introduces a taxonomy of ERM maturity, using a *Beginner, Intermediate*, and *Advanced* maturity levels. Key sources are SRA (2017b), Aven (2018a) and Aven and Kristensen (2019). The last reference establishes a risk management framework based on the distinction between "general knowledge" (GK) and "specific knowledge" (SK), which is highly relevant for ERM. The framework is presented in Section 3.2.

ERM is a special case of risk management, as enterprise risk is defined as risk of an enterprise where the consequences are related to the principal objectives or overall performance judged important for the organization (refer to Section 2.1). Thus, discussions on general principles of risk management, as well as on general concepts, approaches, methods and models, are also relevant for ERM. There are, however, some particular issues and challenges related to ERM, and these are specifically addressed in the coming analysis (see Sections 3.3–3.5).

3.1 General risk management principles

Below some state-of-the-art knowledge on generic risk management principles is presented, based on guidance developed by SRA (2017b):

- Risk management covers all measures and activities carried out to manage risk, balancing developments and exploring opportunities on the one hand, and avoiding losses, accidents and disasters on the other. In general, the proper risk level is a result of a value and evidence/knowledge-informed process, balancing different concerns. To generate value, risk taking is needed. How much risk to accept in pursuit of value depends on context and how values are weighted.
- Three major strategies are needed for managing risk: a) risk-informed strategies, b) cautionary/precautionary/robustness/resilience strategies

(meeting uncertainties and potential surprises), and c) discursive strategies. In most cases the appropriate strategy would be a mixture of these three types of strategies. The higher stakes involved and larger uncertainties, the more weight on the category b) and with more of different views related to the relevant values, the more weight on category c).

- This process of balancing different concerns can be supported by cost-benefit methods, but this type of formal analysis needs to be supplemented with broader judgements of risk and uncertainties, as well as stakeholder involvement processes.
- To protect values like human lives and health, and the environment, the associated risk must be judged to be sufficiently low.
- Risk perception refers to a person's subjective judgment or appraisal of risk, which can involve social, cultural and psychological factors. Risk perceptions need to be carefully considered and incorporated into risk management, as they will influence how people respond to the risks and subsequent management efforts.
- Risk perception studies are important for (i) identifying concerns but not necessarily for measuring their potential impacts and (ii) for providing value judgement with respect to unavoidable trade-offs in the case of conflicting values or objectives.

Simplified, many risk problems can be classified as simple, uncertain and/or value differences (Aven and Renn 2019), inspired by work by IRGC (2005). A simple problem is characterized by "objective" probability distributions, and accurate predictions of future consequences. An example is smoking. Uncertainty is characterized by a potential for extreme consequences and large uncertainties concerning the nature and extent of the consequences. Complexity is an example of an underlying factor leading to uncertainty. An example of this category is climate change. The risk management strategy b) is highlighted. The third category is characterized by a potential for extreme consequences and different values related to the risks (consequences at stake, uncertainties). An example is nuclear industry and climate change. The risk management strategy c) is emphasized. It is common to refer to systemic risk when addressing risk related to a system characterized by uncertainty and/or value differences. To highlight the system being addressed, reference should be made to global systemic risk, financial systemic risk, etc. (Aven and Renn 2019).

We also include some principles for risk communication (SRA 2017b):

- Risk communication can be broadly understood as an iterative exchange or sharing of information related to the characterization, assessment and management of risk between and among different groups, including regulators, stakeholders, consumers, media and general public. It is multi-directional and includes both formal and informal messages and purposeful and unintentional ones. In today's super-mediated environment, risk professionals must also recognize that any risk message they seek to communicate is likely competing with multiple, conflicting messages from unofficial sources.

• Successful risk communication requires an understanding of the target audience, including the best means for reaching the audience: a credible or trusted source; and a message that has ideally been pre-tested to ensure its effectiveness. Those seeking to develop and test risk messages employ host of methods, including surveys, focus groups, interviews and experiments. There is also a vast theoretical literature to inform the practice of risk communication.

• A prerequisite for successful risk communication in many situations is clarity on fundamental risk analysis concepts and principles, for example what uncertainty means in a risk assessment context.

• With few exceptions, such as proprietary information or that which may damage public security, risk professionals should seek an open, transparent and timely risk communication policy. Such a policy not only demonstrates respect for the target audiences and ensures they have the information they need to take risk mitigation actions, if necessary, but it also can help ensure the perceived trustworthiness and legitimacy of the sources (SRA 2017b).

Risk assessment is an important tool in risk management, and some basic principles related to such assessment are (SRA 2017b):

• Risk assessment is the systematic process to identify risk sources, threats, hazards and opportunities; understanding how these can materialize/occur, trigger events/event sequences and what their consequences can be; representing and expressing uncertainties and risk; and determining the significance of the risk using relevant criteria.

• Risk assessment uses the best available data, information and knowledge, within the constraints and frames of the assessment.

• Probability theory and other frameworks for representing, modeling and treating variation and uncertainties, as well as traditional statistical and Bayesian analysis, provide basic tools of risk assessment.

• Quantitative measures of uncertainty (typically, probability and imprecise probabilities) should be supplemented with characterizations of the knowledge that these measures are based on. Such characterizations may cover lists of assumptions and judgments of the strength of the knowledge.

• A high-quality scientific risk assessment meets the following criteria:

  i)   It meets some basic scientific requirements:

      ○   It is solid (complying with all rules, assumptions and constraints; the basis for all choices and judgments are clear; principles and methods are subjected to order and system so that critique can be raised; etc.)

 ° It is relevant and useful (contributing to solving a problem, meeting stakeholders' expectations, etc.)

 ° It is reliable and valid. While reliability is concerned with the consistency of the 'measuring instrument' (analysts, experts, methods, procedures), validity is concerned with the success at "measuring" what one sets out to "measure" in the analysis. A key aspect to be considered in relation to validity is the degree to which the knowledge and lack of knowledge have been properly addressed.

ii) The decision-maker (and other stakeholders) has confidence in the assessment with its results and findings. This confidence will depend on many factors, including the analysts' and scientists' own evaluations of the quality of their assessments, and how the decision-maker judges the competence of the analysts and scientists.

- Peer review is a useful tool for checking and improving the quality of scientific risk assessments (SRA 2017b).

There are many ways of describing the risk management process using risk assessment, but the basic steps are mostly the same in all (see also Figure 3.1):

1 Establish the context and set objectives. This step involves the definition of the entity's key objectives which could be defined in terms of profit, safety, etc.
2 Identify threats/hazards/opportunities that could affect something that the entity values.
3 Analyze associated risks.
4 Evaluate the risks. This step involves judgments as to whether the risks should be adjusted or not; for downside risks we talk about acceptable (tolerable) risk or not.
5 Risk control, risk treatment, risk response. When the risk is judged unacceptable, we can abandon the (potential) activity, we can reduce the risk or we can transfer it to third parties (e.g. insurance).

 In addition, internal and external communication is also often included in this sequence. The process is iterative, not necessarily sequential. We also find these steps in most standards on risk management, including ISO 31000 and ERM documents (COSO 2018). They are relevant for all types of organizations; e.g. profit maximizing enterprises, hospitals and non-governmental organizations (NGOs). The present analysis focuses on profit-maximizing enterprises, although other types of organizations are also covered.

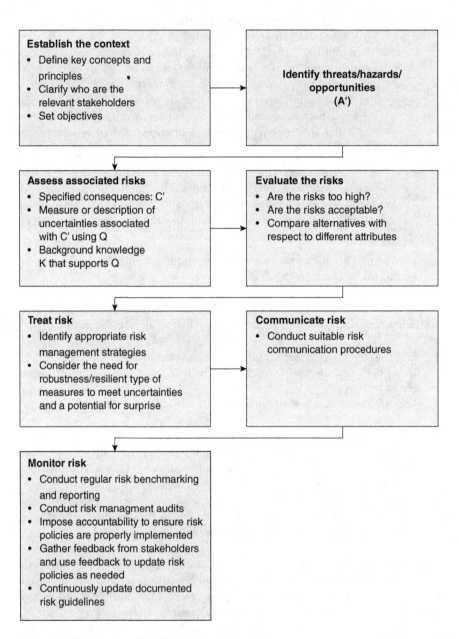

Establish the context
- Define key concepts and principles •
- Clarify who are the relevant stakeholders
- Set objectives

**Identify threats/hazards/
opportunities
(A')**

Assess associated risks
- Specified consequences: C'
- Measure or description of uncertainties associated with C' using Q
- Background knowledge K that supports Q

Evaluate the risks
- Are the risks too high?
- Are the risks acceptable?
- Compare alternatives with respect to different attributes

Treat risk
- Identify appropriate risk management strategies
- Consider the need for robustness/resilient type of measures to meet uncertainties and a potential for surprise

Communicate risk
- Conduct suitable risk communication procedures

Monitor risk
- Conduct regular risk benchmarking and reporting
- Conduct risk managment audits
- Impose accountability to ensure risk policies are properly implemented
- Gather feedback from stakeholders and use feedback to update risk policies as needed
- Continuously update documented risk guidelines

Figure 3.1 High-level outline of risk management process

In addition, we will add some fundamental principles related to concepts and the field and science of risk analysis and management (SRA 2017a, b; Aven 2018a):

• The risk field and science cover two main types of activities:

  A   Risk analysis, communication and management related to specific activities (interpreted in a broad sense covering also natural phenomena) in the real world, for example the use of a medical drug, the design of a process plant or the climate. The aim is to support risk knowledge generation and communication, as well as handling (management, decision-making) of risk problems and issues (applied risk science, applied risk analysis, communication and management).

  B   Development of generic concepts, theories, frameworks, approaches, principles, methods and models to understand, assess, characterize, communicate and (in a broad sense) manage risk (generic risk science). Concrete activities to collect data and establish databases are considered to be type A, whereas methods for how to perform these activities are covered by B.

      Contributions to the risk science mean adding knowledge to A or B, or both.

• We make clear distinctions between variation/variability and uncertainty and imprecision, and different methods are used to represent and/or express these, like frequentist probabilities (and related probability models) and probability and imprecise probability, respectively. Clear and meaningful interpretations are required for these concepts, as summarized in Section 2.2.3, see also Appendix B.

3.2 A risk management framework based on the distinction between general knowledge and specific knowledge

In practical (real-life) situations, the risk management strategies mentioned in the previous section need to be supplemented with a strategy which may be labelled "risk-based requirement strategy". This strategy is typically used when the knowledge is strong – the situations considered are well-understood and there is nothing new or unusual about the system or activity under study. Experience, statistical analysis and traditional risk assessment may have been used to establish the "risk-based requirement strategy". The idea is reflected in standards, for example the risk-related decision-making framework by ISO 17776 (ISO 2016). In this standard, the "risk-based requirement strategy" is labelled "good practice" and is added to the other two basic risk management strategies (risk assessment informed and cautionary approaches) referred to in Section 3.1.

Depending on the decision context considered, these management strategies are, to varying degrees, adopted. With strong knowledge and minimal uncertainties, the "good practice" approach is justified, whereas if the values at stake are high and the uncertainties are large, all strategies are required. For other situations, with fewer uncertainties, the cautionary and precautionary strategy is not given the same weight.

To illustrate this discussion, consider the offshore industry in Norway. In the early years of this industry, there was little knowledge about the hazards and potential accidental events that this industry faced. Risk assessment methods were introduced, and they matured as the industry expanded, contributing to increasing the general knowledge (GK) about the associated risks. The industry also gained knowledge about the safety and control measures needed, and how to design and operate the facilities in a safe manner. It learned from successes, failures, near misses and accidents.

To a large extent today, the same hazards remain on an offshore facility as in the early days. The main difference is the increased GK about the hazards and an increased GK of how to manage them.

Due to this increased GK in the offshore industry gained through experience, improvements and years of conducting risk assessments, the basic strategies (risk assessment informed and cautionary) have largely been replaced by a "risk-based requirement" strategy with the use of codes and specific requirements that need to be met. An example of this is the specific requirements established for how to design and operate safety (barrier) systems. If these requirements are fulfilled, no further risk assessments are needed for the hazards and safety systems covered by the requirements.

However, when new technical concepts and arrangements are introduced, for example when moving the control rooms for offshore facilities from offshore to office buildings onshore, a more thorough and traditional risk assessment strategy, combined with a robustness/resilience strategy, is required.

We are led to a classification system, based on three types of risk management strategies:

a)   Risk-based requirements strategy
b)   Risk assessments (risk-informed) strategy
c)   Cautionary (use of robust/resilient arrangements and measures) strategy

In addition to strategies a)-c), dialogue and discursive strategies need to be mentioned (refer Section 3.1). These strategies use measures to build confidence and trustworthiness, through clarifications of facts, reduction of uncertainties, involvement of affected people, deliberation and accountability (Renn 2008; SRA 2015b). A successful example of the use of such strategies is the three-party dialogue introduced in the Norwegian petroleum industry, where formal collaboration is established between the industry, the unions and the authorities (Bang and Thuestad 2014; Lindøe and Engen 2013; Rosness and Forseth 2014; Aven and Renn 2018).

The practical implementation of a risk management system based on these strategies is, however, not straightforward. What are the conditions that must be fulfilled for a situation or activity to be classified as one of the "risk-based requirements strategy"? When is the knowledge strong enough? When can we ignore the potential for surprise? Knowledge is basically justified beliefs (SRA 2015a), established on the basis of data and information, testing, argumentation, modeling, etc. The knowledge can be more or less strong, but that is based on judgements by someone, and these judgements can also be wrong. How should we take such aspects into account in the risk management? When is the robustness/resilience strategy actually justified?

The present discussion aims to contribute to meeting these challenges. We seek to do this by making a distinction between two types of knowledge: GK and SK. For the above offshore example, the former type of knowledge relates to over 40 years of experience from the oil and gas industry, while the latter type of knowledge relates to concrete knowledge for the installation considered, for example concerning design features, operational constraints, targets and experience. Using these two types of knowledge, we formulate key features and requirements for the risk management, for example by stating that risk management is the process of making sure that the GK is sufficiently strong to be used for the planning, procedures and requirements for the activity studied, and that we have sufficient SK and control at all times.

Based on the dichotomy between GK and SK, as well as recent developments in risk science, the risk-related decision-making framework presented by ISO 17776 (ISO 2016) is enhanced. These developments relate to our understanding of the link between risk, uncertainties and knowledge, and how we can use this to improve risk assessment and management as discussed in this book (see e.g. Flage et al. 2014; SRA 2015b; Aven 2016a).

Different types of risk management systems exist. On a general level, we have systems described in overall standards like ISO 31000 and ISO 17776 (ISO 2016, 2018). More specific systems are presented and discussed in the scientific literature, in textbooks and papers on risk management (e.g. Aven and Renn 2010; Meyer and Reniers 2013; Haimes 2015; SRA 2015a). Over the years, we have seen a gradual development of these, from pure probability-based risk assessment approaches to broader risk-management frameworks, highlighting both risk assessments and robust/resilient strategies. A main driver for this development has been the acknowledgement of the importance of uncertainties and knowledge for the proper understanding, assessment and management of risk.

An important source for this acknowledgment has been the insights developed over the last 20–30 years by the safety science literature (e.g. Rasmussen 1997; Hollnagel et al. 2006; Dekker 2012). A key point made is that, for complex systems, full control of the risks cannot be achieved. Surprises will occur. If complexity is not fully acknowledged, the result will be blind zones and poor understanding of uncertainty (Årstad and Aven 2017).

Another source is the literature on black swans in risk management, which captures similar ideas, linking risk, knowledge and uncertainties (Taleb 2007; Aven 2015b); refer to Chapter 5. It is argued that, if the risk assessment restricts its focus on probabilities, important aspects of risk could be covered or concealed, as the risk characterizations are conditional on some knowledge and this knowledge is associated with uncertainties and risk. Blacks swans are understood as surprises relative to this knowledge, for example so-called unknown knowns (some, but not the current analysts, have the knowledge) (Aven 2015b).

In the following we will present and discuss various features of this framework:

1   Overall model
2   Risk management in different stages of a project
3   Using and controlling assumptions
4   Classifications of threats and risks
5   Decision-making, choice of alternatives and measures
6   Discussion
7   Conclusions

3.2.1 A model for the risk-related decision-making

We define three states:

S: Successful realization of the activity, for example production as planned or increased production
I: Intermediate state (because of a threat, i.e. a risk source or an event)
F: A serious failure state, for example as a result of a major accident occurring.

Risk management is defined in relation to two possible situations:

a)   That S is not achieved
b)   That F occurs.

For a), the key questions to ask are: what are the visions and goals defining S? What are the key instruments to be used to meet these visions and goals? How do we ensure that the system quickly returns to state S if it happens to visit state I; in other words, how do we ensure that the system is able to regain or restore performance (and even improve) in case of changes in the system (due to stressors, disturbances, opportunities), i.e. that the system is resilient? What are the main threats and risks related to not being able to obtain the S state?

For b), the key questions are: how do we prevent this state F from occurring? What are the key instruments to be used? What are the main threats and risks of F occurring?

At first glance, the difference between a) and b) may seem minor. However, it matters greatly whether the focus is on accident prevention or on not meeting some business objectives. Some events could lead to long periods of state

I occurring, but with minor or no effect on the likelihood of a serious failure state F occurring.

The risk management tasks and responsibilities include:

- Make sure that the relevant actors have sufficiently strong knowledge about the (RS,A,B,C), where RS: risk sources, A: events, B: barriers, C: consequences – what could go wrong (that S is not achieved or F occurs) and why (necessary GK).
- Make sure that the necessary and right measures are in place – and that they are functioning as intended (necessary SK).
- Make sure that the relevant actors have sufficiently strong knowledge (GK + SK) to conclude that they are sufficiently sure that state S will be the normal state and F will not occur.

The GK is the starting point for the risk management. If it is strong and has been reflected in relevant solutions and measures, we can focus on the SK. If not, the GK needs to be strengthened and/or measures for ensuring that the knowledge is properly reflected in solutions and measures implemented. To evaluate the strength of the GK, the risks related to unknown knowns is a key problem, as discussed in Section 2.2. Thus, although the GK could be strong, we need to consider who knows what and how well they know/understand it.

The GK provides a frame for understanding the SK related to the system or activity studied, concerning technical conditions, competences, experiences, training and exercises, planning and preparations, planning processes, etc. The SK needs to be "transferred" back to the GK, in order to make a decision on its criticality and to find the required and suitable measures. For example, if the test of a system or component during an operation results in a failure, we need to decide what should be done, by whom and when. We also need to decide what should be done if a test has been delayed/not performed. How long a delay can be accepted before it is no longer safe to operate? The GK provides input to this.

Sufficient SK and control means a judgement that the risk associated with the activity is considered sufficiently low and is acceptable.

In Figure 3.2, a model for selection of appropriate risk management strategies is presented, using the concepts of GK and SK. It can be seen as a version of the framework presented by ISO 17776 (ISO 2016). A key message from Figure 3.2 is that when the GK, as well as the SK, is strong, risk-based requirement strategy can be implemented. If, however, the SK is weak (but the GK is still strong), weight needs to be given to robustness/resilience, as the activity considered could have special features and there is a potential for surprises relative to the GK. Using feedback loops, the model allows for differentiations between situations where it is possible to increase the knowledge – for example by performing analysis, testing, modeling, decision-making and the use of assumptions – and where this is not possible. If the GK is weak, a robustness/resilience-based strategy is always needed, as the SK has a poor foundation. If

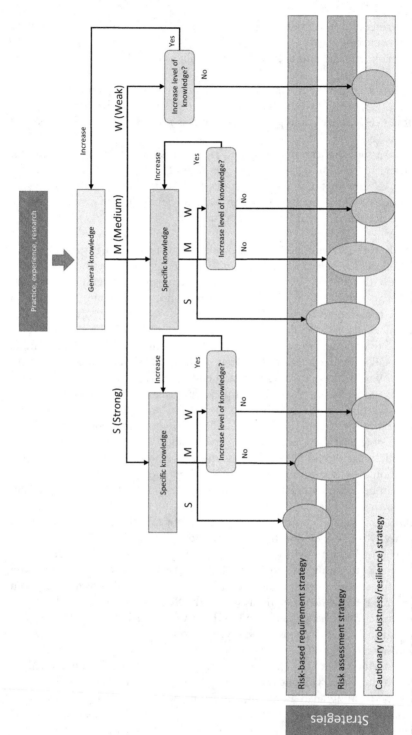

Figure 3.2 A model for defining main risk management strategy, based on categorizations of GK and SK (Aven and Kristensen 2019).

the GK is medium strong, risk assessments will provide useful decision support, except in cases with weak SK. In the case of weak SK, the risk assessment will have rather limited information value and is therefore not highlighted in the model in Figure 3.2.

When faced with a situation where the level of knowledge (GK or SK) is medium or weak, one should always consider the questions: Can and, if yes, should the level of knowledge be increased before a decision on the risk management strategies is made? This is founded on the thesis that increased level of knowledge will provide a better decision basis, and less costly (less conservative) risk management strategies and measures. Aspects to be included in such considerations could be: the timeframe (before the decision(s) has to be made), what can be done (consult with external experts vs. the need for extensive research work) and cost (will the increased knowledge be worth the cost needed to gain it?).

There are several other simplified features in this model. In fact, some types of risk assessments are always conducted. For instance, it is important to identify risks related to assumptions made, and, in the case of large uncertainties, risk assessment is a useful tool to systematize the knowledge available and identify knowledge gaps, although no attempts are made to quantify risk.

The model illustrated in Figure 3.2 is to be considered as a conceptual model rather than a fixed process/evaluation to be performed at specific times with a fixed set-up for how it should be done. The main idea with the figure is to increase the reflection on the level of knowledge (GK and SK), and how the different levels should influence the selection of the risk management strategy/strategies to be used. "Unconscious" approaches or approaches based on traditions ("we have always done it like this"), such as always using the risk assessment strategy without reflecting on whether the outcome will provide a better/needed decision support and/or whether the input needed is available (i.e. sufficient level of SK in order to conduct the assessment), is not beneficial to any party. It can be considered a misuse of the decision–makers time and money, and it may jeopardize the importance of doing, for example, an extensive risk assessment when that is the suitable and best strategy.

3.2.2 Risk management in different stages of a project

For decisions at the early stages of a development project, the GK provides the basis for the decisions. As the project develops, the SK becomes more important, and, in the operational stages, when making a decision about the operation of a system, the SK is central. However, in most situations, the GK is important for placing the observations and measurements of the specific system in context, and the GK provides this context, with its general theories, experiences, practices, etc.; the GK will always provide guidance on how to understand and use the SK.

For example, at the early stages of an offshore development project, for proven development concepts such as fully integrated topside facilities and subsea tie-back developments, the GK provides the basis for the identification of hazards, accidental events and the risk control measures (barriers) needed. To perform traditional risk assessments, starting by asking what can happen/ go wrong and thereafter continuing to assess why, how often, what the consequences will be, etc., will, for proven development projects, not provide any new knowledge. Thus, the main purpose of performing such assessments in such cases will not be to gain more insight about the risks associated with the concepts but to reproduce it (which could be relevant, in order to give the decision-makers this knowledge).

The GK provides guidance on the need for risk assessments and the type of such assessments, including the methods and models that should be used.

A main strategy for managing the risk through different stages is to use and "control" assumptions. In the early stages of a development project, the SK is weak, and assumptions are introduced as discussed in the following section.

3.2.3 Using and controlling assumptions as a strategy to deal with weak specific knowledge

Consider a case where strong or medium strong GK exists (e.g. fires in buildings). A specific building is to be constructed. The developers want to get the building up as fast as possible, but they do not yet know what the building will contain when it is completed. They do not know whether it is going to be used for housing, partly housing and partly offices/industry, or only industry purposes.

The building's main load-bearing structure, the divisions between the floors, the construction materials, the firefighting equipment, etc., will to a large extent be governed by what the building is going to be used for (due to, for example, regulatory requirements). So, do the developers have to wait until the building is fully rented out before they can start the building process?

No, they need to make some decisions, and these are often formulated as assumptions, for example that the building is going to be a flexible housing/ office building, and that only the lowest floors shall have the possibility to be used for either housing or offices, while the rest of the building is going to be used only for housing.

To choose the combined housing and office concept for the building would most likely eliminate the possibility of allowing future industry activities in the building. This is a risk the decision-makers must take into consideration when they decide on the type of building they want to build.

Using a traditional risk assessment approach, one may argue that details related to the final building, i.e. its combination of flats, offices and/or industry activities, need to be in place in order to conduct a proper hazard identification, risk characterizations and evaluations. In other words, the building needs to be specified in detail before it can be assessed properly. When such detailed specifications cannot be made (due to lack of knowledge), assumptions can be used in order to continue the project. The alternative is to stop or delay the project. Such assumptions can, for example, relate to the overall features of the building, as discussed above, or to the load capacity of walls, in the case of fires and/or explosions. As modifying, for example, the load-bearing structure or the fire divisions will be very costly (often impossible) after the building is finalized, the choice of assumptions is critical. Figure 3.3 presents a simple model for how to use assumptions in the risk management by considering differences in the level of GK and SK, refining the scheme in Figure 3.2.

If the GK is strong but the SK is medium and weak, the use of assumptions (which will often be decisions that limit the flexibility in the way forward) will allow for a shift towards more weight given to the a) and b) strategies, "risk-based requirement strategy" and risk assessment strategy, for example from a mainly cautionary approach to a combined risk assessment and a partly cautionary approach, if the GK is strong and the SK is weak, or from a cautionary/risk assessment approach to a combined 'risk-based requirement strategy', risk assessment and cautionary approach, if the GK is medium and the SK is medium.

A key feature of this approach, based on assumptions to compensate for lack of SK, is that the decision-makers ensure that the assumptions are fulfilled (e.g. making sure that industry activities are not allowed in the building in the future, in the building example presented above). There will always be risk related to the assumptions actually being met in practice.

3.2.4 Classifications and judgements of the severity of threats and risks

Threats and risks can be classified according to three categories: high, medium and low. The category "high" is typically associated with an unacceptable risk, requiring additional measures in order to proceed, whereas "low" is typically associated with an acceptable risk, where no additional measures are needed. The "medium" category is associated with situations where the risk is acceptable but additional measures should be implemented if possible. Management considerations are needed to decide which measures to implement.

To classify a threat or the risk as high, the following criteria need to be considered (minimum one of these criteria applies):

a) The risk is judged to be high when considering consequences and probability
b) The risk is judged as high when considering the potential for severe consequences and significant uncertainty (relatively weak knowledge)
c) Lack of robustness/resilience
d) Weak GK about (RS, A, B, C)
e) Weak SK about (RS, A, B, C)
f) Strong GK about undesirable features of (RS, A, B, C)
g) Strong SK about undesirable features of (RS, A, B, C)

For example, the risk is classified as high if a critical failure on the Blowout Preventor (BOP) has been revealed through testing, by reference to a), c) and g).

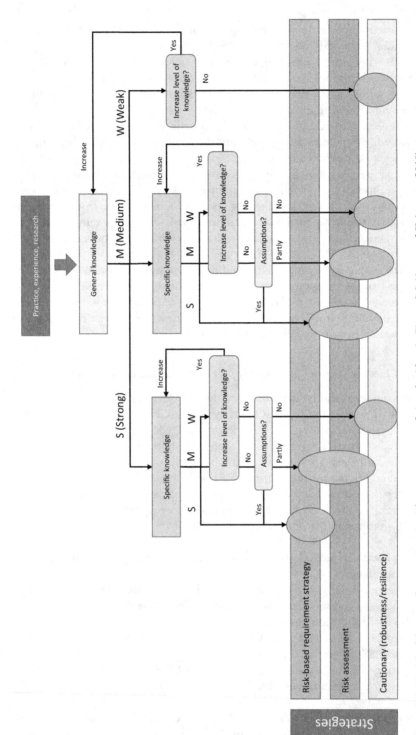

Figure 3.3 Model of the use of assumptions in risk management, refining the ideas in Figure 3.2 (Aven and Kristensen 2019)

We can also classify the risk as high if the BOP has not been tested, with reference to b), c) and e).

In the former example, we argued according to what we know and, in the latter, to what we did not know.

Analogously, we can define criteria for low (all relevant criteria apply):

h) No potential for serious consequences
i) The risk is judged to be low when considering consequences and probability, and supporting knowledge is strong
j) Solid robustness/resilience
k) Strong GK about (RS, A, B, C)
l) Strong SK about (RS, A, B, C)

Medium applies to all other cases.

To evaluate the strength of the knowledge, we need to address issues such as defined in Section 2.2.3 (Flage et al. 2014; Aven and Flage 2018; Aven 2017b):

- The reasonability of assumptions made
- The amount and relevancy of data/information
- The degree of agreement among experts
- The degree to which the phenomena involved are understood and accurate models exist
- The degree to which the knowledge has been thoroughly examined (for example, with respect to unknown knowns; i.e. others, but not the analysis group, have the knowledge).

The last point relates to potential surprise issues like (refer to Section 2.2.4 and Bjerga and Aven 2016):

- The possibility of unknown knowns. Have special measures been implemented to check for this type of event (for example, the use of an independent review of the analysis)?
- The possibility that events are disregarded because of very low probabilities, although these probabilities are based on critical assumptions. Have special measures been implemented to check for this type of event (for example, signals and warnings influencing the existing knowledge basis)?
- Risk related to deviations from assumptions made
- Changes in knowledge over time

Examples

How to make judgements about risk and use the GK and SK depends on the situation considered. We consider three examples to illustrate this point:

1   A company buys a product from a manufacturer. There is no need to perform a probabilistic analysis and calculate risk metrics, as the company has

well-documented strong GK in relation to the performance of the product, established on the basis of work done by the manufacturer, as well as operational experience with this type of product. The manufacturer has conducted a risk assessment of the product and implemented risk-reducing measures, and reference can also be made to practical use of the product, demonstrating its high reliability. The company has strong knowledge expressing that the reliability is high. However, there is always a potential for surprises, and the risk related to such surprises needs to be addressed, through, for example, checks of key assumptions made.

2   In the above example, the manufacturer, on the other hand, may find it useful to use a probabilistic analysis to characterize the reliability and risks. Uncertainties and the strength of knowledge supporting this analysis need to be reflected. Bayesian analysis can provide a suitable framework for updating the probabilities, given new information.

3   In this final example, consider a situation where a product is used in a completely new context. The GK for the product may be strong, but it is not relevant for this new context. Hence, we are led to SK judgments. An analysis of what characterizes this new context compared to the standard one is conducted. This analysis may, for example, reveal that the new context involves a higher exposure level from a specific risk source. Measures will then be considered to meet this risk factor. Probabilistic analysis is not recommended, as the knowledge supporting the probabilities is so weak. However, qualitative probability judgements or interval probabilities could be useful to communicate experts' degree of beliefs: Is this a likely event or not? Is it higher than 50%? Negligible probability?

These examples show that different situations call for different weights on the three main components of a performance-uncertainty characterization. Compared to common risk assessment practice, the proposed framework has a stronger focus on the knowledge dimension.

3.2.5 Decision-making, choice of alternatives and measures

When facing many potential solutions and measures, we need to evaluate these. A key aspect to consider in relation to this is the *manageability* of a risk event (for example "low oil price") or measures meeting this risk event, which is a concept that relates to how difficult it is to reduce the risk and depends on technical feasibility, time aspects, costs, etc. (Aven 2017b). It is often informative to present a matrix with, for example, three categories (high, medium, low) based on manageability on the one axis, and effect on risk on the other. The latter axis relates to how large an effect the measures have on risk: consequences, probability and strength of knowledge; or how large an effect the risk event has on risk. Measures which score relatively highly on manageability and risk are clear candidates for implementation. Such matrices need to be used with care.

For example, if the risk event considered for an oil company is "low oil price", it may, at first glance, be tempting to express the manageability as low, leading to the conclusion that no measures are required. However, the risk is not only related to the price changes, equally important are measures implemented for meeting a low oil price, for example reducing operational expenditure. This risk event could therefore be classified as relatively high as regards manageability, and the main focus is on measures that could reduce the negative effects for the company if such an event should occur. In general, the following risk-reduction process is recommended (Aven 2017b):

1 Implement measures in the case of high risks, as defined above.
2 If the costs are small, implement the measure if it is considered to have a positive effect in relation to risk and performance in a wide sense (medium or even low risk).
3 If the costs are significant, make an assessment of all relevant pros and cons of the measure. If the expected net present value (or corresponding indices) can be meaningfully calculated, implement the measure if this value is positive.
4 Also consider implementing the measure if it generates a considerable positive effect on the risk and/or other conditions, for example:

  ° Reducing uncertainty, strengthening knowledge
  ° Strengthening the robustness in the case of hazards/threats, strengthening the resilience

The approach aims to balance the need for cost-effectiveness and being cautious in the face of threats with potential negative consequences. See also Chapter 7.

3.2.6 An illustrating example

Consider a house development project during spring and summer, with an issue of radon risk. The owner has currently not been able to make proper radon measurements in the house as it needs to be measured in the winter. Based on a radon map, the owner observes that there are high radon concentrations in the area where the house is located. The GK concerning radon risk is strong and the risk is judged high according to the scheme presented in Section 3.2.4, for example by referring to criterion f). The GK recommends some protection barriers to be installed. The SK is judged to be rather weak, and to strengthen this knowledge the owner needs to defer the project some 6–9 months to make detailed measurements. The results of such measurements could potentially show that the radon exposure for the house is small, and no special protection is required. However, a delay of 6–9 is considered too costly for the owner, and the conclusion is that the protection barriers are installed on the basis of the GK, in line with Figure 3.1 which points to the cautionary principle and the implementation of robust/resilient measures.

3.2.7 Discussion

The distinction between GK and SK to assess risk leads to a new type of approach. We find, however, similar ideas in the Bayesian method, where a prior distribution and the underlying probability model are established on the basis of generic knowledge and combined with observations and measurements representing SK, to produce an integrated distribution reflecting the total knowledge. The Bayesian method has a strong theoretical foundation and can be useful in many cases to systematically update knowledge. The approach presented above differs, however, from the Bayesian approach in many ways. First, it is a qualitative approach, not a quantitative approach as the Bayesian one. The strengths of quantitative analysis are well known, as are the weaknesses of qualitative studies. Probabilistic quantification and the use of Bayes' formula make it possible to systematically combine knowledge about unknown quantities and observations (measurements). Using qualitative approaches, the stringency of the probability theory is lost, and it is not possible to ensure the same level of coherency in judgements. However, quantification also has strong limitations. To use a probability to represent uncertainty means that important aspects of risk are not reflected, aspects that are important to properly evaluate the significance of the risk and make the right decisions. The argumentation for this assertion is well known (see, for example, Flage et al. 2014; Aven 2014) but, to quickly recap, a probability representing or expressing uncertainty is conditional on some knowledge, and this knowledge could be more or less strong and even erroneous. For the proper use of the risk assessment, it is not enough to only report the probability numbers, as these reflect "conditional risk". The assessment may, for example, be based on a belief that the system studied has some specified properties, but in real life it could, in fact, have others, and this can lead to negative surprises (see examples in Aven 2017b). The use of imprecise probability or interval probabilities (Flage et al. 2014, Section 2.2.2) makes the transformation from knowledge to the probabilities more objective but does not eliminate the issue of the underlying knowledge being weak or wrong. Such intervals will also reduce the information value of the assessments, as the intervals seek to avoid incorporating analysts' judgements.

A probabilistic quantitative risk assessment produces a risk description $(C',P\,|\,K)$ using the notation introduced in Section 2.2.3. The method presented above describes risk using the triplet (C',Q,K). Thus, the knowledge supporting the uncertainty description Q is a part of the risk description. In $(C',P\,|\,K)$, the probabilistic metrics are to be seen as conditional on some knowledge, whereas, in (C',Q,K), the knowledge is subject to scrutiny. The aim is not only to describe the strength of this knowledge but also to strengthen it when the knowledge is weak. An objective transformation of the knowledge from the evidence to the risk description is attractive and has a value, but the price paid is that the assessment becomes rather uninformative for the decision-makers if the evidence is not strong. We may, for example, have some signals indicating a failure in the system, but if we are not able to understand these signals they are of little importance. The proposed risk assessment method presented above seeks to stimulate processes to strengthen the knowledge generation where the knowledge is judged as weak, and also to reveal knowledge gaps, in particular unknown knowns. If the risk description at some stage of the analysis is (C',Q,K), the study at a later time could be (C',Q,K$_1$), where K$_1$ is stronger than K. The assessment may, for example, have revealed that an assumption used is questionable and should be replaced by a more nuanced analysis, adding new knowledge to the table. The split into GK and SK can be useful in this respect. For example, it is important to distinguish between what are GK gaps and what are SK gaps. The former case may trigger some generic research projects, whereas the latter case could lead to broader involvement of operational personnel in the risk assessment.

The subjectivity of the analysis must be acknowledged. The analysts may consider the knowledge to be strong, but they could be wrong. It is about beliefs and justifications of these beliefs. We know that scientists and analysts often have strong confidence in relation to their own knowledge, but history has shown that incorrect conclusions are made. The limitations of the method need to be taken into account in the risk management. These problems particularly apply to quantitative analysis but are also an issue when it comes to qualitative studies. The approach proposed above seeks to meet this challenge through its checklists and reviews, but it is still based on judgements which could be wrong. The way of dealing with this challenge is to recognize the importance of robustness and resilience-based strategies. Such strategies constitute a main category of risk measures justified by the imperfection of the risk assessments, whether they are quantitative, qualitative or a mixture. All industries have built in some degree of robustness and resilience, but the risk assessment rationality is often seen as the superior one; see, for example, discussions in O'Brien (2000), Pasman et al. (2017) and Aven (2011). However, in the face of uncertainties, there is theoretical strong justification of the robustness and resilience-based strategies; see, for example, Renn (2008) and Aven (2019b).

A main challenge with the approach presented above is that it is based on qualitative judgements regarding what is high, medium, or low risk. Different analyst groups could come to different conclusions about the magnitude of the risk, as there is no clearly defined scale. However, the idea that such a scale exists can be disputed; risk is more than a probability number (see also Flage et al. 2014) and, to be able to include all relevant risk aspects, we are faced with a dilemma. We either present a rather narrow risk description based on risk numbers as the basis for the decision-making, which does not incorporate important aspects of risk, or we use a qualitative approach, which lacks scale precision but is more complete. Also, metrics based on quantification can be used to support the qualitative approach, but these metrics are not viewed as final results but as input to the overall qualitative judgements to be made. To make a judgement that, for example, the risk is "high", criteria as outlined in Section 3.2.4 are introduced. The judgement does not automatically prescribe a decision to act to reduce risk; considerations are needed to check for the feasibility of measures, costs and other concerns, but commonly the classification "high" leads to conclusions about unacceptable risk and the need for risk-reducing measures. This presumes, however, that the "perspective" and "references" of the analysis are clarified. For example, the perspective or reference for the conclusions could be overall technical criteria in the company and the industry, regulations, etc. In other cases, the study team includes managers with proper authority, and the conclusions could then also be influenced by the value judgements of these managers. Think of the planning of a technical operation on an offshore installation. Here, the decision-maker could be a part of the analysis team, and conclusions can be made about risk being too high and unacceptable as a part of the assessment.

The approach presented is based on the split between GK and SK, but also about knowledge and lack of knowledge. Uncertainty is about lack of knowledge, and the risk concept highlights uncertainties. However, the traditional risk assessments often focus on the available knowledge. The probabilities assessed reflect the analysts' knowledge, not the lack of knowledge. When making judgements about the strength of knowledge, we also focus mainly on the existing knowledge. Lack of knowledge is more the issue when addressing potential surprises and the unforeseen. The presented approach also aims to give weight to this risk aspect. It represents a challenge, as it extends beyond the analysis as such, and it has traditionally not been given much attention in risk assessments. Recently, it has, however, been more emphasized – references to black swan types of events are relatively common today. How to best deal with this type of risk is not straightforward, as the issue cannot be solved by calculations. The presented approach highlights some tools in this regard, but there are many others that could be useful in relation to the approach; see, for example, Aven (2015) and the references therein. See also Chapter 5.

3.2.8 Conclusions

Using the dichotomy between GK and SK, risk management is viewed as the process of making sure that the GK is sufficiently strong to be used for the planning, procedures and requirements of the activity studied, and that we have sufficient SK and control at all times. Based on this idea, a framework is presented that shows how risk can be evaluated and managed, giving due attention to potential surprises and the unforeseen. The framework builds on current risk science, which acknowledges the importance of using both risk assessment and robustness/resilience-based strategies to properly handle risk. In contrast to many other risk management frameworks, it is mainly qualitative, and it does not make a sharp distinction between assessment and risk descriptions, on the one hand, and the handling of the risk, on the other. The main focus is on the actions and decisions to be made, not on the risk characterizations as such. For the purpose of making the right decisions, detailed and nuanced risk descriptions are not always needed (refer to, for example, Lambert et al. (2012) and Karvetski and Lambert (2012)). The key is to identify the measures that are needed to make the activity safe and the risk tolerable/acceptable. Risk quantification can be useful in many cases to systematically assess risk-related information and knowledge, but qualitative judgements are always needed to be able to properly consider all aspects of risk of importance for the decision-makers. Qualitative judgements have their limitations, but they can still be useful. The challenge is to establish some suitable guidance on how to conduct these qualitative risk analyses. The main aim of the above analysis has been to provide such guidance, using the concept of GK and SK

3.3 More specific ERM principles

According to COSO (COSO 2004, Moeller 2018), ERM encompasses:

- Aligning risk appetite and strategy – Management considers the entity's risk appetite in evaluating strategic alternatives, setting related objectives and developing mechanisms to manage related risks.
- Enhancing risk response decisions – ERM provides the rigor to identify and select among alternative risk responses, such as risk avoidance, reduction, sharing and acceptance.
- Reducing operational surprises and losses – Entities gain enhanced capability to identify potential events and establish responses, reducing surprises and associated costs or losses.
- Identifying and managing multiple and cross-enterprise risks – Every enterprise faces a myriad of risks affecting different parts of the organization, and ERM facilitates effective responses to the interrelated impacts, and integrated responses to multiple risks.
- Seizing opportunities – By considering a full range of potential events, management is positioned to identify and proactively realize opportunities.
- Improving deployment of capital – Obtaining robust risk information allows management to effectively assess overall capital needs and enhance capital allocation (ERM 2018).

In sum, "ERM risk management helps an entity get to where it wants to go and avoid pitfalls and surprises along the way" (ERM 2018). A general overview of basic ERM theory, as defined by COSO (Moeller 2018) can be found in Appendix C.

Current literature provides substance and guidance when it comes to all of the topics mentioned above. The present book seeks to provide further insights on some aspects as outlined in the preface. More specifically, we highlight the following ideas and principles:

1 Distinguishing between ERM and TRM (Task Risk Management)
2 Paying due attention to uncertainties and the potential for surprises (black swans)
3 Integrating risk assessments and resilience-based thinking and methods

4   Balancing different concerns, by seeing beyond traditional cost-benefit types of analysis using expected values

These topics will be followed up in coming chapters.

3.4 ERM program

A risk program is a set of documented activities necessary for the implementation of ERM. These risk program activities primarily involve oversight and implementation of the risk management, including the hazard/threat/opportunity identification, risk assessment and the risk treatment. A risk program is created to ensure that the risk management process is performed in an effective manner and in line with the fundamental principles presented in Sections 3.1 and 3.3. The program provides clear and concise steps for systematic planning of risk activities, including clear project milestones, goals and responsible parties. Based on the COSO framework (Moeller 2011) and risk principles described in this section, a risk program should contain the following items:

1   Introduction. This should articulate the following:

- Why a risk program is needed for the organization
- The need for widespread adoption of the risk program and coordination among stakeholders
- The scope of the risk program (what types of risks are included, justification for what specifically is not included)
- Leadership levels that have approved and adopted the risk program, including leadership's commitment to ensuring the risk program has the resources and executive support necessary for a successful implementation

2   Risk policies

- Standardized processes for how to address risk (see Section 3.1 for details)
- Templates or forms to be used for documenting risk policies and implementation activities. For example, documentation could include output of the steps shown in Section 3.1, standardized communication with parties responsible for implementing risk treatment plans, and other documentation needed for audit purposes.

3   Criteria for evaluation of risks. This should include guidance on the organization's risk appetite, broad priorities for risk assessment (e.g. safety, financial, etc.), and any related strategic initiatives that can influence how risk is treated in the organization.

4   Risk activities. This should contain clear guidelines for the following elements:

- Specification of risk activities, including a process for selecting responsible parties for implementing risk activities; setting deadlines for risk activities; and monitoring of implementation

- Evaluation and monitoring of the current risk program, recognizing that the risk program should adapt to current conditions (strategic, economic, etc.)

5   Related documentation. Any requirements for paperwork and regular meetings should be balanced with any organizational efforts toward minimizing (or increasing) bureaucracy. Over-burdensome documentation can lead to a lack of efficiency, while the use of some documentation can improve standardization. Related documentation can include guidelines for:

- Responsible parties for managing the risk program
- Responsible parties for implementing risk treatment activities
- Responsible parties for overseeing coordinated activities among business units
- Guidelines for reporting and transparency of risk activities
- Guidelines for the risk program evaluation process, including a timeline for evaluation (e.g. annually, every five years, etc.). In some cases, it may be more appropriate to recommend a risk program evaluation following major events that can signal major changes in the operating environment. Examples of major events include changes in political leadership and associated initiatives, advancements in technology capabilities, political conflicts, changes in organizational leadership/ownership, etc.
- Guidelines for effective governance/oversight of risk activities. This oversight should carefully monitor effectiveness, support internal auditing, and promote transparency of risk practices. This oversight should also include continuous improvement and re-evaluation of risk program.

The risk program defined above requires that the program is supported by all levels of organizational leadership, includes adequate coordination of activities, and ensures that risk goals are recognized and maintained. The risk program, as part of larger ERM activities is a management process that involves stakeholders from all levels of the organization. While it cannot operate alone as a standalone process, it should instead be embedded into all business processes.

3.5 A taxonomy of ERM maturity

This section introduces a taxonomy of ERM maturity in an organization. It is based on three levels of maturity, *Beginner*, *Intermediate*, and *Advanced* maturity levels. While the overall ERM principles are the same for all three maturity levels, increased levels of maturity involve more sophisticated approaches. The assumption is that organizations that are new to risk management practices start at the *Beginner* level. Then, with experience and increased resources, organizations can achieve higher levels of maturity.

Table 3.1 presents the taxonomy of ERM maturity. The types of maturity are defined by the following types of characteristics: *Resources* in the organization

Table 3.1 Taxonomy of ERM maturity

	Characteristic	Beginner	Intermediate	Advanced
Resources				
	R.1. Dedicated risk manager		✓	✓
	R.2 Dedicated risk management business unit (proportional to size/importance of organization)			✓
	R.3 Documented risk guidelines and policies, available to all organizational stakeholders			✓
	R.4 Clear and detailed risk strategies (risk-informed strategies, cautionary/precautionary/robustness/resilience strategies, and discursive strategies)	✓	✓	✓
	R.5 Resources for regular risk management benchmarking and reporting		✓	✓
Expertise				
	E.1 Some employees trained on risk management practices	✓	✓	✓
	E.2 All employees trained on risk management practices, with training aligned with each role's function in risk management processes		✓	✓
Culture				
	C.1. Agreement among board and other leadership on the organization's risk appetite	✓	✓	✓
	C.2 Regular assessment and accountability at all levels of the organization, to ensure risk policies are properly implemented	✓	✓	✓
	C.3 Risk perception studies to identify major risk concerns, including social, cultural and psychological factors in risk judgment		✓	✓
	C.4 Implementation of open, transparent and timely risk communication procedures	✓	✓	✓
	C.5 Invite feedback from stakeholders engaged in the risk practices and incorporate in risk policies as needed	✓	✓	✓
Practices				
	P.1 Meets local and industry-specific regulations	✓	✓	✓

(Continued)

Table 3.1 (Continued)

Characteristic	Beginner	Intermediate	Advanced
P.2 Meets local and industry-specific non-regulatory risk and safety guidelines	✓	✓	✓
P.3 Knowledge-dependent prioritization of risk informed by formal tools	✓	✓	✓
P.4 Formal procedures for balancing risk concerns, such as cost-benefit methods		✓	✓
P.5 Formal procedures for identifying appropriate risk control, risk treatment and risk response strategies that are in agreement with the overall risk appetite of the organization		✓	✓
P.6 Active stakeholder involvement in risk management processes		✓	✓
P.7 Formal processes for assessing risk for high uncertainty and black swan surprises			✓
P.8 Continuously monitor and audit the ERM process, while adapting to changing conditions and stakeholder feedback	✓	✓	✓

that are responsible for ERM; *Expertise* that is gained through training; *Culture* that involves organizational support for ERM and the creation of a risk-conscious workforce; and *Practices* involving the ERM procedures in place. In the table, each characteristic is followed by a check mark, designating whether the presence of that characteristic is deemed to be at the *Beginner, Intermediate,* or *Advanced* level. Some characteristics may apply to multiple maturity levels.

Each maturity characteristic is described as follows:

Resources: Mature ERM processes require a variety of resources including personnel, technology and documentation. The necessary resources to oversee ERM tasks are typically proportional to the size of the organization. Larger organizations may have the ability to devote more dedicated resources to ERM tasks. However, smaller organizations can also achieve ERM maturity by adopting the practices outlined in Table 3.1, and by having some cohort of organizational members be fully or partially responsible for overseeing ERM tasks.

A first and critical responsibility for ERM leaders is to develop a set of documented risk guidelines and policies that are agreed upon by organizational leaders. The guidelines and policies should include formalization of the characteristics described in Table 3.1. This documentation should also include the organization's risk strategies, with reference to the use of risk assessments, cautionary/precautionary/robustness/resilience strategies, as well as discursive strategies. These guidelines and policies should be clear and available to all relevant stakeholders, including the board, executives, managers and other decision-makers. The resources should also have in place policies/guidelines for risk benchmarking and reporting that are available to all members of the organization.

Expertise: Ideally, all members of the organization should be trained on all risk management guidelines and policies. However, it is often impractical to do this in organizations with wide ranges of responsibilities. Instead, we suggest that the most mature organizations tailor ERM training with each role in the organization. For example, it is most important for executive leadership to be trained on understanding high-level risk strategies, with particular focus on expressing the overarching values of the organization, how those values translate into the risk appetite, and how the values and risk appetite factor into major decisions and investments. Field level members of the organization may instead be trained on actionable risk decisions, such as involving quality control, occupational safety and emergency response training.

Culture: Risk culture is here understood as shared beliefs, norms, values and practices with respect to risk in an organization. A strong risk culture relies on wide organizational support of risk policies. An important step in achieving support of risk policies is to include organizational perspectives in the policy-making process. These organizational perspectives may be widely varying, such that consensus is not obtained. However, disagreement and debate can allow for effective decision-making and problem-solving (Hong and Page 2004).

In addition to meeting Resource R.5 (benchmarking and reporting), it is important for the risk culture to embrace risk accountability by having policies in place to address any lapses in risk practices, while also following organizational policies and regulatory policies for whistleblowing. The regular use of risk perception studies can be used to identify major risk concerns while also resonating the importance of risk-consciousness throughout the organization. These studies may be conducted in an anonymous manner to allow for confidentiality. They can also be conducted in group settings in various business units. Results of these studies can later be used to articulate social, cultural, and psychological values when making risk judgments. The most risk-conscious organizations will regularly communicate risk policies and practices in an open, transparent and timely manner.

Practices: As a minimum requirement, it is important to meet local and industry-specific risk and safety regulations. In addition, there are many local and industry-specific non-regulatory risk and safety guidelines an organization may choose to follow, including ISO standards. Current risk standards should be used with care as their scientific bases vary considerably. Risk matrices are, for example, commonly used in practice, but there are strong arguments that this practice is dangerous and misleading. Instead, we suggest the use of methods described in Chapter 2, including the extended risk matrix that covers consequences, likelihood and the strength of knowledge supporting the likelihood judgments, as discussed in Section 2.2.4.

Many organizations have already-existing procedures for balancing risk concerns, such as cost-benefit methods. As Section 3.1 and Chapter 7 describe, cost-benefit analyses do not adequately reflect risk and uncertainties. These analyses require decision-makers to assign a monetary value to aspects such as the value of a statistical life (VSL). For example, the US Department of Transportation uses this term aimed at instituting a common monetary value for fatalities, while also applying a fraction of VSL computation for various types of injuries. Applications also include monetization of travel time savings and air pollutant emissions for various transportation investments (US Department of Transportation 2016).

As part of the risk prioritization process, organizations should adopt formal procedures for identifying appropriate risk management strategies that are in agreement with the overall risk appetite of the organization. All risk decisions should be informed by relevant stakeholder involvement, such as from the board and executive leadership. It is also important to include input from other levels of the organization, and possibly from local communities, with recognition that policies will impact and require support from a broad variety of stakeholders. Maturity can also involve formal processes for assessing risk for high uncertainty and black swan surprises, as described in Chapter 5 of this book.

4 Distinguishing between ERM and Task (project) Risk Management (TRM)

Consider the following goals specified in a company:

a) Increasing the value next year by 10% compared to this year
b) A specific production loss due to equipment failures and repairs

Such formulations are to a large extent motivated by the common use of Management By Objectives (MBO) and standards such as the ISO 31000 standard on risk management which defines risk in relation to objectives (risk is the effect of uncertainties on objectives) – see discussion in Section 2.1.

Now suppose the company considers an objective of say 15% value increase next year instead of 10%. Enterprise risk can be defined in relation to the value increase. We can also define risk in relation to b). However, care has to be shown as the change from 10% to 15% in a) could cause higher risks and uncertainties in meeting criterion b). There is clearly a hierarchy of objectives, and concentrating on risk management in the sense of meeting objectives without understanding this hierarchy could lead to poor results, in the sense that the risk management on a lower organizational level could show excellent results and meet all goals, but has not contributed to the main overall performance and objectives of the organization.

Often there is a weak, or no clear, link between the principal objective and the sub-goals in the organization. In addition, interdependencies between goals could generate inconsistencies and lower levels of performance than expected. Increasing the ambition set for the overall performance of the organization may lead to higher risk seen in relation to lower-level objectives. In the following, this challenge is described in more detail, applying the analysis and framework developed by Aven and Aven (2015).

4.1 A framework for ERM

We divide the risk into three categories: enterprise risk, task risk and personal risk; see Figure 4.1. For the enterprise risk, the deviation is explicitly expressed through the impact dimensions defined by the enterprise – here, change in monetary value and occurrence of incidents. In the coming discussion, we assume a value generating enterprise with principal objectives formulated in relation to monetary values and occurrences of incidents, but the concepts and

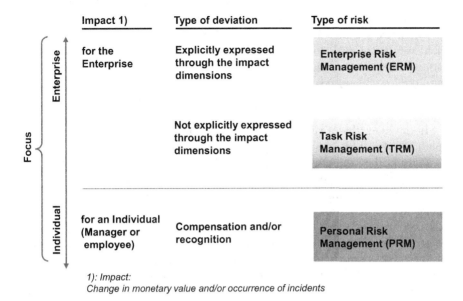

Figure 4.1 Types of risks and risk management

Source: Aven and Aven 2015

analysis are relevant for all organizations with possibly different types of principal and strategic objectives.

For the task, the deviation is not directly expressed through these impact
dimensions - the deviation could for example be linked to delays in a project.
For the personal risk, the deviation is linked to compensation and/or recognition. Distinguishing between these types of risk is essential in order to be able
to understand the incentives behind the risk management.

In ERM the focus is the enterprise and its principal objectives. A number
of tasks/projects are carried out in the enterprise, but the risks and related
deviations are not explicitly linked to these impact dimensions. We speak about
TRM. The long-term aim of these tasks/projects could be to contribute to
meeting the principal objectives, but as discussed above, there is not always a
clear link between the task goals and these impacts. In some cases, we may even
experience the tasks having a negative influence on the principal objectives of
the enterprise. We speak about goal-induced actions when the TRM induces
actions aimed at satisfying the project goals.

In addition, we use the concept of personal risk and PRM. A manager may,
for example, have a goal of increasing his/her income by 50%, and the satisfaction of this goal is seen as dependent on meeting a specific task goal. It could
also be that a bonus scheme is directly linked to the achievement of specific
goals for which the manager is responsible.

The PRM is not a formal part of the management of an enterprise, but, as
it could strongly affect the TRM and ERM, it needs to be given due attention.

The challenge is to design the enterprise's incentive scheme to ensure consistency between the PRM and the TRM/ERM.

Often we see that ERM is juxtaposed with managing risk related to the achievement of goals and objectives. Such a perspective is, however, problematic as there is not a one-to-one relationship between the principal objectives and the lower-level goals. In line with our terminology, if you cannot explicitly express the goal through the impact dimensions of the enterprise, it is not ERM, but TRM.

In the hierarchy of risk management types, the ERM must always overrule both TRM and PRM in order to ensure fulfilment of the principal objectives.

Current thinking on performance and risk management do not capture the above conflicts. Strategic objectives are set as desired future states, actions are put in place to move towards these objectives and the deliveries are measured via Key Performance Indicators (KPIs). Based on the measured KPIs, actions are put into effect to increase the probability of meeting the objectives and increase performance. This approach is also supported by the ISO 31000 where risk is defined as the effect of uncertainty on objectives. Thus, risk is linked to the achievement of objectives. An example may illustrate the point: Company X states that their future desired state is to have a strong market position and actions have been put in place to increase the probability to reach the objective. The progress is measured by market share in % (the KPI). The underlying principal objective is still to create value, but when actions are decided, the principal objective has no or little impact. Increasing the market share becomes a goal in itself and the risk management is about increasing the probability to achieve the goal. The typical question in this approach is: "What is threatening the goal fulfillment?"

In this approach a more holistic process is sought – the decisions have to be checked against the principal objectives, i.e. higher market share is not necessarily good if it does not create value or another level of market shares of the products are more profitable. By this holistic approach, the strategic objectives will have to be seen in relation to the principal objectives in order to reduce any conflicts of interests. The principal objectives are set at the highest level in the organization and will normally remain unchanged over time, while the strategic objectives will change over time.

The process is similar to the quality circle (Plan, Do, Check, Act) in quality management (Deming 2000). When the process issues – the Plan-Do-Check-Act – relate to enterprise risk, the performance management is also ERM. However, many performance management activities are not ERM, as shown above. The risk management process is, nevertheless, in line with ISO 31000. This interplay between the performance process and the risk management process is critical for the development of the enterprise. Disconnected processes will easily lead to KPIs which have weak links to the principal objectives. Figure 4.2 illustrates current practice versus the recommended approach on how we suggest ERM should be accomplished. In current practice the KPIs often become goals themselves and the risk management is about increasing the probability for achieving the targeted KPI. The link to the principal objectives

Figure 4.2 Current versus proposed focus in ERM

Source: Aven and Aven 2015

is often weak or missing, but in the approach described here the focus is on how actions can increase the likelihood of achieving the strategic objectives in a value creation perspective. Thus, "sub-optimal" risk management decisions can be avoided.

4.2 The ship metaphor

Figure 4.3 presents a ship metaphor to illustrate the relationship between performance and risk. Specifically, the purpose of the model is to provide an improved understanding of the linkages between TRM and ERM and to use this insight to provide guidance on how to best structure and plan the management of an enterprise in situations involving risk and uncertainties.

Based on the ambition level, risk appetite and strategic considerations the enterprise decides on its strategic objectives. Questions like "What does success look like?" and "Where are we going?" are important questions to answer when stating ambition level. It must also be assured that the concrete strategic objectives are in line with the principal objectives. The risk appetite expresses the amount of risk the enterprise intends to take in pursuing value creating opportunities (Aven 2013b, Appendix B). Running a business involves taking risks, thus the risk appetite is about risk/reward considerations. Finally, the strategy for achieving state III has to be worked out.

The point of departure for the model is thus an enterprise that is planning for some future activities based on its strategic objectives. The consideration will conclude in concrete strategic objectives stating the future desired position, e.g., a profitable market leader within its core activities or a profitable player

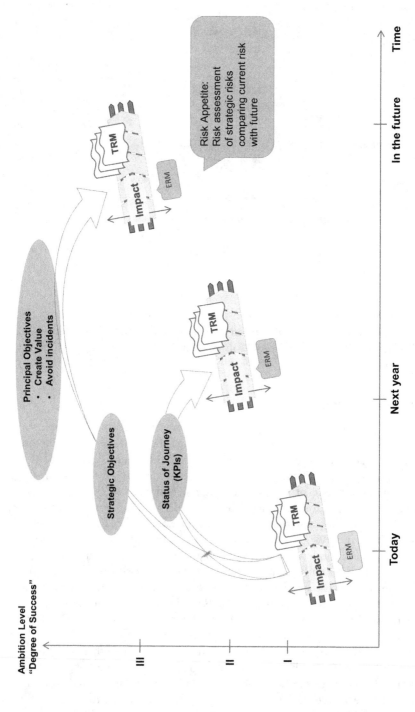

Figure 4.3 The ship metaphor describing the links between performance and risk

Source: Aven and Aven 2015

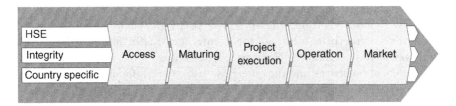

Figure 4.4 A model of the value chain of an enterprise, with risk themes (access, maturing, etc.) and specific risks crossing the value chain (HSE, etc.)

Source: Aven and Aven 2015

with a certain portfolio mix of assets in a specified risk and reward balance. The KPIs are specified in order to measure the development towards achievement of the strategic objectives, e.g., market share in % (focus on increases) or %-share in pre-defined asset classes (focus on specific classes). These KPIs are often also supplemented by specific points in time as targets, e.g. market share of x% within 20XX.

The enterprise is represented by a ship having the form of the value chain of Figure 4.4, with arrows indicating that there is uncertainty about the outcomes of the activities, upwards and downwards. ERM is about managing all of the organization's risks related to its activities in the value chain, and in order to ensure completeness, the risks could be sorted in risk themes covering all activities in the whole value chain. These themes could, for example, cover: access, project maturation, project execution, operation and market, as shown in Figure 4.4. In addition, in order to capture specific risks going across the value chain, risk themes such as HSE, integrity and country specific risks could be used.

To utilize the capabilities of the organization and to increase the value of the enterprise, the top level in the organization develops strategic objectives, which are aimed at transferring the performance of the enterprise from the level today (I) "to the next level" some years in the future, level III (the level represents the future desired position). The ship is consequently moved upwards in the figure reflecting the degree of success related to its ambition level. Currently, the ship is sailing at a certain speed towards ambition level I (the speed represents the pace of which the target is met), but if the strategic objectives are implemented, the ship will change course towards ambition level III and adjust its speed in order to reach the target within 20XX.

Assessments of these changes in the position and speed of the ship need to be carried out to support the top management's strategic decision-making. What are the events that can threaten the changes, what are the consequences of these events, and what about uncertainties and likelihoods? Furthermore, we also need in advance to assess the risks in the new position at level III; how will they change compared to the current level and is the new position in line with the stated risk appetite? This risk assessment could lead to changes in the ambition level and strategic objectives.

ERM is about managing the enterprise risk, i.e. deviations from reference levels for the enterprise value and the occurrence of HSE and integrity events and associated uncertainties. The strategic objectives should be consistent with the principal objectives, and the enterprise risk can thus focus on deviations in the ship's position, relative to the plans established, as well as on possible deviations in the value development at specific positions. A concrete example could be the deviation from the strategic objective of being a profitable market player with a certain market share increase in the years to come (measured by KPIs). To describe the risk, probabilities would typically be used to express the uncertainties and degrees of belief, supplemented by judgments about the strength of knowledge on which the probabilities are based. While we are sailing, we will also have enterprise risks originating from the value chain activities, and these may result in risk-induced actions in line with risk appetite policies and other relevant criteria and targets.

During the journey, the performance will typically be monitored using KPIs, see Figure 4.3. At a specific point in time they may, for example, reveal that the ship seems to be on the wrong course, and actions are required. This is TRM, but it is also ERM when assessing the risks in the ERM impact dimensions. A number of TRM activities are carried out to ensure that specific tasks are executed and meet defined objectives, plans, etc. Some of these activities are TRM, but not ERM, as the deviations addressed are not directly linked to the principal objectives of monetary value and incidents. ERM must always have priority over TRM as the principal objectives are more important than the TRM goals. The goals of the TRM are only indirectly linked to the ship's course and speed and could be "sub-optimal" in relation to the principal objectives. In the example above, the strategic objective states being a profitable market player while the KPIs measure progress on market share and timing only. Even if these KPIs are indicators only, they often become targets. In a TRM perspective, the focus will then be to decide on risk adjusting actions to increase the probability of reaching these KPI targets. In an ERM context, this decision could easily be "sub-optimal" because a more profitable solution exists and the KPIs should be revisited. To avoid a "sub-optimal" TRM, the goal hierarchy has to be defined and understood – in our example a better solution for the enterprise could be to change the targets for the KPIs somewhat to ensure a better decision from a ERM perspective.

To ensure that ERM actually overrules the TRM perspective in an enterprise, its governing documentation must define both these risk management approaches and a prioritization rule (the ERM overrule property) must be clearly formulated. The top management has to confirm the approach in the decision-making – at this level the risk management focus is always on the enterprise (ERM) and not task or personal objectives as in TRM and PRM, respectively. The ISO 31000 – with its risk concept linked to objectives – does not address this challenge of ERM, but by adding the ERM overrule property, the desired focus on achievement of principal objectives can also be ensured when adopting the ISO perspective.

4.3 Cases showing why ERM must overrule TRM

We consider a case from the oil industry to illustrate some of the issues raised in the previous section. The executive committee and board of an international oil company are looking into how to create value for the shareholders, and alternative strategic objectives are being discussed and evaluated. Two formulations of strategic objectives are considered: "build a globally competitive oil company" and "create value as an upstream and midstream oriented and technology-based energy company". Let us assume that the latter strategic objective has been chosen and a portfolio of investment projects is planned to be executed in order to fulfil the objective. The Business Areas in the oil company assess investment proposals according to profitability criteria and relevance to strategic objectives. The entity in the company responsible for securing a good and consistent investment decision basis is defined as the Asset Owner.

A final decision has been made by the Asset Owner to realize an investment project by performing detail design, construction and preparation for operations. The construction will be delivered by an in-house Delivery entity. The two main elements that need to be constructed are the facilities (platforms, subsea solutions, etc.) and the wells (drilling and well). We denote these as Facilities and D&W. In the overall plan, a date for when the asset can produce oil and gas is set and a delivery agreement is signed between the suppliers (Delivery entities Facilities and D&W) and the Asset Owner. The main objectives of the Delivery entities are then to deliver on time, cost and quality (the task).

In line with the ship metaphor, the Asset Owner represents the enterprise which decided to realize an investment project as one element in the fulfillment of its strategic objectives. The Asset Owner has the overview on how the execution of this project creates value for the enterprise and which risk management decisions that support it. The KPIs are set to reflect delivery on time, cost and quality. The enterprise has a portfolio of such projects going on all the time which aims to fulfill the strategic objectives and corresponding value creation.

In order to manage the risk related to the assigned task, the Delivery entity performs a TRM where the impact dimensions are expressed as deviation from the task and not expressed through the enterprise's impact dimensions. The Asset Owner manages the risk according to ERM principles, i.e. deciding upon risk adjusting actions using a cost-benefit approach for creating value in monetary terms for the enterprise, and paying due attention to relevant risks and uncertainties, in particular related to the major incidents. For this purpose, the Asset Owner needs to get relevant risk information from the Delivery entities.

Let us assume that the Delivery entities shall execute their tasks within 1 January Year 3 and both have to finish their tasks for the project to be able to start production from this date. During Year 1 the Facilities has received new information and has realized that the schedule will be tight or almost impossible to meet – their risk assessment shows a high probability for not reaching the target (the Delivery entity's impact dimension). An updated estimate for delivery date without any further adjusting actions is three months delay, i.e. 1 April Year 3. We can simplify this situation for the Facilities by assuming that they face only two main decision alternatives:

a) increase manpower significantly to accelerate progress to finalize within original delivery date (increase cost considerably); or
b) focus strongly on critical lines and avoid any further delays.

The goals have already been set for the Facility management and a compensation scheme has been attached to it. The incentives for alternative a) are then strong – both for fulfilment of the task and compensation to the Facility management. The risk management approaches here are TRM and PRM.

In a narrow risk management context, i.e. risk is related to meeting the objectives, the Facility management is doing exactly what it should do; it decides to go for alternative a) since this alternative reduces the probability for not delivering according to the agreed task delivery.

However, in an ERM context, the risk management incentives at project and project manager level could be in conflict with the interest of the enterprise. The Asset Owner performs ERM and manages risk where the impact dimensions are seen relative to the enterprise. The Asset Owner has to broaden up the considerations and take into account aspects not covered by the task management. A key question to ask for the ERM is whether more cost should be incurred in order to increase the probability of meeting the strategic objective. It turned out in this case that the D&W was also delayed (with an estimate of at least 6–9 months) and the ERM decision would then obviously be to go for alternative b) (no need to accelerate Facilities when D&W is even more delayed) since this is in the interest of the enterprise and its shareholders – as opposed to the "optimal" decision of the TRM and PRM.

Returning to the ship metaphor, the TRM would indicate a need for a changed course for the Facilities due to the KPIs showing the delay. Following the ERM perspective, the change in course observed is not large and no strong change of the course is needed. The change in course required by the TRM would be costly and not in line with the ERM objectives. Hence the course of the ship is not adjusted as requested by the TRM.

The KPIs from the D&W would also show negative signs due to the delay and generate similar decision alternatives as above (a) and (b). Since the focus of the Delivery entities is the agreed delivery and risks related to the task, they can only do TRM. However, it is crucial that important and relevant risk information flows from the Delivery entities to the Asset Owner enabling them to do ERM. The Asset Owner conducts then a risk assessment of the relevant activities in the context of the principal objectives, and, based on a judgment of the overall performance and risk related to the delay and increased cost, it finds that case a) is the preferred alternative. For oil projects, delays are often very costly in value terms due to the NPV effect from the whole revenue stream being shifted in time. The ERM related to the D&W delay may thus require a change in the ship course.

The hierarchy of objectives is important in the risk management – the ERM has to overrule the TRM to ensure "optimal" risk management decisions. Managing the risk related to the tasks with their focus on meeting their "local" objectives, must be executed with care. Reducing risk and uncertainties on the TRM level must always be seen in relation to the ERM objectives. This requires great flexibility and coordination in the organizations as decisions need to be made to simplify the management of complex activities. The key here is to highlight the different types of risk faced and acknowledge that the really important risk is the enterprise performance and risk, and not the task performance and risk. TRM is a just a tool in ERM. The effectiveness of the TRM is dependent on a well-functioning ERM to ensure parallel incentives since the Delivery entities only see the TRM dimension and cannot optimize on behalf of the enterprise. To prevent "sub-optimal" risk management the Delivery entities have to rely on relevant and updated delivery goals at all times from the ERM.

In Year 1, when the Asset Owner realizes that the ship is out of course, necessary actions will be decided to get it on track again, based on the information then available. A revised course is specified to support the fulfilment of the current strategic objectives. The revised course includes updated delivery goals to reflect the new realities, and risk assessments are carried out to support decisions on new risk adjusting actions, supporting both principal objectives and revised task objectives.

Here is another oil industry case that illustrates the ship metaphor and differences between TRM and ERM; it is related to one of the core activities – exploration. The chosen strategic objective was as above to "create value as an upstream and midstream oriented and technology-based energy company". Drilling cost is identified as a core parameter in this and KPI targets are set, e.g. drilling cost per meter at X. This KPI is seen as a good indicator supporting both the principal and strategic objectives.

However, a further look into the case would reveal that the TRM of achieving the chosen KPI target could have negative impact on the principal objectives. One-dimensional focus on drilling cost does not capture the differences in complexity of wells and prospectivity. In the TRM, risk adjusting actions increasing the probability for reaching the cost targets will be appreciated, while in the ERM, the creating value dimension and the balance risk versus reward will be added, i.e. more expensive wells could be preferred due to the attractiveness in the reservoir. The ERM and TRM could easily imply opposite decisions and the ERM overrule property should then apply. The ship metaphor highlights the importance of the ship position – the state relative to the strategic and principal objectives, and how the TRM and KPIs can be more or less linked to these objectives. The KPI in this case was only partly able to reflect the ship's position.

A third example is the oil company's earlier focus on reserves or production as strategic objectives. All actions increasing the probability for achieving stated targets for oil reserve or production were appreciated risk management activities. The risk management decisions were primarily goal-induced and as such would have been categorized as TRM since the link to the ERM impact dimension value creation is unclear. Even though the individual decisions could create value, it is not clear how to ensure maximum value creation of the portfolio of projects if the primary focus is on reserve or production growth and not maximum value. In an ERM context the interaction between strategic and principal objectives would influence the risk management decision and ensuring maximum value creation of the portfolio. This portfolio may not be the same as the one that satisfies reserve or production targets.

4.4 Discussion

Ideally, the aim is that every sub-goal supports the principal objectives, but in real life the linkages could be indirect or even lacking completely if the sub-goals have not been calibrated well enough. The statement "no goal, no risk" is a common misconception used in this context: if goals have not been formulated, there are no risks, as there is no reference for judging the degree of compliance. However, deviation needs not only to be considered in relation to goals. What we need is a reference value, and this could be delivery according to a specific project plan or just the normal or planned production level. If the risk is related to such a normal production level, we get focus on high and low values, not only whether the production meets a specific target level.

For an enterprise, it is essential to be considered competitive, for example being cost-efficient, as this makes the company more attractive as a partner and increases its profit opportunities. The cost development over time can be measured using various performance indices and hopefully they will show a positive trend. Some of the cost cutting could have a negative impact on principal objectives linked to safety and security, and thus care has to be shown in managing the activities to avoid unacceptable safety and security levels. To control the safety and security levels, risk studies have to be performed that see beyond the expected net present value calculations and highlight the probabilities of occurrences of these events, the strength of knowledge of the probability assignments and potential surprises, as discussed in the previous chapters.

As the example about drilling costs showed, the understanding of the drivers of the performance measures is an important element of the risk management. A reduction in the production unit cost does not necessarily support the principal objective of creating value, i.e. higher profits. If the focus is to reach a certain unit cost level, this can be achieved by being more cost-efficient, and, everything else being equal, this would generate value. However, the goal could also be achieved by prioritizing fields with a low degree of complexity, for example low-cost production wells. The latter will certainly show a lower production cost per barrel produced, but this strategy need not be the best alternative when it comes to value creation. The strategy could mean lost opportunities compared to a strategy based on complex wells which could have a large potential for high rewards. A risk management approach focusing on uncertainty on non-principal objectives only (e.g. unit cost level) without considering the principal objectives of the enterprise could easily imply sub-optimization and value destruction. For example, the risk assessment would typically show lower downside probability for a strategy a) going for plain vanilla wells compared with a strategy b) adopting complex wells. Combining this with a stronger background knowledge for the risk assessment in the a) strategy, it is likely that this strategy will be chosen. However, as stressed above, such a perspective is too narrow – the principal ERM objectives need to be taken into account, both when it comes to risk and reward.

ERM and MBO at the highest level, or MBO with a clear link to principal objectives, are consistent activities. Often MBO has no direct link to value creation, and risk management in this context is by definition TRM. An enhanced MBO approach can be developed by looking beyond the TRM results and focusing on holistic performance evaluation. However, to ensure that the TRM is in line with the ERM, the key question to ask is, as discussed and illustrated by the above case: "does the TRM-induced action support the principal objectives of the enterprise?" This is a question the top management in an enterprise must consider before the action is taken and not in retrospect as part of a performance review. Processes need to be established where the TRM goals are seen in relation to the goals of the ERM. Top-level risk committees could play an important role here to discuss such questions and influencing the enterprise to ensure consistency between MBOs and ERM.

4.5 Conclusions

We have discussed risk in relation to strategic objectives and performance management in an enterprise risk setting. We have presented and discussed a set-up and model for describing the links between performance and risk, using the metaphor of a ship, where the ship is loaded with cash-generating activities and has a direction over time determined by the overall strategic objectives. To obtain clarity in communication about risk in the enterprise and to ensure the right approach in supporting the enterprise principal objectives, we recommend the use of the terms "Enterprise Risk Management", "Task Risk Management" and "Personal Risk Management", defined as in Section 4.1. The enterprise risk is defined by deviations from reference values expressed through the impact dimensions of the principal objectives (change in monetary value and occurrence of incidents), and associated uncertainties. The TRM is to be seen as a tool supporting the ERM. The TRM, as well as the PRM, must be carefully supervised to see that it leads to the desired results meeting the enterprise's principal objectives, i.e. the ERM has to overrule both the TRM and PRM in the management of an enterprise.

Hierarchies and different type of management levels in an ERM context are not new. However, the ERM–TRM–PRM scheme here suggested with its risk conceptualization and characterizations based on deviations from relevant reference values, and associated uncertainties, represent a new way of thinking for the management of such organizations. Current risk management perspectives, for example based on ISO 31000 and COSO have different building blocks and are not in the same way highlighting the "sub-optimization of risk" associated with the MBO thinking in an enterprise. Compared to the suggested approach here presented, these standards and the current ERM practice place less emphasis on the knowledge dimension. Probability is used to describe uncertainties without incorporating the strength of knowledge that these probabilities are based on. By the same token, decision analysis and portfolio theory do not represent an alternative to the approach here presented. A pure probability-based approach with specified utility functions is inadequate for supporting decisions in an ERM context as here studied. See also discussion in Chapter 7.

5 Potential surprises and the unforeseen (black swans)

It is now common to hear people referring to a "black swan" when a surprising or unforeseen event occurs; this metaphor was made popular by Nassib Talib through his book, *The Black Swan*, in 2007 (Taleb 2007). We need metaphors to make our field and science interesting and relevant for people, and the "black swan" metaphor does exactly that. The effect is in fact remarkable. It quickly leads us into reflections of what risk actually is, how we can assess and describe risk and what the limitations are when measuring risk using historical data and traditional methods based on available knowledge. It also makes us rapidly see the importance of reading signals and being resilient in case something surprising should occur. A black swan is not an excuse for not intervening and reducing risk; rather, it is a means to get the right focus – to extend the risk management beyond narrow risk assessments and their follow-up and use new and creative approaches for assessing and handling the risk.

The black swan metaphor motivates further discussions and analysis of the knowledge supporting the judgements, the beliefs and assumptions. As argued for in this book, current risk analysis practice pays too little attention to these aspects of risk. The knowledge aspect of risk is not sufficiently incorporated in the methods and techniques used. There is a common belief that probability is sufficient for expressing uncertainties, but this idea fails to acknowledge that any probability used to express uncertainties is conditional on some knowledge. The strength and correctness of this knowledge need to be given attention, not only the probabilities, as discussed in Section 2.2.

Some risk analysts would like to restrict the black swan metaphor to unknown unknowns – events that nobody has experienced before they occur. However, such an understanding of the metaphor would make it more or less uninteresting, as such events are so rare. The attractiveness of the black swan concept is that it relates to something that we face daily: that surprising events occur relative to our knowledge. It is a main aspect of risk, and we need to improve current risk analysis methods to better meet this type of risk.

In this chapter we look closer into the black swan metaphor, and the processes that it focuses on. First in Section 5.1 we look closer at the concept of black swans. The we discuss how to assess and manage these types of events. The chapter is partly based on Aven (2013c, 2015b, 2015d, 2018b) and Khorsandi and Aven (2019).

5.1 Clarification of concepts. Different types of surprises

In this book, a black swan is understood as a surprising, extreme event relative to one's knowledge/beliefs, and can be of different types: a) unknown unknowns, b) unknown knowns (we do not have the knowledge but others do) and c) events that are judged to have a negligible probability of occurrence and thus are not believed to occur (Aven 2015b). We will motivate and discuss this terminology and basis in the following.

Taleb (2007) refers to a black swan as an event with the following three attributes. Firstly, it is an outlier, as it lies outside the realm of regular expectations, because nothing in the past can convincingly point to its possibility. Secondly, it carries an extreme impact. Thirdly, in spite of its outlier status, human nature makes us concoct explanations for its occurrence after the fact, making it explainable and predictable. The essential point for the discussion in this book is the second criterion, which is considered in line with the definition of a black swan referred to above.

There are strong feelings associated with the use of the black swan metaphor among professionals working with risk. A main discussion point is what type of events the black swans should capture. The essential point is, however, not the term black swan but how to get increased focus on and properly meet potential surprises and the unforeseen. As will be shown below our basic ideas are in line with the origin of the metaphor and that of Taleb. As mentioned in the introduction of this chapter the metaphor would be far less interesting if we restricted it to unknown unknowns only. We could have chosen to refer to different nuances of black swans (pure black, light black, black gray, etc), but that would not change the message and the motivation for introducing the metaphor; to get an increased focus on the "risk" not captured by the standard probabilistic approaches to risk assessment and management.

Professor Dennis Lindley, one of the strongest advocators of the Bayesian approach to probability, statistics and decision-making, has been very clear on the use of the black swan metaphor (Lindley 2008): Taleb talks nonsense; the calculus of probability is adequate for all kind of uncertainty and randomness. Lindley presents an example where he considers a sequence of independent trials with a constant unknown chance of success, and he shows that a black swan (failure of trial) is almost certain to arise if you are to see a lot of swans, although the probability that the next swan observed is white (success of trial) is nearly one. Aven (2013) shows that this analysis is misleading, a key assumption made is not adequate, and that with another and more meaningful assumption, the probability of a black swan occurring in a huge population of swans is extremely small when the analyst has observed many white swans. Thus, the occurrence of a black swan will come as a big surprise relative to the probability assignments. Having in mind the origin of the metaphor (Taleb 2007; Aven 2013c), from the perspective of people of the Old World, the discovery of black swans in Australia came as a big surprise relative to their probability judgments. One could not rule out that black swans exist, but the probability based on the observations were miniscule. We would also here mention John Stuart Mill who argued in 1843 that regardless of how many white swans we observed, that still did not prove that black swans did not exist.

Hence the black swan was a surprise for us (people living in the Old World), but not for all (people living in Australia); it can be labelled as an unknown known (unknown to us, known to others), not an unknown unknown (unknown for all).

Alternatively we may argue as above that the probability, as seen from the perspective from the Old World, of a black swan occurring was so small that it was not believed to occur and that it consequently came as a big surprise when discovered in Australia; a big surprise relative to the available knowledge/beliefs.

Hence the metaphor is linked to surprises relative to our knowledge/beliefs. The occurrence of the surprising event need not be an unknown unknown – and it was not in the case of the black swans in Australia – as it was known by many people that swans could be black.

Taleb (2007) provides a number of examples of black swans:

> Just imagine how little your understanding of the world on the eve of the events of 1914 would have helped you guess what was to happen next. (Don't cheat by using the explanations drilled into your cranium by your dull high school teacher). How about the rise of Hitler and the subsequent war? How about the precipitous demise of the Soviet bloc? How about the rise of Islamic fundamentalism? How about the spread of the Internet? How about the market crash of 1987 (and the more unexpected recovery)? Fads, epidemics, fashion, ideas, the emergence of art genres and schools. All follow these Black Swan dynamics. Literally, just about everything of significance around you might qualify.
>
> (Taleb 2007, p. x)

Few or none of these events can be characterized as unknown unknowns, although they were not easy to foresee. Taleb also refers to the events on September 11, 2001, as a black swan. He writes

> Think of the terrorist attack of September 11, 2001: had the risk been reasonably *conceivable* on September 10, it would not have happened. If such a possibility were deemed worthy of attention, fighter planes would have circled the sky above the twin towers, airplanes would have had locked bulletproof doors, and the attack would not have taken place, period.
>
> (Taleb 2007, p. x)

An attack such as the one on September 11, was not a new type of event. It was not an unknown unknown. Clearly some (the terrorists) had the knowledge, showing that the event could be considered an unknown known, alternatively as a type c) event. Similar type of events had occurred before, see e.g. Bazerman and Watkins (2008) who discuss this in detail on pages 28–29. In 1998, a risk analysis was conducted for the Federal Aviation Administration (FAA) in the USA by two university experts where events like terrorists crashing planes into, inter alia, the World Trade Center and Pentagon were studied. And in 1999, Al Qaeda terrorists armed with knives hijacked an Indian airliner to Kandahar, Afghanistan. To remain in control during the hijacking, the terrorists cut the throat of a young passenger and let him bleed to death – a tactic that the September 11 terrorists are suspected to have used on flight attendants (Bazerman and Watkins 2008).

Hence, we can categorize the September 11 event both as an unknown known (type b)) and as a type c) – a known type of event but not believed to occur because of low judged probability.

As another example, take the bombings and killings in Oslo and at Utøya on July 22, 2011. These events were of course not unknown unknowns, they were unknown knowns in the sense that they were unknown to us and known by someone (the terrorist). But we could also say that they were black swans of type c) as we knew that a single person could do extreme events (solo terrorism), but we judged it to be so unlikely that we did not believe it would occur. We can apply the same type of reasoning for many other examples, like the demise of the Soviet bloc mentioned by Taleb. Of course, we knew that such an event could occur if we took a historical perspective on the rise and fall of states, but knowing when and how would be difficult. If we looked into the future in, say, 1985 and were to predict something about the future, we would say that the demise of the Soviet bloc could happen, but it would be very unlikely to occur during, say, the next 10 years. Given our knowledge, we would not believe it would occur. But it did occur, despite our beliefs.

The key idea of the work on black swans is to get the proper focus on such events. And we see that we are naturally led to the three categories a)-c) defined above.

This brings us to a discussion about why addressing black swans are important in risk management.

First, many events of this type – unknown knowns and events not believed to occur because of low judged probability – do in fact occur (e.g. September 11, 2001, July 22, 2011). Surprises occur relative to our knowledge/beliefs. Hence this type of event needs to be addressed. The black swan metaphor with the three categories a)-c) is helping us to get focus on this issue – that we can get surprising outcomes relative to our knowledge and beliefs. It is not an excuse for not doing anything – rather the opposite – namely to get focus on a special type of risk linked to our limited ability to foresee what can happen using methods that are more or less good in seeing what can happen.

Some examples from the oil and gas industry demonstrate this. In recent years we have experienced several incidents that nearly resulted in major accidents (e.g. NOG 2019). Some people in the organizations had the necessary knowledge to foresee and prevent these events, but not the ones who planned the critical operations and assessed their risk. The events were of the unknown knowns type or of type c), negligible probability – not believed to occur, from the point of view of the operating team. The incident shows the importance of addressing potential surprises relative to the present knowledge/beliefs. And that is what we seek to obtain by the focus on surprises and black swans. The assigned probabilities made by the operating personnel may show that the risk is negligible, but their risk understandings were based on poor knowledge about the system. The traditional risk matrix could show acceptable risk according to common procedures, but the risk matrix does not reveal this poor knowledge. This fact represents a challenge for the risk management, but we are confident that by increased focus on this type of risk, and by providing adequate concepts and methods, the related risk management can be improved. The focus on black swan type of events (a), b) and c)) goes hand in hand with an acknowledgment that the traditional probability-based approaches to risk analysis and management need to be extended to adequately take into account the knowledge and surprise dimensions of risk.

Think about the Deepwater Horizon accident as an example (see Aven 2015b). The accident was a result of a combination of events and conditions occurring, that probably came as a surprise to those involved in the management of the activity. In this case, this combination includes (NC 2011):

- Erroneous assessments of the results of pressure tests
- Failure to identify that the formation fluid penetrated the well, in spite of the fact that log data showed that this was the case
- The diverter system was unable to divert gas
- The cutting valve (Blind Shear Ram) in the BOP did not seal the well

The accident could be a black swan for them. It came as a surprise that such a sequence of events could occur; they had not thought of such a scenario. It is a black swan of type b). If they had thought of it, they would have concluded that it was so unlikely that one could ignore the scenario occurring. It would have been a black swan of type c).

Now let us take a macro perspective – looking at a large number of such activities, for example the whole oil industry. Risk is now linked to the occurrence of any major accident in the industry; where and how the event occurs is not the issue. A risk assessment is conducted. It is concluded that there is a relatively high probability that such an accident could occur. Thus, one cannot say that it is a black swan if such an event actually occurs. From a macro perspective, a realistic analysis would state that we must expect that a major accident will occur somewhere during the next 10 years. However, there is no law that expresses that it will actually happen. We are not subject to fate or destiny. Each unit (organization, company, installation) works hard to prevent such an accident from actually occurring. It is believed that with systematic safety work, this goal can be achieved. Accordingly, any such serious accident normally comes as a surprise (as discussed by, for example, Turner and Pidgeon 1997); it is a black swan for those involved in the operation and management of the activity. Hence, one must be careful in describing the perspective when discussing whether an event is a black swan. What is a black swan – a surprise – depends on whose knowledge/beliefs we refer to, refer also discussion in Aven (2016b).

5.2 Assessing and managing black swans

Black swan types of risk needs more attention, and the present book points to and highlights concepts, principles and methods for how we should think to obtain this. A key thesis is that by adopting the new risk perspectives as discussed in this book, there is a potential for improved understanding, assessment and management of risk, surprises and black swans. These perspectives can help analysts and decision-makers in providing appropriate concepts and a foundation for a deeper understanding of what the risk associated with surprises and the unforeseen (black swans) is all about. They also provide assessment and management principles that can prevent, or at least reduce the likelihood of, black swan type of events (which have undesirable consequences). In addition, they stimulate and lay a platform for the development of suitable methods that can achieve such an effect (Aven 2014, p. 207).

The easiest case relates to rare events where the uncertainties are small – the knowledge base is strong and accurate predictions can be conducted; i.e., the situation is characterized by "perfect storms" (Aven 2015b). For this type of issue and problem, standard risk assessment using statistical methods, as described, for example, by Paté-Cornell (2012), can be applied to make rational decisions, as seen for instance in the traffic and health areas. Unfortunately, few problems in practice can be seen as perfect storms; surprises and black swans may occur, and the challenge is how to meet this type of risk.

A number of management strategies are used for meeting surprises and black swans (Cox 2012; Renn 2008; Aven 2014), including adaptive risk analysis, robustness and resilience-based approaches. Adaptive analysis is founded on the acknowledgement that one best decision cannot be made, but rather a set of alternatives should be dynamically tracked to gain information and knowledge about the effects of different courses of action (Aven 2015b). On an overarching level, the basic process is straightforward: one chooses an action based on broad considerations of risk and other aspects, monitors the effect, and adjusts the action based on the monitored results (Linkov et al. 2006). Measures to improve robustness include (Renn 2008; Aven and Renn 2010) inserting conservatisms or safety factors as an assurance against variation, introducing redundant and diverse safety systems to meet multiple stress situations and establishing building codes and zoning laws to protect against specific hazards. See Joshi and Lambert (2011) for an example of such a "robust management strategy" using diversification of engineering infrastructure investments. Resilience is a protective strategy against unforeseen or unthinkable events, and key instruments for it include "the strengthening of the immune system, diversification of the means for approaching identical or similar ends, design of systems with flexible response options and the improvement of conditions for emergency management and system adaptation" (Aven and Renn 2010, p. 129).

We will discuss these strategies in more detail in the coming sections. They can be viewed as responding to the cautionary principle, as defined in Section 3.1. As an example of other types of such strategies, we will mention the substitution principle (Löfstedt 2014), which can be defined as:

> Substitution is the replacement of one substance by another with the aim of achieving a lower level of risk
>
> (CEFIC 2005, p. 1)

where "substance" is viewed in a broad sense. For situations with large uncertainties, we often face a dilemma: should we avoid or ban a substance that has an intrinsic ability to cause harm, or should we further examine it to reduce uncertainties and be able to produce more reliable predictions and avoid negative surprises? Ideally, we should of course perform thorough risk assessment – giving due attention to the uncertainties – but there is always a trade-off to be made. We need to find a proper balance between the desire for reducing risk and other concerns, such as costs and value generation. Finding the right balance is not a scientific issue, but about the weight to be given to the cautionary principle, refer to Chapter 7.

A number of specific assessment methods exist for identifying hazards and threats (e.g. HAZOP, HazId, Failure mode and effects analysis (FMEA)). These methods have been shown to be effective for many type of applications, but there is a potential for improvements as discussed in, for example, Aven (2014) and Zio (2018). Event identification represents a key part of risk assessment and management, as if the event is left out, the risk management will also easily leave it out. A non-traditional method worth mentioning here is anticipatory failure determination (AFD) (Kaplan et al. 1999; Aven 2014; Jensen and Aven 2018). It is a hazard/threat identification and analysis approach which uses so-called creative methods (e.g. I-TRIZ): Instead of asking, "How can this failure happen?", the AFD approach questions, "If I wanted to create this particular failure, how could I do it?" The strength of the method comes from the process of deliberately "inventing" failure events and scenarios (Masys 2012). Another commonly used method is scenario analysis (Chermack 2011). Here, there is no search for completeness and characterizations of uncertainties and risks as in traditional risk assessment. The anticipatory backwards scenarios are of special importance – starting from a future imagined state or event of the total system or activity considered, the question is asked: "What is needed for this to occur?" (Aven 2015b).

A key task of the risk assessment is to challenge more or less clear assumptions, hypotheses and explanations. A method often used for this purpose is red teaming, which serves as a devil's advocate, offering alternative interpretations and challenging established thinking (Masys 2012; Aven 2015b). For example, "businesses use red teams to simulate the competition; government organizations use red teams as 'hackers' to test the security of information stored on computers or transmitted through networks; the military uses red teams to address and anticipate enemy courses of action" (Ambrose and Ahern 2008, p. 136). Red teaming challenges assumptions, generalizations, pictures or images that influence how we understand the world and how we take action, i.e. our mental models (Senge 1990). An example of a how a red-team analysis can be used to improve a standard event (scenario) identification, is presented in Aven (2015b).

In addition, the quality discourse (quality management), with its link to "common-cause variation" and "special-cause variation", and the continuous focus on learning and improvements, needs to be mentioned when discussing approaches and methods handling surprises and black swans (Aven and Krohn 2014; Aven 2015b). The focus on improvements leads us to the concept of anti-fragility (Taleb 2012), which we will come back to in Chapter 6. According to Taleb, the antifragile is seen as a blueprint for living in a "black swan world", the key being to love randomness, variation and uncertainty to some degree, and thus also errors. To be in top shape and improve our bodies and minds, we know that there is a need for some stressors; the same is true for other activities and systems (Aven and Krohn 2014).

Here is a checklist for aspects to consider to ensure that the surprise dimension of risk is given due attention (Aven 2014, p. 208; NOG 2019):

1 Has an overview been provided of the assumptions made (concerning system, data, models, expert assessments, etc.)?
2 Has a risk assessment been conducted of deviations from the assumptions – an assumption deviation risk assessment (individually and by looking at combinations of variations from several assumptions simultaneously)? See Section 2.2.3.
3 Have efforts been made to reduce the risk contributions from the assumptions with the highest deviation risk?
4 Has the quality of the models used been assessed? Have the model errors (differences between the correct value and the outcome of the models) been found acceptable?
5 Has an assessment been made of the strength of the knowledge which forms the basis for the probabilities?
6 Is this strength incorporated in the risk description?
7 Have efforts been made to strengthen the knowledge where it is not considered strong?
8 Have special measures been adopted to identify unknown knowns?
9 Have special measures been adopted to identify possible weaknesses (gaps) in the knowledge which the analysis team has based its analysis on?
10 Have special measures been adopted to assess the validity of assessments where events are in practice ignored because of judged negligible probability?
11 Have people and expertise outside the analysis team been used to identify such conditions as those mentioned above?
12 If expected values of a certain quantity have been specified, has the uncertainty related to this quantity been assessed?

Confronting black swans is difficult as they extend beyond current knowledge, but there exist a number of different approaches, strategies and measures that can be applied to meet such events. In the following, we seek further insights by specifically addressing the three types of surprises (black swans) a)-c) referred to in this section. The discussion follows Khorsandi and Aven (2019) who build their analysis on a so-called High Reliability Organization (HRO) perspective.

5.2.1 Unknown unknowns

It is difficult to be prepared for unknown unknowns as these are events that were completely unknown. In general, resilience, as well as signals and warnings, provide useful general means, in addition to knowledge generation of relevant phenomena and processes. Increased knowledge will, as a general rule, reduce the probability of a black swan of this type. Testing and research are generic measures to confront this black swan type of risk.

While organizations cannot prepare for these events directly, they can, however, do so indirectly by shifting their focus from strategies aimed at improving predictive models to those that acknowledge the presence of uncertainties and aim to better manage them. By acknowledging the potential for surprises to occur that are rooted in causes that lie beyond our understanding, the focus of risk management efforts can then be directed at limiting a system's vulnerabilities to surprises so as to prevent them from becoming disasters.

Strategies for limiting a system's vulnerabilities – and thus enhancing their survivability – are typically of two types. The first involves designing systems that are tolerant to disruptions and otherwise ultimately reduce the consequences of their failure. This approach would focus on, as a matter of priority, uncovering the failure mechanisms of systems, the outcomes of their failures and ways to reduce the potential for such occurrences. Ideally, using this approach, we would like to develop systems that are immune to catastrophic failures, and thus black swans, by designing them to "fail gracefully rather than catastrophically" (La Porte 2006; see also Park et al. 2011, 2013; Weick and Sutcliffe 2007, p. 70). However, in a world where many of the vulnerability-inducing characteristics of systems may also be their production-enhancing characteristics (such as tight coupling and interconnectedness which allows both efficient transfer of products and services, as well as rapid propagation of failures) the question is whether achieving such limited vulnerability, or perfect protection from grievous failures, for some systems may only be possible to a limited extent.

The second approach, which can be considered an active approach to survivability, focuses on developing resilient systems, and organizations for managing them, that can rapidly detect and effectively respond to threats as they emerge. This approach is based on the belief that despite an organization's best efforts to develop stable systems and processes, systems are still capable of producing surprises (La Porte and Consolini 1991; Schulman 1993; Hollnagel et al. 2006). According to Hollnagel et al. (2006) a resilient system has the ability to:

- respond to regular and irregular threats in a robust yet flexible (adaptive) manner
- monitor what is going on, including its own performance
- anticipate risk events and opportunities
- learn from experience

Through a mix of alertness, quick detection and early response, the failures can be avoided. Considerable work has been conducted on this topic in recent years; see for example Weick and Sutcliffe (2007), Righi et al. (2015) and Bergström et al. (2015). The Weick and Sutcliffe reference addresses the concept of organization/collective mindfulness, linked to HROs, with its five principles: preoccupation with failure, reluctance to simplify, sensitivity to operations, commitment to resilience and deference to expertise. There is a vast amount of literature (see e.g. Weick et al. 1999; Le Coze 2013; Hopkins 2014) providing arguments for organizations to arrange their efforts in line with these principles in order to obtain high performance (high reliability) and effectively manage risks, the unforeseen and potential surprises. Indeed, it was the ability of organizations to have what seemed to be a successful track record in managing inherently complex, tightly coupled, and high-hazard systems that lead to such great interest in high reliability research. As Rochlin (1993, p. 17) describes, "What distinguishes reliability enhancing organizations is not their absolute error or accident rate, but their effective management of innately risky technologies." Weick and Sutcliffe accredit the success of HROs to their deeply embedded culture and mindset towards risk that promotes what they refer to as organizational "mindfulness" (Weick and Sutcliffe 2007, p. 32). Organizational mindfulness is the "capability to induce a rich awareness of discriminatory detail and capacity for action" (Weick et al. 1999). Mindful qualities help organizations obtain a more clear and informed understanding for reducing "blind spots" and uncertainties in their view of a system or organization, so they can better detect and contain threats as they emerge.

Weick and Sutcliffe (2011, p. 63) suggest that emerging threats can be tracked more mindfully when systems, practices and the people who carry them out are preoccupied with the potential for failures, when they are reluctant to simplify details in their descriptions and understandings of systems, and when they maintain heightened levels of sensitivity to their operations. The importance of preoccupation with failure is based on the notion that surprising events are often preceded by precursors, and by maintaining a state of alertness towards the potential for unexpected occurrences to occur, organizations are better positioned to detect their signals earlier to limit their development (Weick and Sutcliffe 2007, p. 37). Further, the reluctance of mindful organizations towards simplification is to preserve the value of information and incoming signals by resisting crude and general categorizations of information. This is of particular importance when previously un-encountered events begin to unfold so that important details are maintained such that they can be effectively communicated and evaluated. Moreover, maintaining heightened levels of sensitivity to – and awareness of – operations allows for more meaningful actions to be developed that are in line with the intentions of those actions. This reduces the gap between what organizations hope for and what they actually plan for and achieve (Weick and Sutcliffe 2011).

Once a threat is detected, HROs make use of flexible organizational structures that enable them to adapt to a wide range of potential contingencies, and defer decisions to those with expertise, to make use of local knowledge where surprises emerge (Roberts 1990). This supports the performance variability that resilience demands, as resilience depends on the repertoire of actions and experience from which organizations can draw from and combine in novel ways to develop appropriate responses in the face of unique events (Weick and Sutcliffe 2007, p. 3; see also Hollnagel 2015). But there are inherent risks in deferring decisions down the chain of command. Those granted the right to make critical decisions must also understand the broader implications of the decisions they make, to avoid major accidents resulting from potentially conflicting outcomes in other areas of the system.

The discussion in this section is to large extent also relevant for the two other categories of events, b) and c). Reducing vulnerabilities and increasing resilience are means to confront all types of surprising and unforeseen events.

5.2.2 Unknown knowns

Surprises of this kind (unknown knowns) are considered intelligence failures. They reveal inabilities to effectively transfer and receive knowledge of known threats, which lead to what Turner referred to as organizational "blind spots" (Turner and Pidgeon 1997).

Numerous studies of organizational accidents describe how information failures are a significant contributing factor to the occurrence of accidents (Reason 1997; Turner and Pidgeon 1997; Pidgeon and O'Leary 2000). In his studies of disasters, Turner (1976) found several issues as to why organizations fail to notice what, in hindsight, were considered signs of imminent threat with potential for disaster. Among findings particularly relevant to this category of surprises are conditions such as rigid organizational perceptions and beliefs, neglect of outside complaints and challenges in handling multiple sources of information that can impede the flow of necessary information to relevant persons (Turner 1976). These problems are likely to be exacerbated with the increased specialization and fragmentation of organizations. These challenges are becoming more apparent in an age where the task of ensuring the safety and reliability of many of today's systems, including some of those originally studied as part of HRO research, is no longer limited to single vertically integrated organizations that maintain high levels of control over their large scale and tightly integrated systems (Rochlin 2001, p. 72; Schulman et al. 2004).

Even within organizations, fragmentation based on the "divide and conquer" approach to problem solving can lead to an organization that is designed to achieve local optimums, where each segment is focused on achieving its own targets. If the target of one segment is in conflict with that of another, this leads to impediments in the flow of valuable information. Under this scenario, local optimums may be achieved (e.g. reducing preventive maintenance cost, or short term cost savings through low quality or leaner designs), which may be in conflict with the global optimums, putting undue stresses in other areas of the organizations (e.g., increased long term costs outweighing the initial cost savings achieved, or reduced margins for error in complex systems with large uncertainties – see Carroll et al. 1998). See also discussion in Chapter 4. However, such lessons are hard to learn when individuals rarely – if ever – directly experience the ramifications of many of their most important decisions, as the time the average individual spends in a specific organizational position is short lived relative to the time it takes for the consequences of their decisions to become evident (Senge 1990, p. 23).

Reducing the potential for these surprises requires improving communication links between those with knowledge of threats, those assessing the risk of threats and those exposed to threats, so that the ever-changing domains of information and knowledge can be continuously reflected in the risk assessments and communicated to relevant persons. Roberts and Rousseau (1989) refer to this as the concept of "having the big picture" or :having the bubble", where knowledge is shared across an organization in such a way that includes necessary details while maintaining the broader scope of the situation. Efforts for improving such communication links, and in effect organizational awareness, must not only focus on transferring information across geographic boundaries within and across organizations and industries, but they must also focus on ways to transfer information across time frames, such that the lessons learned from one generation can be effectively transferred to the next generation.

Overcoming information asymmetries however, is an enormous challenge as moving from individual to joint sense-making efforts can be complicated by numerous technical, operational, organizational and cultural factors (e.g., Boin and Renaud 2013). Individual biases, the potential for groupthink among members of an organization, the lack of empathy and understanding of decision consequences and potential competition among members of an organization all create barriers to flow of vital information.

Perhaps the most significant aspects to be addressed for overcoming asymmetries of information is the underlying organizational culture and structure, as it influences the value placed on information, and the associated information sharing and gathering practices (Turner and Pidgeon 1997, p. 47). HROs create a climate in which people are on the constant lookout for potential failures and are reluctant to simplify their understanding of the world.

Although simplification is an inevitable aspect of analysis: organizational mindfulness aims to reduce the liabilities of simplification by developing deeper understandings of systems and the environments in which they operate in order to reduce organizational blind spots to otherwise potentially knowable threats. The liabilities of simplification hold both for how knowledge is transmitted and how it is received (see e.g., Hopkins 2012). How information is labeled, categorized and communicated, and what people choose to report and omit in their analysis, can limit an organization's ability to identify and respond to potential threats (Weick et al. 1999; Bea et al. 2009).

While their preoccupation with failure implies that HROs do not expect to obtain complete knowledge of their systems and environment, it also implies that they take deliberate steps to obtain more comprehensive models of their surroundings (Weick et al. 1999). According to Weick and Sutcliffe (2007, p. 20), HROs revise their understandings more often than most organizations, and seek out information regarding the limitations of their knowledge in order to "know more about what they don't know" (Weick et al. 1999; Roberts et al. 2001). To broaden the scope of their analysis, HROs encourage what Schulman (1993) refers to as "conceptual slack" as a means for instituting redundancy in observations and variety in viewpoints aimed at encouraging a broader awareness to threats. As Schulman (1993) describes, "Conceptual slack is a divergence in analytical perspectives among members of an organization over theories, models, or causal assumptions pertaining to its technology or production processes."

Furthermore, HROs take deliberate steps to encourage the reporting of errors and incidents (Tamuz 1994), and so called "bad news". Weick et al. (1999) (in reference to Westrum 1992, pp. 405–406) describe the case of the Redstone missile's mid-flight test failure, where troubleshooters had ordered corrective action based on the likeliest cause of the failure from their investigation. However, as Ward (2006) describes, following the investigation, one of the engineers requested to see Von Braun and reported to him that during pre-launch testing he may have caused a short-circuit, which could have led to the loss of control of the system. However, since the system seemed to be working following the checks, he did not think anything of it. After it was found that this was the cause of the loss, Wernher Von Braun sent a bottle of champagne to the engineer in appreciation for such news, as it meant that expensive and unnecessary corrective actions were avoided. According to Ward (2006), "He wanted everyone to know that honesty pays off, even at the risk of incriminating oneself."

Where data is limited, HROs devote significant resources to encourage a richer analysis of the failures reported (Weick et al. 1999; Bierly and Spender 1995, p. 644). Moreover, HROs maximize opportunities for learning by looking to other organizations and industries to explore similarities, draw analogies, identify opportunities and potentially uncover latent organizational flaws (Weick et al. 1999, p. 54). However, since not all information is directly transferrable, nor can it always be transferred in a timely manner, the resilience of organizations in the face of surprises is critically dependent on the level of expertise of each individual and the familiarity ("knowability") of the threat (Boin and Renaud 2013). In HROs, the experience of professionals is actively sought out, and asymmetries of information are overcome by developing flexible organizational structures as previously described, that can be rearranged around their expertise in times of crises (Roberts 1990; Rochlin et al. 1987).

While the factors necessary to achieve such a mindful culture of information seeking and sharing remain unclear, Vogus et al. (2014) suggest that organizational mindfulness is more likely to occur when individuals are motivated to act in the interest of others (prosocial motivation), and are more receptive to alternative perspectives as a result of their emotional ambivalence.

5.2.3 Events judged to have negligible probability of occurrence

This third type of surprise event (black swan) is a known event where the probability of occurrence is considered negligible, and consequently is not believed to occur. Nonetheless such events do occur as discussed in Section 5.1, and the question is how we should best confront them.

These events can be caused by what Turner (1976) describes as the tendency to minimize emergent danger, where signs of threat are undervalued or neglected. There can be numerous reasons for why the threat of such events were ignored or misjudged. A critical aspect when looking back to such events is that signals of problems brewing underneath the surface are only acknowledged and understood as indications of disaster when one understands their disaster potential (Reason 1997, p. 39). According to psychologists Wagenaar and Groeneweg (1987), "accidents do not occur because people gamble and lose, they occur because people do not believe that the accident that is about to occur is at all possible". Surprises of this type can occur when decision contexts are clouded by ambiguities, or when a decision-maker's concerns are misaligned with what knowledgeable and independent observers would consider as the nature of the risk involved in the decision context ('t Hardt 2013). As Brugnach et al. (2008) describe, multiple or conflicting views of a system can create challenges in how information and the associated knowledge extracted from it is integrated or reconciled. Such events can also be due to rigidities in an organization's perceptions and beliefs, which is among the other common causal features of disasters as identified by Turner (1976), and previously described as relevant for category (b) type of events in Section 5.2.2. Long established cultural and institutional beliefs within an organization influence the attitudes and perceptions of its members towards risk. The perception of risk influences which threats receive attention within an organization and which are deemed unproblematic. This in turn affects the perceived value of available information, and whether the information is worth acknowledging, sharing or ignoring.

How decisions are framed can elicit different preferences, affecting the value placed on various outcomes and courses of action to be taken (Tversky and Kahneman 1981). Weick et al. (1999) discuss how success in achieving long periods of high reliability and the absence of failure itself can lead to a different kind of failure, which is failure of mindfulness, as the temptations that arise from long periods of failure-free operations can lead to low levels of mindfulness.

Failures of this type can include, for example, restricted efforts towards seeking out new information, reduced levels of attention, complacency, and homogeneity which can arise "because people expect success to repeat itself" (Weick et al. 1999 in reference to Sitkin 1992, pp. 234–236). Research also suggests that it can be challenging for an organization to learn from near misses when such events are evaluated as successes, as it can lead to a lower perceived or judged risk of the threats, and in turn increased risk taking (Dillion and Tinsley 2008).

An essential challenge for managing the risk of these events thus lies in overcoming a mindset of complacency and inattention, where assumptions are not questioned, sources of errors and failures are not detected, and, if they are, efforts for correcting them are not implemented. The importance of resisting complacency and inattention in the management of safety-related risk has long been recognized in the literature on HROs. Rochlin (1993, p. 14) describes how there is a "suspicion of quiet periods" in the absence of surprises, where rather than justifying reasons for complacency, HROs find reason for anxiety. Even in cases where risk reducing options are implemented, a high reliability mindset demands a "chronic unease" about the potential for errors in the analyses of operations (Weick et al. 1999). This is similar to what Westrum (2008) refers to as a "restless mind" in resilient organizations. According to Weick et al. (1999), "In the more effective HROs, complacency is interpreted as a failure of striving, inattention is interpreted as a failure of vigilance, and habituation is interpreted as a failure of continuous adjustment".

Creating and sustaining a dedicated culture of mindfulness to overcome tendencies towards complacency, however, can be a challenge. Being overly suspicious and overly preoccupied with the potential for failures can lead to a state of "debilitating paranoia" (Weick and Sutcliffe 2007, Beck 1992). Nurturing healthy levels of skepticism thus requires balanced learning processes. Critical challenges of balanced learning lie in understanding what information can and cannot be ignored, and where to draw the line (Turner 1976, p. 379). These issues raise difficulty when accident precursor signals are weak or ambiguous. As noted by Paté-Cornell (2012), deciding whether and when to take action involves managing the trade-off between false positives and false negatives, or in other words "between the credibility of the signal (and the severity of the potential event that it reveals) and the risk of a false alert". The tradeoff involves the level of concern about risk as it influences the degree of investment in systems and actions for managing risk.

The organizational values of HROs provide guidance for such decision-making and reliability are not treated as measures that can be traded against marginal gains in efficiency and market competitiveness (Boin and Schulman 2012). As Rochlin (2001) suggests, the nature of HROs is such that safety is non-fungible. It has been argued, however, that HROs are exceptional in that many organizations today are not as shielded from public and market pressures as some of the original studied HROs (Boin and Schulman 2008), which have led to criticisms in expecting the same prioritization of safety from other organizations. While the nature of many organizations today is inherently different from the original HROs studied, there are important lessons to be drawn from the HRO theory, which are of particular importance for organizations in which the stakes of errors and failures are so high that they would not only threaten the survival of the organization itself, but could also lead to large scale damages to the public and environment in which the organizations operate.

Sustaining mindfulness requires effective management of what psychologist Festinger (1957) refers to as cognitive dissonance. Cognitive dissonance is a form of mental stress experienced when confronted with new information or ideas that go against pre-existing assumptions and expectations. Such information goes against peoples' need for what Festinger (1957) refers to as "internal consistency", which is the need for information we receive to align with our perceptions of reality. Our internal consistency is reestablished by either rejecting the signals provided by new information, or by updating our perceptions to acknowledge that there are alternative views to what we consider as reality. This need for consistency can potentially give rise to irrational behavior and maladaptation in the face of changing threats.

To understand how HROs manage cognitive dissonance, we refer to Weick and Sutcliffe's (2007, p. 29) description of what it takes to forestall surprises, which in most situations involves "mindful practices that encourage imagination, foster enriched expectations, raise doubts about all expectations, increase the ability to make novel sense of small interruptions and expectations, and facilitate learning that intensifies and deepens alertness". Based on this description, we argue that a mindful approach to risk analysis and management distinguishes between historical frequencies of past events occurring, and the probability for future events to occur. Mindful approaches to risk analysis and management are also concerned with the knowledge basis upon which judgments of probabilities and risk are made, and focus on developing a deeper understanding of the limitations of any models used in risk analyses. Furthermore, the preoccupation of HROs with failure implies that where major consequences are of concern, discounting the danger of events on the basis of low historical frequencies may not necessarily be justifiable.

Based on the above, it can be said that HROs resist what Hopkins (2000) refers to as a "Culture of Denial". Instead, effective sense-making resembles the characteristics found in a generative culture (Westrum 1993), which involves actively seeking out the potential for errors in order to enhance the detection of early warning signs of unexpected changes or errors in the system

5.2.4 Conclusions

Managing the risk of surprises, those so-called black swan events, is fraught with challenges. As systems become more complex and interconnected, they present hazards, some of which may lie outside the domains of current knowledge. The knowledge that exists is often dispersed, which in large part is due to the complexity of the systems extending beyond the understanding of a single individual or organization. Furthermore, the available information may present ambiguities, yet organizations need to understand the value of that information and what can and cannot be ignored among the potentially vast amounts of data available. All the while the demands for safety continue to rise. Each of these challenges creates a potential for surprises to occur.

While the fundamental lack of understanding regarding precise explanations and causations of high reliability, and how long organizations can successfully persevere these characteristics implies that high reliability may be an ideal of which organizations seek but never expect to achieve (Rochlin 1993; Boin and Schulman 2008), nevertheless there are valuable lessons that can be extracted from the existing literature on HROs which provides a way forward towards developing more informed decisions for reducing the potential for black swans. We conclude by highlighting three of them.

First, despite how many surprises were previously uncovered and successfully controlled, mindful organizations skeptically question existing beliefs and practices based on an understanding of human fallibility and limited knowledge. The ability to reflect on the existing knowledge basis and to ask skeptical questions is perhaps the first step towards uncovering potential surprises, and better preparing against those that eventually reveal themselves. The need for integrating multiple sources of information in the search for answers to such questions enhances collective sense-making efforts. The notion of collective sense-making not only allows decision-makers to better appreciate the degree of uncertainty and potential ambiguity involved in judgments of risk, but it also gives risk analysts a greater appreciation of the complexity of the decision problem at hand, through a mutual appreciation of the numerous perspectives and influencing factors affecting the analysis. If and when changes occur, those with a better understanding of the effect of changes on the analysis, and an appreciation of its limitations, would be in a better position to respond to them.

Second, strategies are needed that promote continuous learning, knowledge sharing, and rapid information feedback loops for disseminating knowledge both within and across organizations and industries. Barriers to learning and the flow of valuable information should be identified and removed in order to develop meaningful risk assessments and associated decisions. Removing such barriers requires an understanding of the values and incentives at the global and local levels of the organization, and among the individuals both within the organization and across the various organizations supporting it. Because executives, system planners, managers and regulators largely operate through setting and influencing organizational incentives, such an understanding helps them achieve compatibility between local and global objectives through developing incentives that nurture learning, information sharing and collective sense-making efforts (see also, Ackoff 1970).

Third, as long as our knowledge of the world and our efforts to eliminate vulnerabilities remains incomplete, a domain of threats will continue to exist of which their occurrence will come as a surprise. Even if potential surprises were uncovered, actions taken to mitigate their occurrence would introduce changes, which can themselves create the potential for new black swans to occur. A balance is thus needed between strategies of anticipation and those of resilience, to both mitigate the occurrence of anticipated threats and strengthen capabilities for managing the consequences of unanticipated threats as they unfold. Finding this balance is perhaps one of the most difficult challenges facing risk managers today. Ultimately, the level of risk taking in organizations should be seen in proportion to the level of risk society is willing to accept in pursuit of the benefits to be gained from such operations. Whether the surprises go un-accommodated due to a) b) or c) type of events, the excuse that such events were unforeseen would miss a critical point, which is that high reliable organizations anticipate surprises and focus efforts on managing them in early stages (Schulman 1993; Weick et al. 1999). This is not to imply that all surprises can be eliminated. Rather, the anticipation of surprise warrants a shift in focus from eliminating surprises in their entirety to finding ways to reduce the potential for surprises from becoming black swans, through early detection and containment. As mentioned, a key focus should be on nurturing a culture of inquiry in which vulnerabilities and ways to reduce them are continuously revisited. One area of particular focus for reducing systems vulnerabilities should be on understanding the conditions that both support and hinder the work and sensemaking abilities of professionals who are tasked with managing threats in real time (Schulman and Roe 2007). The work of these professionals is critical in detecting threats as they occur, and preventing surprises from escalating beyond control.

6 Integrating performance, risk and resilience-based thinking and methods

This chapter discusses performance, risk, uncertainty, resilience and related concepts. Using recent developments in the risk analysis field as described in previous chapters of this book, we develop a unified ERM perspective – a framework – for how to think in relation to performance and risk, from fundamental concepts to characterizations, assessments and management. A case example involving three types of systems is used to illustrate the perspective. The chapter is to large extent based on Thekdi and Aven (2017, 2019).

6.1 Background and context

Performance management is becoming an increasingly critical component of an effective business strategy. Aspects of performance management drive essential functions, such as setting shareholder expectations, managing reliability, managing quality, and benchmarking efficiencies. These tasks are critical because they serve as a communication of expectations while guiding organizational decisions. In parallel, it is common for organizations to make dedicated efforts towards understanding risk associated with adverse events such as production loss, accidents, changing climate conditions and cyberterrorism. This type of risk management is essential for strategic policymaking and actions to protect organizational performance.

Uncertainty is a fundamental concept in both performance and risk management. For example, consider the case of a major oil company. Performance management principles provide a justification for initiatives to increase efficiency or output in production operations. Risk management principles provide a justification for initiatives to avoid disruptions of these same operations due to adverse events. Performance management initiatives can and should acknowledge that the attainment of performance goals is subject to risk and vulnerable to a variety of uncertain conditions, such as climate, political landscapes, economy, etc. These are the same uncertain conditions or scenarios that would be commonly considered during the risk assessment process.

Often, performance and risk reduction are viewed as competing objectives. Performance management is to a large extent considered the management of *opportunity*. Increased performance can result from taking advantage of increased efficiencies, strategic investments that contribute to organizational objectives, or possibly even what is considered "good luck". The field of risk also addresses performance, but with the main objective of protecting against undesirable events. Risk management is often seen as the study of missed or *lost opportunity*. Thus both performance and risk management address organizational opportunity and related uncertainties.

Consider a profit maximizing enterprise, like an oil company. Its principal objectives are to create value and at the same time to avoid HSE and integrity incidents, see Chapter 4. Performance management is conducted to run the business activities effectively and meet the value objective. In addition, risk and HSE management are implemented to avoid such incidents and ensure that the risks related to them are acceptably low. These two sets of management processes are often separated, run by different organizational sectors and built on different scientific and professional schools and ways of thinking. They are commonly considered incompatible and in conflict: a value focus easily leads to an increase of the HSE risks, or vice versa, an improved HSE level could hamper value generation processes. On the other hand, it is also common to associate good HSE management with improving business efficiencies and productivity.

Because performance and risk are so closely intertwined, it is in place to look closer into their relationship and explore synergies both with respect to basic ideas and management methods and tools. Although there is limited research on integrating performance and risk (Thekdi and Aven 2016), there is now a rich source of concepts and principles that provide a platform for possible developments in this direction. We leverage the latest glossary from the SRA (SRA 2015a), which provides new ideas about how to define and understand risk; refer to Chapter 2. In line with measurement theory, the glossary makes a clear distinction between the concept of risk and how it is described. Uncertainty is a key component of the concept, whereas probability and the supporting knowledge are key components of the risk description. Similar ideas can be used for performance-based concepts. The thinking clarifies the different aspects of uncertainty and knowledge related to performance and risk, and stresses the need for always questioning how well the concepts are measured or described. Using these research advances as a foundation, we are able to clarify and contrast performance and risk concepts and principles.

The proposed framework intends to fill the gap in existing research by clarifying distinctions between performance and risk. First, in Sections 6.2 and 6.3, we seek to create a platform for understanding key concepts of performance management and risk management through identification of common and disagreeing ideas and principles. This includes an exploration of the historical impetus for why the fields diverged on particular principles. Then in Section 6.4, we present the framework which defines performance concepts and principles inspired by the ideas on risk referred to above. This includes a detailed perspective on performance characterization, assessment and management as related to concepts of risk, uncertainty and opportunity. This perspective allows for a nuanced definition of performance that incorporates Future Performance (FP), Current Performance (CP), and Historic Performance (HP) in relation to a reference value. Finally, we relate the perspective and definitions to two practical case examples in Sections 6.5 and 6.6. Section 6.7 provides some concluding remarks.

6.2 Historical impetus for the risk and performance fields to diverge

Formal and modern performance management began with the relevance of scientific management during the industrial revolution of the late 1800s and early 1900s. A noted leader in this movement included Frederick Taylor, known for using performance management to increase labor productivity and economic efficiency. Another leader in this movement, WD Scott, introduced the rating of workers, leading to formalized rating systems for military personnel (Armstrong 2017). The MBO regime introduced by Peter Drucker in 1954 improved the work environment by allowing workers to share responsibility in setting objectives and track actual individual performance with objectives (Drucker 2012). In more recent history, there is increased discussion on how to relate financial performance, operational performance and the concept of organizational effectiveness (Venkatraman and Ramanujam 1986). More recent performance evaluation literature considers non-financial stakeholder concerns (Freeman 1999). These non-financial metrics contribute to the notion of the "triple bottom line", recognizing that organizations should value both financial and non-financial performance aspects of the organization. While there is no accepted practice for quantifying this triple bottom line, components may include aspects of pollution, energy consumption, quality of life, health and well-being, in addition to other more commonly used financial metrics (Slaper and Hall 2011).

Risk analysis is rooted in probability theory with applications related to insurance and also linking health conditions with hazardous activities (Covellow and Mumpower 1985). Modern risk management is also rooted in manufacturing origins, but with focus on safety-oriented measurements, in compliance with trade union initiatives and in regulation with the 1970 Occupational Safety and Health Act in the United States. The study of extreme event risk has been focused in relation to, for example, the safety of nuclear installations and process plants, and, after September 11, 2001, we have also seen a momentum in security-related studies. More recent literature focuses on extreme events associated with natural hazards, such as hydro-meteorological, geophysical and climatological events (IFRC 2018). With increased emphasis on evaluating multi-objective and multi-stakeholder systems, there is growing interest in investing resources toward building system resilience (Hosseini et al. 2016; Francis and Bekera 2014). There is also a movement toward recognizing the management of risk as the management of uncertainty (Aven 2016a).

Common in risk approaches is the classification of types of uncertainty. Aleatory uncertainty involves natural variability that is often described by probability models. Epistemic uncertainty is rooted in limited data or knowledge of the systems and activities studied (Paté-Cornell 1996; Aven 2012b). It has become increasingly common for the performance management discipline to embrace concepts of aleatory uncertainty. For example, modern portfolio theory relies on quantifying risk as defined by an asset's variance (Markowitz 2014). Similarly, the risk management discipline embraces concepts of aleatory uncertainty by using probability distributions to represent model inputs. The distributions model the physical phenomena and related variation, whereas the "true" values of the distribution parameters are subject to epistemic uncertainties. Epistemic uncertainty is sometimes addressed in modern performance and risk management applications using methods of scenario analysis, allowing researchers to study related decision-making for a wide variety of possible future events (Thekdi and Lambert 2012). Similarly, decision tree analysis relates to both performance and risk management, and is often used for financial planning, machine-learning models, and many other applications (Parnell et al. 2013). Decision tree analysis is most effective in situations of high-knowledge, allowing decision analysts to identify solid probabilities to each uncertain outcome.

There is a considerable amount of literature on sensitivity analysis and uncertainty importance analysis, where the challenge is to identify the most critical and essential contributors to output uncertainties and risk; see e.g. Borgonovo and Plischke (2015). This type of analysis is useful in identifying critical assumptions and risk (influencing) factors, which is a key aspect of ERM.

As both performance and risk models grow in complexity and are applied to diverse applications, it is becoming increasingly challenging to identify commonalities between these two disciplines. Although these two disciplines are often studied in isolation during organizational planning, we argue that with a broadened uncertainty-informed approach to performance management, the performance and risk fields can be viewed within a singular performance-risk domain for some contexts. This singular performance-risk domain has potential to facilitate a comprehensive performance-risk approach to organizational management, allowing for innovation in strategic performance-related decision-making.

6.3 Common and disagreeing principles for performance and risk

The first step in characterizing performance with regard to risk is to identify the key principles. Table 6.1 provides a summary of common and disagreeing principles between performance and risk. In the table, a "+" sign denotes that a given principle is typically adopted in the application of the given management type. A "−" sign denotes that the given principle is either not adopted

Table 6.1 Common and disagreeing principles between performance and risk

Principle Type		Principle	Performance Management	Risk Management
Conceptual				
	C.1	Reliance on quantitative assessment	+	+
	C.2	Evaluated as a deviation from a reference value	−	−
	C.3	Study of loss	−	+
	C.4	Study of opportunity	+	−
	C.5	Often relies on expected values	+	+
	C.6	Involves aleatory uncertainty	+	+
	C.7	Involves epistemic uncertainty	+	+
Application				
	A.1	Employ the use of scenarios	+	+
	A.2	Focus on financial and operational efficiencies	+	−
	A.3	Requires cost/benefit analysis to evaluate effectiveness	+	+

Source: Based on Thekdi and Aven (2019)

Note: A "+" sign denotes that a given principle is typically adopted in the application of the given management type, whereas a "−" sign denotes that the given principle is either not adopted or not consistently adopted in the given management).

or not consistently adopted in the given management type. The "+" and "−" designations represent the state of current practice. While we argue for a convergence of both performance and risk management disciplines, we recognize that disagreement on certain principles currently exists. Most notably, principle *C.2 Evaluated as a deviation from a reference value* shows a "−" sign for both performance and risk management. However, the concepts and case study of the present analysis suggest that this principle should be adopted to support an integrated perspective for both performance and risk management.

Both performance and risk are heavily reliant on data analysis for quantitative measurements. Performance management generally uses these quantitative measurements for benchmarking, strategic planning and tracking progress. Risk management uses these quantitative measurements for risk assessments and decision-making for risk management strategies. Both performance and risk involve the study of uncertainty, with aleatory uncertainty most commonly represented by probabilistic models. Decision-making for supporting system investments may acknowledge uncertainties in various ways, for example through sensitivity analysis or scenario analysis, and may contain some balancing of costs and benefits.

The study of performance and risk is notably different in the following aspects. First, risk is primarily the study of loss, while performance is primarily the study of opportunity. Both commonly involve the use of expected values, for example the expected return on a portfolio or the expected loss due to accidents. However, with risk management, the distribution of the loss and its severity is highlighted. The problems of using expected values to describe risk are recognized in risk management (e.g. SRA 2015a; Aven 2012a), refer Appendix B, yet it is commonly adopted in practice. Its suitability very much depends on the application. The expected value may provide useful insights for an insurance company but rather limited information for a company concerned with the safe operation of a specific installation. Using an aleatory interpretation, one can interpret the expected value as the long-run average of outcomes for a large population of similar situations to the one studied. In general, the expected value is to be interpreted as the center of gravity of the relevant probability distribution.

Established and accepted industry practices exist for both performance and risk, as shown in Figure 6.1. For example, when studying potential losses to a system that is well understood, safety and reliability modeling tools are accepted practice. When studying extreme events associated with high consequences, tools such as vulnerability and resilience analysis are commonly used. When studying opportunity, the scenario-based projections and proactive management decisions are commonly used. While each of these tools are designed to address particular facets of opportunity and risk, few tools currently exist for addressing situations of low knowledge of system organization in cases of potential opportunity. This is a main gap filled by the performance-risk perspective and framework presented in this chapter.

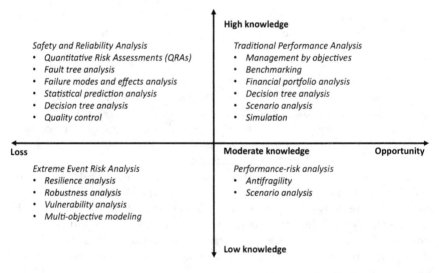

Figure 6.1 Commonly used models and tools (examples) based on knowledge versus opportunity and loss

Source: Based on Thekdi and Aven (2019)

6.4 Proposed performance-risk perspective

The topic of performance-risk applies to all types of situations, but we have a special focus on situations of moderate or low knowledge and in cases of opportunity. Any definitions or models must be compatible with existing principles in both the performance and risk fields. We expand traditional principles within the performance field and adapt uncertainty-informed principles from the risk field. We then consider how these new principles align with needs for associated assessment, communication and management.

The basic idea of the performance-risk perspective is illustrated in Figure 6.2. It is based on relating the performance – the future, current and historic – to a reference level. The FP is affected by events (stressors, opportunities), which can lead to performance output O above or below the reference level. There are uncertainties associated with both the occurrence of these events and the actual performance output. To characterize the performance, the uncertainties are assessed using a suitable measure Q, typically covering probability (or imprecise probability) and associated strength of knowledge judgments. The background knowledge K on which Q is based constitutes an element of the performance characterization. See below and Chapter 2 for detailed discussion of these concepts.

The management of performance is based on two pillars: (i) Performance-risk analysis as outlined above informs decision-makers about performance and risk related to the relevant decision alternatives, and (ii) robust/resilient/

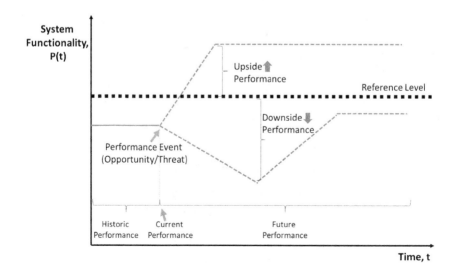

Figure 6.2 HP, CP and FP as compared to a performance Reference Level

Source: Based on Thekdi and Aven (2019)

antifragility-based thinking which aims to provide solutions and arrangements that are robust, resilient and antifragile, i.e. able to properly deal with changes in conditions or events (stressors, disturbances, opportunities) of known and unknown types, and improve performance over time. The robust/resilient/ antifragility-based thinking represents a broad frame of concepts (discussed below) that are not necessarily interchangeable. Instead, we argue that all of these concepts are relevant and should be employed and explored, while recognizing that some concepts may have greater importance or priority for particular applications.

The second pillar is justified in the same way as in risk management. Performance analysis in general provides conditional performance characterizations given some knowledge, and this knowledge could cover aspects of risk and uncertainties – surprises can occur. To meet these risks, uncertainties and surprises, and also learn from them, there is a need for processes as highlighted by resilience engineering and antifragility-based frames. These processes should then be coordinated with communication, allowing for efficient dissemination of risk-related knowledge and decisions to relevant stakeholders.

The management of performance-risk should include decision-support mechanisms to enable decision-makers to choose system investments with consideration of issues like competing performance-risk objectives and different views among stakeholders. The system investments should be carefully constructed to acknowledge uncertainties related to both upside and downside performance. For example, an organization can choose to do nothing, accepting the potential upside or downside performance; they can choose to invest in strategic changes that can avoid potential downside performance or attract upside performance; they can transfer, allowing them to divest from practices associated with downside performance; they can mitigate, limiting the impact of downside performance; or they can exploit, allowing them to take advantage of potential upside performance.

This performance-risk management requires updated definitions of risk and performance principles to be able to reflect both upside and downside performance. The following definitions apply:

Risk is defined as a deviation relative to a reference level and associated uncertainties (SRA 2015a, Section 2.1, Appendix A). Risk is in general described by the triplet (C',Q,K) where C' is some specified consequence (seen in relation to the reference values), Q is a measure of uncertainty associated with C', and K is the background knowledge that supports C' and Q (SRA 2015a).

Performance-risk is defined as deviation in performance relative to a reference level and associated uncertainties. FP is generally described by the triplet (O, Q, K) where O is a specified system output, Q is a measure of uncertainty associated with O, and K is the background knowledge that supports O and Q (Thekdi and Aven 2016).

Performance can be divided into FP, CP, and HP, as shown in Figure 6.2. Depending on whether the performance is above or below the reference value, we are led to upside performance (risk) and downside performance (risk).

Performance Exposure: Being subject to an opportunity or loss.

Performance Event: An event affecting the system's performance.

Performance Resilience: The ability to regain/restore the performance Reference Level following a change in condition or event (known or unknown type of change or event).

Performance Antifragility: The ability to improve performance relative to the performance Reference Level over time following a sequence of changes in condition or events (known or unknown type of changes or events).

Performance Improvement Capability: The ability to improve performance relative to the Performance Reference Level over time.

Performance Vulnerability: The degree performance is affected by a change in condition or event.

Performance Robustness: The opposite of Performance Vulnerability

Performance Competitive Advantage: The ability to be in a superior operating position due to high levels of Performance Resilience and/or Performance Antifragility

The above definitions describe performance concepts for FP, CP, and HP. It can be argued that all three performance concepts are subject to uncertainty. HP and CP can be subject to uncertainty, for example, because of poor performance measurement techniques. CP can also be subject to aleatory uncertainty if a metric reflecting variation is considered. FP is subject to both aleatory and epistemic uncertainty as described in Section 6.1. To address uncertainty related to FP, we use the deviation from a Performance Reference Level and associated uncertainties to define concurrent performance-risk concepts. This reconciled understanding of performance and risk provides a basis for how deviations under uncertainty can be assessed and managed to concurrently protect and improve a system's performance level. This includes understanding the difference between upside performance and downside performance, depending on whether the FP is above or below the Performance Reference Level.

We also introduce several risk-related concepts that are redefined to apply to performance management. For example, the definition of Performance Exposure, suggests that some systems may be more subject to performance events and losses/opportunities compared to others, depending on their level of exposure. We also introduce the concept of Performance Resilience, highlighting the degree to which systems are able to restore the Performance Reference Level following a change in condition or event. In comparison, we introduce Performance Antifragility, describing the capability for a system to improve performance relative to the Performance Reference

Level over time following a sequence of changes in condition or events. The concept of antifragility was introduced by Taleb (2012) and studied by Aven (2015a). The idea is that by "loving" some level of variation, uncertainty and risk, longer-term improvements to performance can be obtained. The concept of Performance Improvement Capability describes the ability to improve performance relative to the Performance Reference Level over time. The concept of Performance Competitive Advantage describes how Performance Resilience and Performance Antifragility can offer an advantage over competitors.

A key aspect of the above performance-risk-uncertainty set-up is that it sees beyond a strict quantitative assessment and characterization. Such assessments and characterizations are used and provide important input, but are not sufficient to capture all relevant aspects of the performance and risk and related uncertainties. The proposed approach is based on a semi-quantitative approach. To illustrate, two examples will be shown. First, when knowledge-based probabilities are used to describe risk and uncertainties, there is a need to address also the strength of the knowledge that these probabilities are founded on. This is not possible to do mathematically. This strength is relevant for practical performance-risk-uncertainty management, but cannot be captured by mathematical frameworks. Also, the potential for surprises is highly relevant for performance-risk-uncertainty management, but cannot be an aspect of a mathematical set-up.

The framework acknowledges the balance to be made between protection and value generation, and examines how various instruments work in relation to this balance. For example, expected net present value metrics are highly value-focused, as will be discussed in more detail in Chapter 7. Although metrics make use of probabilities, they do not account for other types of uncertainties beyond expected values. Thus, the instrument does not serve as protection or provide cautionary or precautionary purposes. Instead, the proposed framework will highlight both probability and the uncertainty concepts within the management and decision-making processes.

The framework should acknowledge the importance of collective mindfulness within management processes. As introduced by Weick et al. (1999), this should include *reluctance to simplify interpretations, preoccupation with failure, sensitivity to operations, commitment to resilience, and deference to expertise*, refer to Section 5.2. These principles emphasize the need for organizations to consider failure and risk within all levels of organizational hierarchies. This includes developing a proactive culture that is sensitive to warning signs for systemic organizational deficiencies. In an environment with open communication, managers can benefit from obtaining a realistic view of organizational performance. Most importantly, collective mindfulness principles complement risk anticipation with investment in resilience, which can help the organization recover from a wide variety of initiating events (Aven and Krohn 2014).

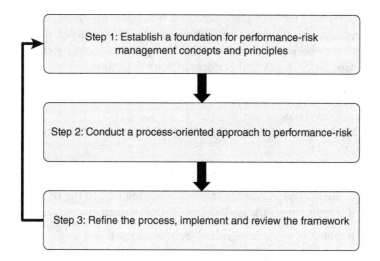

Figure 6.3 Process-oriented approach to risk-performance

Source: Based on Thekdi and Aven (2017)

6.4.1 A process-oriented approach to risk-performance

The above perspective provides a foundation for a process-oriented approach as shown in Figure 6.3, based on Thekdi and Aven (2016). It comprises three main steps. In the first step, concepts and principles are presented for concurrent performance and risk management in line with the above presentation. Second, the main features of the process-oriented approach are defined to address both performance and risk, using the ISO 31000 guidelines as a model. Third, methods are defined for monitoring and continuously reviewing the performance-risk policies. Although this framework can be conducted informally during executive planning activities, a more formalized initiative should include the implementation of software support. A formal web-based software tool can guide discussions, facilitate interaction among stakeholders, store data from past sessions and share information.

> *Step 1: Establish a foundation for performance-risk management concepts and principles – see presentation above*
> *Step 2: Process-oriented approach to risk-performance*

The process-oriented approach supports broad principles for managing risk while also protecting value. This is in agreement with the ISO standard which states that "risk management contributes to the demonstrable achievement of objectives and improvement of performance in, for example, human health and safety, security, legal and regulatory compliance, public acceptance, environmental protection, product quality, project management, efficiency in operations, governance and reputation". However, the ISO standard does little to integrate the concepts. Below detailed sub-steps to perform process-oriented management for both risk and performance are described:

> Step 2.1) Mandate a risk-performance approach with commitment from acting stakeholders
>
> Step 2.2) Define organizational goals and risk-performance goals, objectives and policies
>
> > a Understand the organization and context
> >
> > > i   Identify performance and risk issues relevant to the organization
> > > ii Define overall, high-level qualitative performance-risk goals
> >
> > b Establish performance-risk objectives and policies
> >
> > > i   Develop policies for addressing risk, incorporating the need for agility, resilience and collective mindfulness
> > > ii Develop guidelines for addressing performance, incorporating quantitative performance objectives
> > > iii Identify quantitative performance-risk objectives, define factors that could impact the objectives, and define a policy for protection vs. value generation
> > > iv Develop strategy to integrate performance and risk.

Step 2.1 consists of first considering the many stakeholders and entities responsible for implementing the risk-performance framework. Once the stakeholders have been identified, it is imperative for stakeholders to be committed to the framework while fostering a culture of transparency in the policy-making process.

Step 2.2 consists of defining the overall high-level qualitative organizational goals and the associated risk-performance objectives and policies to meet those goals. This can be performed by meeting with stakeholders to identify the top performance and risk concerns within the current environment and consequently translating those issues into general conceptualized goals. Then, specific measurable objectives and policies can be developed to include principles such as performance, agility, resilience and collective mindfulness as described above. Once policies are agreed upon, it is important to consider how the meeting of goals can be influenced by events or scenarios. For example, this includes defining events, such as natural disasters, that can influence the organization's ability to meet risk and performance goals. As a result, policies can be defined to determine the organization's attitude towards protection from risk and the possibly competing objective of value generation.

Finally, the organization can develop strategies to integrate performance and risk. Using a set of alternative strategies to address performance-risk problems, principles can be defined for selection of the most appropriate strategy. Decision-support methods can then be used to incorporate multiple, and possibly competing, objectives defined earlier in the process.

Step 3: Refine the process, implement risk-performance management and review framework

The following steps of the framework are common for any organizational process and not specific to any particular risk-performance guidelines:

Step 3.1. Standardize framework components with organizational structure

   a   Build Accountability
   b   Integrate into organizational processes
   c   Acquire resources
   d   Establish internal communication and reporting mechanisms
   e   Establish external communication and reporting mechanisms

Step 3.2. Continuously improve
Step 3.3. Implement risk management
Step 3.4. Monitor and review the framework

Steps 3.1–3.4 are in agreement with the ISO 31000 process, requiring firms to incorporate the performance-risk framework into the firm's operations. This includes mandating accountability of stakeholders and responsible entities, communicating both internally and externally, and implementing the agreed-upon framework. This includes continuous improvement and monitoring of the framework in order to refine the process. Often, yearly review is necessary to determine if current practices are sufficient. There may be a need to adapt the framework above to broaden the scope, identify additional objectives, re-prioritize objectives and reconsider performance-risk strategies.

6.5 Case study I

To demonstrate both the theoretical and applied contribution of the above framework, the perspectives and concepts are applied to three firms in different industries, based on Thekdi and Aven (2019). Each industry has unique characteristics that involve widely varying standards for both performance and risk. Additionally, these three industries commonly manage performance and risk in isolated manners, calling for a need to integrate these principles into a single holistic management regime. The case study discussion below will demonstrate that this holistic performance-risk framework promotes significant competitive advantages for the industry.

   Firm A is a major oil and gas company responsible for drilling and transport of their product. Several oil and gas companies have been impacted by consequences related to performance-risk in recent years. For example, the BP Deepwater Horizon spill is an example of downside performance (Skogdalen and Vinnem 2012). High-level measurement of performance for this firm includes the following aspects:

- Shareholder value
- Production
- Loss of primary containment (unplanned or uncontrolled release of oil, gas or other hazardous material)
- Safety incidents
- Greenhouse gas emissions

Firm B is an automotive manufacturer responsible for engineering, production, and transport of their product. The automotive industry has also been impacted by consequences related to performance-risk in recent years. For example, the automotive industry crisis of 2008 resulting from economic downturn combined with changing product demand. Major automakers in the United States received a $25 billion government loan to enable reorganization, allowing the automakers to attempt to regain competitive advantage. High-level measurement of performance includes the following aspects:

- Shareholder value
- Production
- Defect rate for vehicles
- Customer satisfaction
- Fleet fuel economy
- Fleet CO_2 emissions
- Facility energy consumption
- Global water use
- Employee satisfaction
- Community philanthropy

Firm C is a construction product retailer. This industry has also been impacted by consequences related to performance-risk in recent years. It is most notable for benefiting from natural disasters and climate events that may negatively impact Firm A and Firm B. For example, in cases of hurricanes or other natural disasters, consumers purchase rebuilding supplies from these "big box" retailers. High-level measurement of performance includes the following aspects:

- Shareholder value
- Sales
- Carbon footprint
- Community philanthropy

Because Firms A, B and C have unique objectives, operating models and characteristics, they may apply the definitions of performance-risk differently. Tables 6.2–6.9 describe aspects that are important for defining the elements of performance-risk discussed in the previous section. As the performance-risk elements can be overlapping, some measures may be relevant for multiple performance-risk definitions. The Performance Expectation section describes potential aspects of performance measurement, such as financial and sustainability goals. The Performance Exposure section describes potential factors that expose either upside or downside performance, such as economic conditions. The Performance Events or Changes in Conditions section provides potential opportunities and threats that can impact the firm's performance. The Performance Resilience section describes investments that can be used to influence or improve the firm's ability to restore the target Performance Reference Level after a change in condition or event, such as purchasing insurance. The Performance Antifragility section describes potential initiatives that can improve performance relative to the Performance Reference Level over time following some event or change in condition, such as agility and adaptability. The Performance Improvement Capability section describes factors that can improve performance relative to the Performance Reference value, such as building a culture of continuous improvement. The Performance Vulnerability section describes Performance Events or Changes in Conditions that can expose the firm's vulnerability to upside or downside performance. Performance Competitive Advantage section describes characteristics of a firm's performance-risk goals that allows for a superior operating condition.

Table 6.2 Performance Events: Performance-risk concepts and principles applied to Firms A, B and C

	Firm A (Oil and Gas)	*Firm B (Automotive)*	*Firm C (Construction Product Retailer)*
Performance Events or Changes in Conditions	Examples of Events or Changes in Conditions: • Political pressures • Global supply changes • Global demand changes • Changes in regulation • Changes in climate • Human error • Accidents • Natural disasters • Interest rate changes • Cyber-terrorism	Examples of Events or Changes in Conditions: • Economic upturn or downturn • Fuel price changes • Changes in fuel efficiency regulations • Supply chain disruptions • Boycotts • Changes in regulation • Competition • Natural disasters • Interest rate changes • Changes in consumer expectations	Examples of Events or Changes in Conditions: • Economic upturn or downturn • Natural disasters • Interest rate fluctuations • Economic downturn • Regulatory changes • Competition • Changes in consumer shopping habits • Data breach • Supplier delays

Source: Based on Thekdi and Aven (2019)

Table 6.3 Performance Expectation: Performance-risk concepts and principles applied to Firms A, B and C

Performance Expectation	Examples of Performance Expectation:	Examples of Performance Expectation:	Examples of Performance Expectation:
	• Financial goals (based on public or private sector standards) • Sustainability goals, though goals extending beyond regulatory goals are not binding • Safety goals, for example based on industry and organized labor standards • Shareholder expectations • Quotas and/ or geopolitical expectations	• Financial goals, expressed as shareholder expectation • Sustainability goals, though goals extending beyond regulatory goals are not binding • Safety goals (internal or organized labor standards) • Shareholder expectations	• Financial goals, expressed as shareholder expectation • Sustainability goals, though goals extending beyond regulatory goals are not binding • Safety goals • Shareholder expectations • Customer expectations

Source: Based on Thekdi and Aven (2019)

Table 6.4 Performance Exposure: Performance-risk concepts and principles applied to Firms A, B and C

Performance Exposure	Examples of Assessment:	Examples of Assessment:	Examples of Assessment
	• Threat/hazard/ opportunity analysis • Root cause analysis of past incidents within the organization and within the energy sector • Near-miss analysis • Analysis of past opportunities Measures to reduce exposure to downside performance: • Internal and external process audits • Build relationship with workforce	• Threat/hazard/ opportunity analysis • Economic analysis • Simulations • Root cause analysis of past incidents within the organization and within the automotive sector • Analysis of past opportunities Measures to reduce exposure to downside performance: • Internal and external process audits • Build supply chain transparency	• Threat/hazard/ opportunity analysis • Customer surveys • Root cause analysis of past incidents within the organization and in the retail sector • Analysis of past opportunities Measures to reduce exposure to downside performance: • Internal and external process audits • Train workforce • Build relationship with workforce

(Continued)

Table 6.4 (Continued)

• Build relationship with suppliers • Insurance Measures to increase exposure to upside performance: • Embrace new and effective technologies • Be adaptable to industry trends and customer expectations • Invest in competitive advantage	• Workforce training • Grow relationships with labor organizations • Insurance Measures to increase exposure to upside performance: • Frequent and detailed input from customer-base • Be adaptable to customer expectations • Invest in competitive advantage	• Build relationships with suppliers • Insurance Measures to increase exposure to upside performance: • Frequent and detailed input from customer-base • Be adaptable to customer expectations • Invest in competitive advantage

Source: Based on Thekdi and Aven (2019)

Table 6.5 Performance Resilience: Performance-risk concepts and principles applied to Firms A, B, and C

Performance Resilience	Examples of measures to improve Performance Resilience: • Invest in worker safety • Invest in insurance • Invest in protection of resources • Logistics and supply chain management (very general)	Examples of measures to improve Performance Resilience: • Invest in operational redundancy • Invest in safe and protected warehousing • Invest in clear communication with suppliers	Examples of measures to improve Performance Resilience: • Invest in optimal operations management policies • Invest in safe and protected warehousing • Invest in clear communication with suppliers

Source: Based on Thekdi and Aven (2019)

Table 6.6 Performance Antifragility: Performance-risk concepts and principles applied to Firms A, B and C

Performance Antifragility	Examples of measures to improve Performance Antifragility: • Invest in rapid and effective incident response • Adaptability in job functions	Examples of measures to improve Performance Antifragility: • Invest in a culture of problem-solving • Invest in adaptability in job functions	Examples of measures to improve Performance Antifragility: • Invest in optimal placement of inventory • Invest in incident response

Source: Based on Thekdi and Aven (2019)

Table 6.7 Performance Improvement Capability: Performance-risk concepts and principles applied to Firms A, B and C

Performance Improvement Capability	Examples of measures to improve performance improvement capability:	Examples of measures to improve performance improvement capability:	Examples of measures to improve performance improvement capability:
	• Invest in a culture of continuous improvement • Embrace mindfulness • Technology	• Invest in ongoing relationships with past customers • Invest in a culture of continuous improvement • Embrace mindfulness • Technology	• Invest in profitable markets • Invest in a culture of continuous improvement • Embrace mindfulness • Technology

Source: Based on Thekdi and Aven (2019)

Table 6.8 Performance Vulnerability: Performance-risk concepts and principles applied to Firms A, B and C

Performance Vulnerability	Examples of measures to improve Performance Vulnerability for potential threats:	Examples of measures to improve Performance Vulnerability for potential threats:	Examples of measures to improve Performance Vulnerability:
	• Invest in scenario analysis of potential disruptions • Ensure adherence to applicable safety standards • Invest in cyber-threat avoidance	• Invest in scenario analysis of potential disruptions • Ensure adherence to best practices for manufacturing • Invest in cyber-threat avoidance	• Invest in scenario analysis of potential disruptions • Ensure adherence to best practices for retail operations • Invest in cyber-threat avoidance
	Examples of measures to improve Performance Vulnerability for potential opportunities: • Invest in engineering capabilities that can embrace emerging technologies and products	Examples of measures to improve Performance Vulnerability for potential opportunities: • Invest in detailed market knowledge for emerging trends • Invest in flexibility, to adapt to changing customer expectations	Examples of measures to improve Performance Vulnerability for potential opportunities: • Invest in detailed market knowledge for emerging trends • Invest in flexibility, to adapt to changing customer expectations

Source: Based on Thekdi and Aven (2019)

Table 6.9 Performance Competitive Advantage: Performance-risk concepts and principles applied to Firms A, B and C

Performance Competitive Advantage	Examples of assessment of Performance Competitive Advantage:	Examples of assessment of Performance Competitive Advantage:	Examples of assessment of Performance Competitive Advantage:
	• Financial performance vs. competitors • Safety ratings • Sustainability ratings Examples of measures to improve Performance Competitive Advantage: • Ability to recognize uncertainty in Future Performance projections	• Financial performance vs. competitors • Sustainability ratings • Brand reputation • Recalls • Fleet miles-per-gallon Examples of measures to improve Performance Competitive Advantage: • Ability to recognize uncertainty in Future Performance projections • Invest in improved customer service	• Financial performance vs. competitors • Sustainability ratings • Brand reputation • Store traffic • Customer service complaints Examples of measures to improve Performance Competitive Advantage: • Ability to recognize uncertainty in Future Performance projections • Invest in brand recognition and outreach to customers • Invest in improved customer service

Source: Based on Thekdi and Aven (2019)

Firms A, B and C should include the preceding principles within their performance-risk communication, assessment and management. Although assessment of performance-risk would vary by each type of firm, all assessments should contain a systematic process to estimate the concurrent performance-risk conditions. Firm A may measure magnitude of loss or opportunity in terms of financial metrics or those related to safety and environment. Background knowledge related to operational aspects may be well-understood. However, knowledge related to aspects such as propensity for natural disasters, current flow and frequency of human error may be poorly understood. Conversely, Firm B may measure magnitude of loss or opportunity in terms of financial metrics as well as those related to public perception. Background knowledge related to market trends may be high, while knowledge related to social aspects or demand patterns may be poorly understood. Similarly, Firm C may measure magnitude of loss or opportunity using shareholder value and customer sentiment. Background knowledge related to market-driven demand may be high in the short term, but low in longer-term projections.

Suppose Firms A, B and C are publicly traded companies. The communication of performance-risk would involve communication with shareholders and other relevant stakeholders. Potential stakeholder involvement may include executive management, employees, potential investors, customers, political entities and the general public. Some stakeholders, such as relevant decision-makers, may require full information, including all studied opportunity/risk sources, knowledge and data.

The management of performance-risk may vary by type of firm. For example, Firm A may seek to invest in risk mitigation strategies related to safety procedures. Conversely, Firm A may choose performance-risk avoidance by no longer drilling for oil in disaster-prone regions. Firm B may exploit the performance-risk by seeking investments in new products that conform to potential new regulations, thereby having an advantage over competitors. Conversely, Firm B may avoid performance-risk by choosing not to do business or manufacture products in regions prone to downside performance. Firm C may also exploit performance-risk by investing heavily in warehousing near disaster-prone regions, thereby being able to more quickly react to surges in market demand.

This case study illustrates the advantages and innovations associated with an uncertainty-informed approach to manage performance-risk. We classify performance concepts as FP, CP and HP, with all concepts being subject to uncertainty, in particular FP. We recognize that Firms A, B and C all have some Performance Reference Level that may change over time. For example, Firm A may change this reference level following any major high-profile accident; Firm B may change this reference level following major changes in fuel pricing; and Firm C may change this reference level following major changes in interest rates. In addition, all firms are expected to adjust this reference level when the firms enter new fiscal years, when there are major changes to economic forecasts, or following a performance event. As FP is subject to uncertainty, these firms are in effect attempting to manage performance versus the reference level.

This approach involves the identification of potential Performance Events or changes in conditions, allowing firms to understand how decisions may change in the event of each scenario. For example, Firm A may consider scenarios related to high-consequence accidents or natural disasters in their planning projections. Scenario analysis has been used as a common research tool across areas of operations, finance and risk (Postma and Liebl 2005; Miller and Waller 2003; Clemons 1995). Firms may then include their own risk appetite in planning decisions, or possibly seek investments that are robust among the set of scenarios.

This uncertainty-informed approach provides several forms of competitive advantage for Firms A, B and C. These insights are as follows:

Competitive Advantage #1: Using the performance-risk approach, Firms A, B and C all seek investments that improve firm resilience. This principle borrowed from resilience engineering disciplines guides investments that allow the firm to absorb or quickly recover from events or changing conditions. There are several types of initiatives that can help achieve firm resilience, aligning with the characteristics of high-reliability organizations (Weick et al. 2008). First, this involves planning exercises, such that firm actors are able to manage roles and responsibilities in the case of unforeseen events. Second, this includes a strategic prioritization of the most important system features, allowing the firm to focus efforts on the highest priorities. This also allows the firm to deflect any negative consequences toward the lowest priority system features. For example, consider modern vehicles designed to contain a "crumple zone", allowing a vehicle to absorb the energy during a crash, thereby protecting passengers. A resilience mindset allows a firm to be protected against a wide variety of potential events or changes in conditions and are consequently capable of addressing unforeseen events, such as black swan situations. The practice of building firm resilience should be seen as complementary to other initiatives used to protect against specific Performance Events or changes in conditions.

As applied to the case study, Firm C may consider several options for managing risk, such as purchasing insurance for financial protection or investing in high inventory levels, to avoid the impact of events or changing conditions. Complementing this approach with investments in resilience may involve conducting scenario-planning exercises to document how the firm should respond to particular types of events or changes in conditions. This may involve planning the movement of inventory to strategically respond to specific scenarios. In the simplest case, this could involve moving inventory of snow shovels to locations that have an impending snowstorm. In more complex cases, this could involve sourcing products from alternative suppliers if there are impending delays from the current supplier. Initiatives for resilience may also involve activities such as modifying product mix to most appropriately respond to events or changes in conditions that are either positive or negative. For example, the firm may choose to maintain insufficient inventory levels for some products in order to expand inventory of necessary items that are essential following some event or change in conditions.

Competitive Advantage #2: Firms that seek investments to improve the Performance Antifragility are able to improve by introducing, or being subject to, events. By embracing Performance Antifragility, firms invite some level of uncertainty, opportunity and risk. The experience of minor events can be beneficial for firms as the experience builds knowledge on events and also the firm's response. There is extensive literature in education research describing the long-term benefits of minor "desirable difficulties" (Brown et al. 2014). Similarly, there is extensive engineering literature describing the importance of studying "near misses" to promote system wide improvements (Phimister et al. 2003). For example, experience with past events, major or minor, builds a knowledge base for signals of impending events, creates a set of best or most effective practices in the firm's response, and identifies system vulnerabilities that should be further studied. Of course, this knowledge can only be created if there is a culture of mindfulness and eagerness to adapt policies based on learnings from past experiences.

As applied to the case study, Firm B can maintain a significant competitive advantage using an antifragility perspective. Suppose this firm has an extensive history of documenting patterns in firm performance. These patterns may be related to a variety of conditions, such as changes in fuel prices, changes in customer expectations or changes in political climate. Every pattern change involves signals. For example, changes in customer demand for large low mile-per-gallon vehicles may have been associated with major increases in fuel prices. Also, every pattern change involves a firm response. For example, recent changes in United States political climate led to automotive industry investments in domestic production of vehicles. The firm can learn from these events in several ways. First, the firm can use historical data to compile a list of signals or "root causes" for past events. These may include economic models that are able to forecast fuel price changes or impending political sentiment. Second, the firm can use past response to events to define a set of strategies to better react or recover from these events. For example, they may be better able to quickly retool manufacturing facilities to react to changing demand or reprioritize issues in labor relations to be more adaptive to changing conditions.

Competitive Advantage #3: By seeking investments that address Performance Vulnerability, firms are able to manage the ability of performance events or changes in conditions (opportunity or threat) to impact firm performance. Risk-based definitions of vulnerability are often viewed as being the opposite of resilience. We define Performance Resilience and Performance Vulnerability with reference to both upside and downside performance. Performance Resilience can be seen as input to Performance Vulnerability. Within this understanding, we recognize the importance of Performance Exposure, such that a firm can benefit from exposing itself to opportunity, while a firm can be disadvantaged by exposing itself to threat. Similarly, the performance-risk approach aims at being open or inviting to Performance Vulnerability related to opportunities, and eliminating those vulnerabilities related to threats. This could also include being adaptive to changing conditions, such that the firm can benefit from uncertainty.

As applied to the case study, Firm A can maintain a competitive advantage by managing Performance Vulnerability. For example, this firm can address vulnerabilities related to threats using traditional risk strategies, such as by supporting continuous improvement of system wide operational safety strategies. Conversely, the firm can address vulnerabilities related to opportunities in several ways. The firm can reduce vulnerability to political agendas for energy sourcing by investing in a portfolio of alternative energy technologies, such as biofuels. With expertise in these alternative energies, the firm can efficiently alter practices to adapt to these changes. Similarly, the firm can reduce vulnerability to cyber-threats with potential for impacting physical operations by investing in cybersecurity and developing a culture of cyber-awareness.

Competitive Advantages #1, #2 and #3 are interrelated in several ways. Competitive Advantage #1 related to resilience is primarily directed toward regaining or restoring performance following an event or change in condition. Conversely, Competitive Advantage #2 related to antifragility is primarily directed toward improving performance following an event or change in condition. Competitive Advantage #3 related to Performance Vulnerability can be interpreted as being the opposite of Performance Resilience, while including both upside and downside performance.

6.6 Case study II

As a motivating example, consider the study of transportation infrastructure managed through a public-private partnership (P3), based on Thekdi and Aven (2016). A P3 implies a service that is managed through an engagement between the private sector and the public sector. These arrangements are contractual often involving private sector being responsible for operating services, financing or assuming certain risks. As P3 agreements are gaining support, for example within the United States MAP-21 initiative (McElroy et al. 2012), there is potential for this type of agreement to show an increasing trend.

Consider the specific example of the $969 million I-95 transportation infrastructure project in the northern Virginia suburbs of Washington, DC, United States. Under this P3 agreement, the private partner assumes risk for construction and operations, but receives toll revenues (US DOT 2014). This project is defined as *Design Build Finance Operate Maintain Concession*, signifying the responsibilities transferred to the private sector partner.

Under this type of agreement, it is apparent that private sector performance is tied to accelerated project delivery, design of an efficient facility and efficient operations. However, this also exposes the private partner to risk related to design, financial, operational and traffic risk (FHWA 2019). This concurrent performance and risk consideration will be explored in the discussion below.

Table 6.10 describes how the framework and, in particular, the process-oriented approach to risk-performance incorporates key strengths from performance management and risk management described in Section 6.4.1. In addition, this table explains how particular framework components are demonstrated in the motivating example explained above. Table 6.11 describes how the framework addresses key weaknesses with both performance management and risk management, while also explaining how the framework components are demonstrated in the motivating example. As this framework is generalized to be adaptable to organizational needs, formalized implementation applied to the motivating example would require detailed analysis that is out of the scope of the present analysis.

Several common themes are presented in the context of the motivating example illustrating both shareholder and jurisdictional motivation to manage both risk and performance, as follows:

1   What are the intricacies of the organizational goals?

First, Step 1 of the framework calls for establishing a foundation for performance-risk management. Managers should consider the foundations from both a shareholder perspective and also a public infrastructure perspective. For example, the managers should first understand how to define performance for this system. From a shareholder perspective, performance can be measured using system revenue, operating costs, usage, etc. Conversely, a public infrastructure perspective requires consideration of safety, public reputation, connectivity for freight movement, impact on system commute time, environmental impact, sustainability and other aspects that may not be easily measured.

2 Who is responsible for the attainment of the goals?

Step 2 of the framework provides a process-oriented approach to performance-risk management. Step 2.1 requires mandating a performance-risk approach that includes identifying relevant stakeholders and calling for commitment from those responsible for system performance. From a shareholder perspective, this includes considering investors, contractors and system users. From a public infrastructure perspective, this includes considering residents within close proximity to the project, economic growth agencies, public utilities mangers, local jurisdictions, neighboring communities, other transportation service providers, local organizations (business, schools, etc.), historic preservation entities and others.

3 What are the quantities of interest?

Step 2.2 of the framework defines the most important performance and risk issues relevant to the organization. From a traditional shareholder perspective, risk can be investigated by considering financial losses due to inadequate system demand, worker safety, opportunity cost for other projects, and potential surprising/unforeseen maintenance costs. Conversely, performance can be investigated by considering revenues, operating costs, system demand and other objective metrics.

From a public infrastructure perspective, risk can be investigated by considering socioeconomic implications of the project design, system response to potential surprising/unforeseen disruptions, vulnerability to system disruptions, system resilience and others. Conversely, performance can be investigated by considering system congestion, economic development, ease of movement for people and freight and other socioeconomic metrics.

4 How does uncertainty impact the efficacy of system investments?

Step 2.2 of the framework also calls for developing a performance-risk policy. Assuming system failure results from a negative deviation from a reference level (e.g. a forecasted prediction), the consideration of uncertainty is key to meeting system goals. A relevant question phrased from a performance perspective is: If system performance does not meet goals, what organizational processes or principles can aid in achieving the goals? Conversely, the question phrased from a risk perspective is: What is the impact of surprising/unforeseen system performance disruptions and how can they be avoided?

A performance-risk policy requires understanding the agility and resilience of the system. From a shareholder perspective, this includes policies to support the ability to withstand short-term financial losses, to implement operational policies to react to demand fluctuations, and to define contingency plans in response to economic changes that can influence system usage. From a public infrastructure perspective, this includes policies to support system capabilities in response to sudden-onset disruptions such as natural disasters, policies to support system performance in response to changes in regional economies and policies to respond to capability changes in connecting or interdependent infrastructure systems.

There are several factors that could impact the system's ability to meet the defined objectives. These factors are common among both a shareholder perspective and public infrastructure perspective. These include global economic conditions, regional economic conditions, natural disasters, acts of terrorism, values of currencies, cybersecurity issues and others.

The most important policy to consider is that of protection vs. value generation. Performance-risk policies should acknowledge that protection initiatives for system risks can be costly and may interfere with value generation objectives. For example, consider investment in protection, such as protecting physical buildings, multimodal terminals, and bridges. The protective actions require an investment of time and monetary resources. Consider these protective investments to be a form of insurance against potential negative consequences. Although these investments may be useful in the case of a disruptive event, they may incur an opportunity cost for performance enhancements. Any added protection to buildings and multimodal terminals may slow operations, thereby impeding system performance. Protection of bridges, including increased use of sensor data, may require significant resources for ongoing study and evaluation of sensor data.

5   How should the performance-risk management be implemented?

Step 3 of the framework calls for a standardization of framework components with the organizational structure. The methods to achieve this standardization are common across both a shareholder perspective and a public infrastructure perspective. This includes the process of encouraging accountability of responsible parties, integration of the developed principles with organizational processes, the procurement of resources and communication.

A refined implementation of this framework would include the use of a software tool that would allow for interaction among participants. This tool would most importantly include the ability for stakeholders to provide input on items such as conceptual definitions and a register of performance-risk issues. Designing this tool with a web-based interface would allow for public dissemination of continuous improvement and monitoring efforts. An enhanced tool would facilitate decision-making and tradeoff analysis for identifying the most appropriate risk-performance investments. The design of this tool is a topic for future research and development.

Table 6.10 How benefits of Performance Management and Risk Management are incorporated into the performance-risk framework and motivating example

Type of Management	Strengths	How the performance-risk framework demonstrates this strength	Use of this strength in the motivating example
Performance Management			
	1) Meeting of shareholder priorities	Step 2.1	Calling for commitment from those responsible for system performance, including investors, contractors, system users, residents of within close proximity to the project, economic growth agencies, public utilities mangers, etc.
	2) Ability to align objectives/ targets/ requirements with existing organizational practices, as shown through the MBO regime	Step 3	Standardizing framework components with the organizational structure and processes, including encouraging accountability, integrating with standards, procuring resources and communicating with responsible parties.
Risk Management			
	1) Consideration of low-likelihood events	Step 2.2.b	Considering quantities of interest such as financial losses due to inadequate system demand, worker safety, potential surprising/ unforeseen maintenance costs, system response to potential surprising/unforeseen disruptions, vulnerability to system disruptions, system resilience and others.
	2) Inclusion of societal context within decision-making processes	Step 2.1 and 2.2, and 3.1	Employing commitment from stakeholders, including societal performance goals/objectives, and communicating with the general public and other external stakeholders

(Continued)

Table 6.10 (Continued)

Type of Management	Strengths	How the performance-risk framework demonstrates this strength	Use of this strength in the motivating example
	3) Use of risk classification with meaningful descriptions (see Section 3.1)	Step 2.2.b	1) Identifying concurrent performance-risk quantitative objectives, such as decreasing crash rates by 10%, decreasing vehicle emissions by 5%, and decreasing congestion by 20%; 2) Defining variables that could impact the objectives, such as economic cycles and weather events; and 3) Defining a policy for protection vs. value generation as aided by decision-support tools
	4) Inclusion of principles for vulnerability, resilience, and antifragility in operations.	Step 2.2.b	1) Defining the most vulnerable components of the network by simulating various disruption scenarios, 2) Investing in initiatives to recover from network disruptions, such as increasing capacities, building for redundancy and increasing security; and 3) Identifying how the network can benefit from variability, such as dynamic pricing and reversible lanes.

Source: Based on Thekdi and Aven (2016)

Table 6.11 How weaknesses of Performance Management and Risk Management are addressed in the performance-risk framework and motivating example

Type of Management	Weakness	How the performance-risk framework addresses this weakness	Use of the enhanced framework in the motivating example
Performance Management			
	1) Overreliance on historical data to predict future performance	Step 2.2.b	Investing in initiatives to promote agility, resilience and collective mindfulness to avoid overreliance on assumptions in historical data, such as investing in dynamic pricing, reversible lanes and other congestion management practices.

(*Continued*)

Table 6.11 (Continued)

Type of Management	Weakness	How the performance-risk framework addresses this weakness	Use of the enhanced framework in the motivating example
	2) Overemphasis on performance to meet objectives, which can undermine true process improvement	Step 3.1	1) Focusing on accountability with management and engineering by combining risk and performance responsibilities, and 2) Integrating performance and risk management into system pricing, maintenance and other organizational processes.
	3) Incentive for managers to overemphasize compliance instead of true process improvement, as described for the total quality management interpretation	Step 3.1	1) Focusing on accountability with stakeholders, such as operational managers, engineers and executive managers; 2) Integrating process improvement with tasks such as capacity planning and maintenance procedures.
	4) Low (but growing) emphasis on non-financial metrics, as evidenced by the socio-economic and sustainability objectives/ targets/ requirements	Step 2.2	Focusing on both risk and performance goals, such as those related to safety, sustainability and social conditions
Risk Management			
	1) Overreliance on meeting minimum standards and regulations for risk policies, as commonly used by risk acceptance criteria and tolerability limits	Step 3.1	1) Focusing on aligning managerial decision-making with performance-risk goals and process improvement initiatives; 2) Integrating performance and risk management activities within the organizational structure, including all levels of management and engineering, and also at the field level; 3) Building accountability with all levels of management and engineering, and at the field level

(*Continued*)

Table 6.11 (Continued)

Type of Management	Weakness	How the performance-risk framework addresses this weakness	Use of the enhanced framework in the motivating example
	2) Vague standards, such as those recommended through ISO guidelines	Step 2.2.b	1) Developing performance-risk policies that are understood at all levels of management, 2) Implementing modeling tools to assess system vulnerability in response to a variety of disruptive scenarios, and 3) Investing in activities to improve network resilience
	3) Narrow perspectives on risk, paying insufficient attention to uncertainties and knowledge	Step 2.2.b	1) Identifying key uncertainties influencing network performance, such as those existing in data resources and future conditions; 2) Defining factors that could impact objectives, such as vulnerability to disruptions (natural disaster, terrorism, etc.); 3) Considering knowledge strength within modeling assumptions; 4) Conduct processes to identify potential surprises
	4) Insufficient emphasis on shareholder value and operational decisions	Step 2.2	Focusing on concurrent risk and performance goals by also including non-monetary goals related to safety, sustainability, social conditions and others.

Source: Based on Thekdi and Aven (2016)

6.7 Conclusions

We have presented an uncertainty-informed approach to performance, which may be associated with financial, safety, reliability and other facets of organizational management. We further define the topic of performance-risk, a topic that integrates performance management and risk management at a conceptual level. We have proposed detailed definitions for performance-risk as related to concepts of risk, uncertainty and opportunity. We have applied the proposed definitions to a practical case example involving firms in the construction product retail, auto manufacturing and oil and gas industries.

The study and management of performance-risk is an essential competitive advantage within both the public and private sector. Consider the importance of this field in the recent industrial revolution, involving cyber-physical systems. As this revolution will involve increased use of data analytics and automation

(Bloem et al. 2014), efficiencies in operations will reach unprecedented levels, allowing organizations to achieve significant research and performance milestones. However, an insufficient ability to address risk and uncertainty can lead to major regret that is measured by lost opportunity or disastrous consequences. Therefore, it is critical for these research innovations to adequately address uncertainty and risk. For example, consider the case of self-driving vehicles. This new cyber-physical technology is expected to result in significant improvements to safety and sustainability (Howard and Dai 2014). Yet, there remains uncertainty related to policy-oriented feasibility. In addition, there are emerging vulnerabilities related to cyber-threats, reliability of the operating systems, infrastructure and many other concerns.

The above analysis identifies a gap in existing assessments of performance in situations of opportunity and low knowledge. Using recent developments in the risk analysis field, we incorporate the elements of performance-risk into a proposed set of concepts and principles for performance-risk assessment, communication and management. We apply concepts and principles to both upside and downside performance, allowing the performance-risk concepts and principles to apply to both opportunities and threats. We include concepts and principles for new performance-risk aspects, including Performance Resilience, Performance Exposure, Performance Vulnerability, Performance Antifragility and others. We are careful to define these principles by delineating between HP, CP, and FP. We then apply the concepts and principles to a case study involving three varied firms within the oil and gas sector, automotive, and construction products. Finally, we demonstrate that these proposed performance-risk aspects promote significant competitive advantage for widely varying industries.

7 Balancing different concerns, by seeing beyond traditional cost-benefit types of analysis using expected values

ERM is simplified about two main tasks: 1) understanding the activity and its performance and risks and then 2) using this understanding to obtain the "right" performance and risk levels by making suitable decisions, for example, on choice of alternatives and measures. This chapter discusses some aspects related to category 2), obtaining the "right" performance and risk level. It builds on and extends the general ERM principles summarized in Chapter 3 as well as the discussion in Chapter 4 on the link between ERM and TRM.

Decision-makers have to make decisions concerning a choice among alternatives, the need for system improvements, accepting arrangements, etc. Performance assessments provide some information relevant to this decision-making, but the decision-makers also need to take into account other aspects than performance, in particular uncertainties and risk, including uncertainties and risks that are not covered by the information provided by the analysts.

Section 7.1 looks specifically into the practice of specifying performance requirements. Section 7.2 addresses cost-benefit type of analysis and shows why it is necessary to see beyond these analyses to provide adequate decision support. Sections 7.3 and 7.4 discuss links between analysts and decision-makers, whereas Section 7.5 provides some conclusions and recommendations. The final Section 7.6 presents and discusses a related case. The chapter is partly based on Aven (2017a, 2017d) and Thekdi and Aven (2018).

7.1 Performance and the need for addressing other aspects – the use of performance requirements

Performance requirements are commonly used in ERM contexts. An example is a requirement of the following form: the performance of a system (for example, defined by a reliability metric) should exceed a specified number, for example 0.98. In this context, performance (reliability) is viewed in isolation from other aspects like risk and costs. Does this mean that there is no need to see performance in relation to these other concerns?

A common response is that the performance requirement developed has taken into account these other concerns. There is some type of "optimization" supporting the choice made. However, this argumentation can be challenged. Let us look at an example.

The producer of a product believes that high reliability is essential in obtaining success in a competitive market, and has formulated a 0.98 reliability requirement as above in the design process. Verification (testing) processes are to be conducted to check whether the requirement is met or not. The requirement guides many choices made in the design process. It leads to the specification of requirements for the reliability of many components of the product. In this way, the reliability of the product is considered ensured during the engineering process. Cost-benefit analyses may have been conducted, showing that 0.98 provides an "optimal" choice for the reliability.

However, the analysis is based on a number of assumptions, as it is conducted at an early planning stage. The uncertainties are large. There is considerable risk related to deviations in these assumptions. It is impossible to know at the time of the specification of the requirement what 0.98 means relative to, say, 0.99 or 0.97, without having done the design in detail. This is impossible at an early planning stage.

This discussion illustrates a general issue. The performance (here, reliability) attribute of a system is difficult to isolate from other concerns. This well-known fact has been demonstrated through many real-life examples, including works related to the design of huge offshore installations. An early example is presented by Aven and Kirkeby (1989) where the project was to produce natural gas from an offshore field and bring it to shore for delivery to purchasers. A target for the reliability (availability) of the production installation was to be determined. However, the whole idea was abandoned after some time as it was concluded that it was not consistent with the primary objectives of the operator, such as profitability. If such requirements are applied, they can hinder sound innovation and judgment, and result in an unnecessarily expensive design. The fundamental problem of the approach is that to be able to justify a specific number properly, one needs to know the details of the design, which is impossible at an early stage of a development project. The key question to be asked is what comes first, the numerical requirements or the alternative arrangements? The above analysis has argued that a requirement-driven performance approach is, in general, problematic. Instead, an option-driven approach is recommended, which is based on the following fundamental ideas and principles:

a) System performance (expressed by, for example, reliability or availability metrics) is not considered an objective in itself, but a benefit to be balanced against other concerns.

b) Qualitative policies should be defined guiding the choice of alternatives, stating, for example, that the system should show high performance (for example, reliability) or that the performance should be at a level comparable to that of similar systems.

c) Understanding and improving the processes that lead to poor performance (such as failure, deviations, etc.) are highlighted.

d) Alternatives are generated and the "goodness" of these, together with their pros and cons, is assessed to provide support for the alternative to be chosen.

When issues are raised in the development project, for example, concerns about the performance of a specific system, an argumentative deliberative process is conducted, considering the pros and cons of the various options available. It could, for example, lead to two options: 1) improve the performance (reliability) by implementing a specific measure or 2) do nothing.

e) Potential vendors of performance (reliability) critical equipment and systems are approached using a similar option-directed thinking.

The above reasoning is in line with fundamental ideas of quality management. This field argues strongly against the MBO approach (Aven 2014), see also discussion in Chapter 4. Following this approach, it is common practice to parcel out the overall organizational objectives to the various divisions or components. The common idea is that if every division or component accomplishes its shares, the whole organization will meet the overall objectives (Deming 2000, p. 30). The problem with this way of reasoning is that there are interdependences, and the efforts of the various components do not necessarily add up. Meeting one goal, reliability in our case, may lead to less flexibility and performance in respect of other dimensions, and the overall gain is lost. There is a need for an overall system thinking, not isolated optimizations.

The quality management discipline emphasizes also the need for highlighting improvement processes rather than focusing on setting numerical goals. The point is that a goal alone accomplishes nothing and can easily lead to distortion and faking (Deming 2000, p. 31). What is important is satisfying the goal, not the long-term losses that it could cause. The arguments are similar to those presented above. A reliability number would contribute little to the overall success of the development project of the system without going into the method of how to obtain the number. The quality field response is to focus on the understanding and improving the processes that lead to failure, deviations, etc. as expressed by item c).

The above discussion also applies to the operational stage of a system. Earlier records of the system can show availability numbers in the region of, say, 0.95 to 0.97, and a requirement or goal of 0.98 may be considered to stimulate improvements and offer a higher level of performance. Often, we also see that the management bonus system is related to meeting such goals. But again, the question is whether the use of such a number really leads to the overall best solutions, the goal being seen in isolation from other concerns. Meeting the availability number of 0.98 the next year could mean higher risk related to a major accident some years in the future or it could lead to a less profitable overall production.

For developments projects, there will in practice always be a need for specification of some types of requirements, refer to discussion in Section 3.2.

7.2 Cost-benefit type of analysis

The recommended approaches a) to e) point to comparisons of alternatives, with assessments of their pros and cons. These pros and cons can be expressed in different ways, by means of both qualitative and quantitative formulations. As we know, there are many methods for organizing the pros and cons of a decision alternative, including multi–attribute analysis, cost–effectiveness analysis, cost-benefit analysis and expected utility theory (Bedford and Cooke 2001; Edwards et al. 2007; Aven 2014). These methods differ with respect to the extent to which one is willing to make the factors and concerns in the problem explicitly comparable.

Traditional cost-benefit analysis is a method used to measure the benefits and costs of a project. Normally the country's currency provides the common scale used to measure benefits and costs. In practice market goods are easy to transform to monetary values since the prices of the market goods reflect society's willingness to pay; however, the willingness to pay for non–market goods is more difficult to estimate. Special methods have been developed for this purpose, including contingent valuation and hedonic price techniques (Hanley and Spash 1993).

When all attributes have been transformed to monetary values, the total performance is summarized by calculating the expected net present value, the E[NPV]. To determine the NPV of a project, the relevant cash flows (the movement of money into and out of the business) are specified, and the time value of money is reflected by discounting future cash flows by the appropriate rate of return. The formula used to compute the NPV is:

$$NPV = \sum_{t=0}^{T} \frac{X_t}{\left(1+r_t\right)^t}$$

where X_t is equal to the cash flow at year t, T is the time period considered (normally denoted in years) and r_t is the required rate of return, or the discount rate, at year t. The terms "capital cost" and "alternative cost" are also commonly used for r_t. As these terms indicate, r_t represents the investor's cost related to not employing the capital in alternative investments. When considering projects where the cash flows are known in advance, the rate of return associated with other risk-free investments, like bank deposits, makes the basis for the discount rate to be used in the NPV calculations. When the cash flows are uncertain, which is normally the case, the cash flows are represented by their expected values E[X] and the rate of return is increased on the basis of the so-called Capital Asset Pricing Model (CAPM) in order to outweigh the possibilities for unfavorable outcomes (Copeland and Weston 1988).

In a cost-effectiveness analysis, we study the effectiveness by a measure by computing a so-called cost-effectiveness ratio. To illustrate, consider a safety measure S aiming at reducing the risk related to loss of lives. The effectiveness ratio for this measure s is then calculated as E[C]/E[N], where E[C] is the expected cost of the measure and E[N] the expected number of saved lives. The ratio is referred to as the Implied Cost of Averting a Fatality (ICAF). The rule is that the measure should be implemented if the decision-maker is willing to pay more to obtain one unit of effectiveness than the cost-effectiveness index expresses. Thus, if the decision-maker is willing to pay $10 million for reducing the expected number of lives by one, the conclusion would be that the measure should be implemented if ICAF ≤ 10. The number 10 is referred to as VSL (Value of a Statistical Life).

The above approaches are based on the use of expected values. The key justification for using the expected value is the law of large numbers. If we have n systems of a specific type, and the future costs associated with these systems are $C_1, C_2, \ldots C_n$, with a common frequentist probability distribution F, the average cost $\bar{C}$ of these n costs would be approximately equal to the expected value of C when n is large, i.e. $E_f C = \int c dF(c)$, where E_f denotes the expectation with respect to the frequentist distribution F. Hence, in this case we can focus on the expected value $E_f C$, and optimization with respect to $E_f C$ means that we automatically optimize the real quantity of interest, namely the average cost $\bar{C}$.

In performance contexts, we have cases which are well-described by the above set-up and expected values provide a suitable criterion for optimization. However, in practice the situations considered in performance management and ERM contexts are often much more challenging; the uncertainties are large, and we do not have huge populations of similar systems. Then the use of expected values to guide the decision-making cannot be justified.

Consider an enterprise running some rather unique projects. To assess the future costs of the projects, subjective probabilities are used; frequentist probabilities cannot be meaningfully defined. Nonetheless, the analysts have some knowledge about the way the system works and can fail, but there are considerable uncertainties. The average cost $\bar{C}$ could still be a main quantity of interest, but now there is no direct link to the expected value EC. If we use EC alone to guide the decision-making, it is obvious that we may seriously mislead the decision-maker as EC could be far away from $\bar{C}$. Hence, we need to think differently.

As another example, consider the situation where we have quite a few systems and the costs are either zero or extremely large (corresponding to system failures with extreme impacts). In this case it is also difficult to justify the use of expected values to guide the decision-making, even in the special situation where frequentist probabilities are available and known. The problem is that the average cost $\bar{C}$ could be far from $E_f C$ since the average cost is likely to be zero or a high number if one or more of these extreme outcomes occur. The case with subjective probabilities or uncertain frequentist probabilities adds another argument for looking beyond the expected values. The background knowledge supporting the subjective probabilities could be weak and the estimation poor; the result is a potentially big gap between the (estimated) expected cost and the average cost $\bar{C}$.

The use of expected utility theory represents an alternative to these expected value-based approaches. The method has a strong rationale but is difficult to implement in practice. The problems relate to the difficulties in specifying both the utilities and the subjective probabilities (Aven 2012b). There are many other approaches, such as the analytical hierarchy process (AHP). Many of these are controversial as the rationale for specifying the numbers can be questioned. Care should be taken if it is not possible to provide meaningful interpretations of the numbers presented.

It is a research challenge to develop suitable approaches for integrating the various concerns, balancing theoretical rationale and usability. For the proper use of these methods it is essential to acknowledge that they are to be seen merely as tools for supporting decision-making, not for prescribing what to do. All methods have limitations and weaknesses, and decision-makers need to take a broad perspective, reflecting also on the implications of these limitations and weaknesses. There is, in general, a gap between the analysis results and the judgments that decision-makers need to make.

The present book provides input to this work by providing concepts and frameworks for what the gap and issues are, as well as ideas for how to deal with them. The main points addressed are the need for seeing beyond expected values, supplementing the quantitative approaches with strength of knowledge judgments, addressing potential surprises relative to the knowledge of the analysts and distinguishing between analysts' and decision-makers' knowledge and concerns – as will also be discussed below. Analytical tools can and should be further developed, along different lines of thinking using alternative types of decision analysis frameworks, but the message here is that caution needs to be shown. Equally important as developing such tools for informing decision-makers, is the acknowledgment of the need for seeing beyond them when making decisions. In cases with large uncertainties, when probability models cannot be justified, and/or the values are difficult to express (for example, related to environmental damage), pros and cons type of judgments are recommended as discussed above. These judgments can use the more detailed analysis tools, such as cost-benefit analysis, as input, but then must give due attention to their limitations.

7.3 Decision-makers' perspective on uncertainties and risks not reflected by analysts

When analysts characterize the performance of a system, they commonly use probabilities and expected values. For example, suppose the analysts have computed the probability that the system will experience a critical failure next year, and found that this probability is below a threshold value, e.g. 1×10^{-4}. The analysts' message is that the analysis has demonstrated the system is reliable.

The question is now whether the decision-maker will come to the same conclusion. The answer is, not necessarily, as the analysts' assessment is, in fact, a conditional judgment about the performance of the system, given their knowledge, data, information and justified beliefs (including models and the hypotheses that they are built on). This knowledge can be more or less strong and can cover beliefs and assumptions that can, in fact, be wrong, as discussed in Chapter 5.

An offshore oil and gas example illustrates this point. A major hydrocarbon leak occurred on an installation in May 2012 in relation to the testing of two emergency shutdown valves (NOG 2019). The pipe section of interest was designed according to an older standard, where the order in which the valves are operated was critical. The operating team presumed a normal new design practice and the incident occurred. Their assessment of the system was based on an assumption that turned out to be wrong.

Many failures in systems occur as surprises relative to the knowledge of the analysts, as in this example. The relevant scenarios are not identified, or they are identified but are considered to represent a negligible risk under more or less tacit assumptions.

Decision-makers are informed by analysts, but the analyses do not report an objective "truth" about performance and risk, only justified judgments and beliefs. The decision-makers consequently need to see beyond the analysis results and take into account the limitations and weaknesses of the analyses, as discussed above.

The decision-makers do not have the competence to evaluate all the details of the analysis. They need to focus on the big picture, including an understanding of the basic ideas of performance and risk analyses. They need to have fundamental insights into what the analyses do and do not provide. A key point is to acknowledge that the analysts produce conditional performance and risk judgments given their knowledge, and this knowledge also needs to be considered.

The decision-makers are thus faced with a situation where they are informed about the performance and risk of the system or activity under consideration, but also need to consider the risks and uncertainties not fully covered by the analyses. They can request more and better analyses, but the fundamental problem will not disappear. Hence, they are in need of a strategy for dealing with these risks and uncertainties.

We are led to common principles for management of risk and uncertainties, and in brief these are as summarized in Chapter 3: risk-informed principles using risk assessments and cautionary/precautionary strategies and discursive strategies. Cautionary/precautionary strategies are also referred to as strategies of robustness and resilience. In most cases, the appropriate strategy is a mixture of these three strategies.

7.4 How can analysts better meet decision-makers' needs?

The above discussion has pointed to some challenges in ERM. Performance and risk analysts can contribute to meet these in several ways. First, they can improve the way in which they support decision-makers by developing better methods and models for understanding performance and risk and determining the right performance and risk levels; refer to tasks 1) and 2) mentioned in the introduction of this chapter. Second, they can provide decision-makers with suitable frameworks for decision-making in relation to performance and risk issues as discussed in this book; see, for example, the following recommendations.

7.5 Conclusions and recommendations

The above analysis has shown and discussed how the foundation and practice of performance and risk management, and hence ERM, can be improved by clarifying concepts and further developing principles, methods and models for determining the "right" performance and risk level. The following list provides some key recommendations on how to obtain these improvements:

*   Establish a clear understanding of the fundamental principles that determine the "right" performance and risk levels.
*   Clarify the difference in perspective between analysts and decision-makers. Be clear on what decision support the analysts produce and what the decision-makers need.
*   Acknowledge the need for balancing different concerns when making decisions related to performance and risk. Look beyond expected values in this process.
*   Acknowledge the need to take into account the full spectrum of risks and uncertainties.
*   Develop suitable frameworks (covering ideas and principles) for decision-makers on how they should think in relation to performance and risk, and how they can be supported to make good decisions.
*   Use performance requirement-driven approaches with care, considering instead option-driven approaches as described in Section 7.1.

The foundation and practice of ERM have partly already reflected and absorbed these points, but still practice is to large extent characterized by approaches and methods based on, for example, expected values and detailed performance requirement-driven approaches.

In general, we recommend the use of a multi-attribute analysis by analyzing the consequences of the various decision alternatives separately for the various attributes. For each decision alternative, attention should be given to attributes such as investment costs, operational costs, safety, environmental issues, etc. For some attributes it may be attractive to use a quantitative analysis, while for others, qualitative analysis would be preferable. To make risk decisions, there is no need to transform all attributes to one common unit. Decision-makers are able to balance different concerns even if they are characterized in different ways and are subject to risks and uncertainties. A common metric, such as E[NPV], can give a higher level of consistency in the decision-making, but at the price of poor guidance in many cases as the criterion does not give proper weight to risk and uncertainties.

In general, a procedure like the following could be useful in many cases when evaluating different alternatives (Aven 2017b; Aven and Flage 2018; Aven and Vinnem 2007), refer to Section 3.2.4:

- If the costs are small, implement the measure if it is considered to have a positive effect in relation to relevant objectives or other reference values.
- If the costs are large, make an assessment of all relevant pros and cons of the measure. If the expected present value (or similar indices) can be meaningfully calculated, implement the measure, provided this value is positive.
- Also, consider implementing the measure if it generates a considerable positive effect on the risk and/or other conditions, for example:
    ○ Reducing uncertainty or strengthening knowledge
    ○ Strengthening the robustness in the case of hazards/threats and/or strengthening the resilience.

This procedure acknowledges that risk management is about balancing development and protection. Cost-benefit type of analysis supports development, as uncertainties and risks are given little weight and need, therefore, to be used in relation to other principles supporting protection.

7.6 Case study

This section will provide a case example to demonstrate the topics discussed in this chapter. We focus this case study on the oil and gas industry, which involves risk related to financial conditions, health and safety, environmental and operational conditions. We address the topic of reputation loss resulting from operational and strategic decisions. One notable example of this type of risk is the BP Deepwater Horizon explosion and oil spill in the Gulf of Mexico causing eleven deaths, almost 5 million barrels of crude oil being released, over $30 billion in economic damages (Smith et al. 2011) and irreparable environmental damage. These types of organizations are committed to safety of workers, community-members and the environment, but these commitments are not all enforceable through detailed prescriptive regulations. This case study will ask: How should an organization select initiatives that address risk from misalignment with organizational values? We adopt a five-step approach to address the topic, with the following text based on Thekdi and Aven (2018):

Step 1: Identify suitable risk metrics with the knowledge supporting the metrics. First, we ask the following questions: 1) *What can go wrong*; 2) *If it does happen, what are the consequences*; 3) *How likely is it that this will happen?* (Kaplan and Garrick 1981). We then introduce risk metrics that consider a probability of event A, $P(A)$, or an expected value of consequence X, $E(X)$. We further characterize the risk by reflecting on the knowledge K supporting these metrics. We write $P(A|K)$ or $E[X|K]$ to highlight that the metrics are conditional on K. The results are as follows:

What can go wrong?: In addition to financial, operational and safety risk concerns, the organization may face risk associated with reputation loss that is associated with events such as environmental damage, deficiencies in safety culture, unpopular political affiliations, unpopular organized labor policies, negative economic impact in communities and other inadequately understood dimensions. For the purpose of this case example, we will focus on studying reputation risk associated with non-accident operations that are deemed legal, but may pose some type of environmental damage.

If it does happen, what are the consequences?: Consequences involving irreparable damage to the organization's reputation include:

- Physical damage to ecosystems
- Loss of customers
- Loss of brand loyalty
- Unavailability of community workforces
- Protest or unrest
- Loss of political support
- Reputation loss for partner organizations

How likely is it that this will happen?: Although probabilities can be elicited from experts, these probabilities would be based on varying levels of knowledge strength, which is further explained in the next step. In this case, probabilities and imprecise interval probabilities are used (Appendix B), and suppose the following probabilities have been assigned:

- $P(A_1 | K) = 0.2$, where A_1 = environmental damage due to operations in ordinary course of business (legal and non-accidental). This low likelihood level is assigned due to advances in the current engineering safety design. This would be based on well-understood stochastic models that use past data and operational knowledge.
- $P(A_2 | K) = [0.4, 0.6]$, where A_2 = loss of reputation in neighboring communities associated with environmental damage due to ordinary course of business operations (legal and non-accidental). This medium likelihood level is assigned partly based on past history showing the frequency of reputation-harming events.

Step 2: Judge the strength of the knowledge K. Our judgement modifies the scheme offered by Flage and Aven (2009) and Aven (2017b) (see Appendix B) by including a detailed assessment of knowledge-strength for data resources. Each type of knowledge is classified using the following criteria whenever relevant, with three categories [strong, medium, or weak]:

- *Assumptions*, with stronger ratings implying that assumptions are justified
- *Data availability*, with stronger ratings implying that more data are available
- *Data integrity*, with stronger ratings implying that the available data are relevant and analyzed using appropriate methods
- *Consensus*, with stronger ratings implying that there is expert agreement on the appropriateness of this knowledge (experts belonging to different "schools")

- *System understanding*, with stronger ratings implying that this system is well understood, with suitable models

We consider the knowledge strength associated with foreseeing the environmental damage associated with non-accident operations:

- *Assumptions:* There is strong support for assumptions associated with understanding the relationship between operations and the environment. For example, there is strong and justified support for assumptions of hydrology and engineering principles (e.g. water current flows, reliability of equipment, etc.). There is strong support for assumptions associated with public behavior patterns that are used to predict how the public perceive an environmental event. There is weak support for assumptions associated with how information would be shared with the public, through news outlets or social media.
- *Data availability:* There is strong data availability associated with environmental conditions, such as water current flows, temperatures, etc. Also, there is strong data availability associated with operational conditions, such as flow rates, outputs, worker presence, etc. There is weak data availability on the current brand reputation of the organization, although unregulated data sources, including social media, are available.
- *Data integrity:* There is strong data integrity for information sourced from sensor technologies. Depending on the management of the organization, there is presumably strong data integrity for information sourced from workers, suppliers, and contracted agencies. Conversely, there is very weak data integrity involving brand reputation, especially for information sourced from social media and biased news outlets.
- *Consensus:* There is strong expert agreement for the acceptance of data sourced from sensor technologies, but there remains strong disagreement on other aspects. For example, there is weak consensus on how the sensor data should be interpreted to acknowledge the impact of operations on the environment, and on the long-term environmental effects of interactions between operations and the environment. Also, there is weak consensus for interpreting public sentiment that describes potential reputational losses, as experts have individual ideologies and understanding of social factors that influence reputation losses.
- *System understanding:* There is strong understanding of the engineering systems created for the studied operations, but a medium strong understanding of how the engineered systems interact with the environment. There is weak understanding of how these operations are perceived by the public, as this is sensitive to current political climates, recent history of environmental disasters, economic need for the industry and possibly previous evidence of the organization's goodwill towards to the public.

We can assume the relative importance of criteria is not known or is not consistent among decision-makers. Also, these knowledge classifications may not be independent. For example, if data integrity is weak, this can influence whether consensus can be reached, or whether assumptions are justified. Conversely, unjustified assumptions may mislead experts, resulting in improperly concluding consensus among experts. If the entire system is insufficiently understood, this questions whether any data or assumptions (whether weak or strong) are relevant for the study.

Any weakness in any single criterion weakens the entire risk study. However, we propose no general rule for judging strength of knowledge across all criteria, referred to as *total knowledge strength*. Alternative strategies or approaches should be used to gain insights. Some potential approaches to judging knowledge strength are provided in Table 7.1. A *conservative* approach may be appropriate for intelligence-gathering operations, in which there is a large penalty for misjudging or misinterpreting knowledge strength. However, this approach would undermine the ability to prioritize types of knowledge, as of the 243 (3^5) combinations of knowledge classifications, only one concludes "weak" and only one concludes "strong" total knowledge strength. An *optimistic* approach may be appropriate for applications involving a relatively lower penalty for insufficient knowledge judgement. Similar to the conservative approach, the *pessimistic* approach may be most appropriate in applications with a large penalty for insufficient knowledge judgement. One can also compare this total knowledge strength to that found using the optimistic approach to measure sensitivity of knowledge judgement. Finally, the *selective* approach allows for more customization that is specific to the application and decision-maker needs.

The knowledge associated with the organization's reputation is weak across all dimensions. While data that illustrate the current reputation conditions are available, they lack integrity. It is also based on an insufficient

Table 7.1 Approaches to judging knowledge strength associated with alignment with organizational values

Approach	Assumptions
Conservative	*Total knowledge strength* is "strong" if all knowledge classifications across relevant criteria are "strong"; the *total knowledge strength* is "weak" if all knowledge classifications across relevant criteria are "weak"; otherwise, the *total knowledge strength* is "medium".
Optimistic	*Total knowledge strength* is the highest strength assigned among all criteria.
Pessimistic	*Total knowledge strength* be the lowest strength assigned among all criteria.
Selective	Assume *total knowledge strength* is "strong" if all of the most important criteria are classified as "strong"; the *total knowledge strength* is "medium" if some (but not all) of the most important criteria are classified as "strong"; otherwise the *total knowledge strength* is "weak".

Source: Thekdi and Aven (2018)

system understanding and can be quickly responsive to many unpredictable external factors. In contrast, knowledge strength associated with scientific factors, such as system design and engineering principles, is strong across all dimensions.

The resulting total knowledge strength for probabilities is as follows:

- $P(A_1 | K)$ for A_1 = environmental damage due to operations in ordinary course of business (legal and non-accidental), total knowledge strength = "strong"
- $P(A_2 | K)$ for A_2 = loss of reputation in neighboring communities associated with environmental damage due to ordinary course of business operations (legal and non-accidental), total knowledge strength = "weak"

Step 3: Address potential surprises and unforeseen events relative to knowledge. Risk studies that are reliant on "weak" or "medium" knowledge across criteria (from the previous step) can be associated with surprises and unforeseen events. For example, knowledge that is founded on poor assumptions and that is inadequately understood inherently implies that related phenomena are too insufficiently understood to be easily detectable, accurately predictable or considered feasible for standard risk management purposes. Previous steps of this case example involved both "weak" and "medium" knowledge. For example, there is "weak" knowledge associated with the organization's reputation. The phenomena of reputation loss are too poorly understood to allow fluctuations to be quickly and easily detectable, and is thereby an avenue for surprises and unforeseen events.

Managing risk for these types of events may include elements of: 1) Management of precursors by investing in quick detection and early response, 2) Adaptive risk management that considers adjusting future actions based on feedback from past decisions, 3) Management of robustness by investing in actions that are effective across a variety of feasible consequences and probabilities and that improve system resilience, and 4) Investing in improved failure identification techniques, for example AFD methods (Kaplan et al. 1999, Section 5.2). An additional option is to regularly seek input on assumptions, data and models. This can include performing public outreach to invite feedback from community members, employees, political groups, specialty groups and other stakeholders. There is also opportunity to invite diverging opinions internally in the organization, through use of, for example, the "devil's advocate".

Step 4: Evaluate the *goodness* of alternative investments. The act of choosing among alternative investments to address risk is common as organizations struggle to balance system needs and investments. It may be feasible to evaluate the goodness of risk investments, with the eventual goal to support the decision-making. An evaluation of goodness of alternative investments first involves identification and assessment of all relevant attributes, like costs, safety and public perception. For the situations characterized by considerable uncertainties and values at stake, a type of multi-attribute approach is recommended, high-lighting for each attribute the above type of elements:

- Suitable metrics
- The knowledge that these are based on
- The strength of this knowledge
- A judgment of the potential for surprises and unforeseen relative to the knowledge

Suppose there are $n = 5$ mutually exclusive potential investments:

> Option 1: Risk avoidance – The organization could choose to divest from any controversial business practices.
>
> Option 2: Third party transfer – The organization could choose to contract out the most controversial business practices.
>
> Option 3: Mitigate – the organization could invest in public outreach pro-grams that build public trust and promote reciprocity in goodwill.
>
> Option 4: Risk acceptance – the organization could choose to accept all risks and continue with as-is business practices.
>
> Option 5: Acquire additional knowledge – the organization could choose to invest in additional knowledge of the system. This can include allow-ing stakeholders a formal and transparent process to voice grievances and form a partnership for solutions. This allows for quick detection and early response in cases of potential reputation-related risk events.

A qualitative goodness rating may be sufficient for decision-makers. For exam-ple, this could include a high, medium, or low rating of goodness for each investment and criterion combination. This would be beneficial for several reasons. First, this avoids needing to quantify a primarily qualitative aspect of the risk problem. Second, it may provide a sufficient level of granularity for decision-makers, such that the assignment of a rating requires only a qualita-tive agreement on the definitions of high, medium, and low levels. Third, this is a simple and transparent rating that may be tractable in later iterations of the method.

Let z_{ij} refer to the impact of investment i and criterion j. While this case study assumes that z_{ij} is measured on an ordinal scale without units, there may be cases when using units is more appropriate. For example, financial organizations may have a precedent established for converting consequences to monetary units. If a unit measurement (such as dollars) is chosen for z_{ij}, the overall goodness rating would also be measured with the chosen units. However, this method requires that a chosen unit for z_{ij} should be consistent across all criteria and scenarios.

It is also important to be cautious when choosing an appropriate scale for z_{ij}. Preliminary or high-level analysis may deem a 1–3 scale to be appropriate. However, a detailed analysis that requires greater precision may require a 1–100 or even wider scale. Any chosen scale for z_{ij} should be capable of representing potential orders of magnitude for relative impact across scenarios, while recognizing that a relative impact may be difficult to predict when little information is known.

Suppose the relative impact of investment i on criterion j is determined and computed as a function of P(A|K) that can be aided by expert elicitation or surveying of the interested parties. Because this case study involves a broad executive-level analysis, we adopt a simple unitless measure for z_{ij}. For demonstration, let z_{ij} be measured on a scale from 1–3, with an assigned value of 1 signifying an investment having the lowest impact on a given criterion, while a value of 3 signifying the highest (most preferred) impact on a given criterion. No units are used for the z_{ij} measurement because no single unit would be applicable to both of the criteria described below. If this method is further refined with business sub-units, participants may elect to use monetary or other units.

Assume Criterion #1 represents the long-term financial incentive that can be based on knowledge of the financial impact of historical decisions. Suppose resulting numbers used for demonstration of Criterion #1 are: $z_{11}=2$, $z_{21}=2$, $z_{31}=2$, $z_{41}=3$, and $z_{51}=2$. The financial impact for Options 1 and 2 involves the organization to no longer be in direct control of some controversial practice. The immediate financial impacts would be defined at the time of pursuing the option. Presumably, these options would only be considered if they offered some form of financial benefit. As a result, these options are assigned a mid-range impact on the criterion (a value of 2). Option 3 also offers a mid-range impact on the criterion, as it promotes stability in the relationship with community-members. Option 4 offers the highest impact on the criterion because it requires no financial investments. Option 5 offers mid-range impact on the criterion because it invests significantly in new knowledge and information, while it is not clear if the newly acquired knowledge would be supportive in decision-making and long-term financial performance.

Assume Criterion #2 represents the impact on sustainability that could be measured by total irreparable degradation to the environment. Suppose resulting numbers used for demonstration of Criterion #2 are: $z_{12}=1$, $z_{22}=1$, $z_{32}=3$, $z_{42}=1$, and $z_{52}=2$. These ratings can be based on scientific knowledge measuring the impact on ecosystems and the climate. However, this scientific knowledge could be controversial and politicized, thereby relying on a weak knowledge strength. Suppose the sustainability impact for Option 1 and 2 are rated as low because the organization would no longer have direct control over the operations. Option 3 involves the highest impact because it allows the organization to more closely monitor and react to any public dissent or opinion. Option 4 involves a low impact because it does not acknowledge the sustainability issue at all and thereby leaves the organization fully exposed. Option 5 involves a mid-range rating because it would involve additional information that would provide clarity on how to improve the impact to sustainability

Table 7.2 summarizes the impact judgements for each studied option and criterion. These judgements alone provide meaningful information for

Table 7.2 Impact judgements and final *goodness* rating for all studied options

	Criterion #1	Criterion #2	Weighted Goodness Rating
OPTION 1	$z_{11}=2$	$z_{12}=1$	$Goodness_1 = 0.5(2)+0.5(1)=1.5$
OPTION 2	$z_{21}=2$	$z_{22}=1$	$Goodness_2 =0.5(2)+0.5(1)=1.5$
OPTION 3	$z_{31}=2$	$z_{32}=3$	$Goodness_3 = 0.5(2)+0.5(3)=2.5$
OPTION 4	$z_{41}=3$	$z_{42}=1$	$Goodness_4 = 0.5(3)+0.5(1)=2$
OPTION 5	$z_{51}=2$	$z_{52}=2$	$Goodness_5 = 0.5(2)+0.5(2)=2$

Source: Thekdi and Aven (2018)

decision-makers. Options 1 and 2 offer mid-range and low impact across criteria, making them the least impactful across studied options. Option 3 offers mid-range and high impact across criteria, making it the most impactful option across criteria. While Option 4 is the most impactful for Criteria #1, it is given the lowest rating for Criteria #2. Option 5 provides the most consistency across options, with a mid-range impact across criteria.

The information formed above provides a sufficient and transparent basis to guide decision-making. For complex risk studies, it is critical to maintain transparency by not aggregating across the studied criteria. However, within certain contexts, such as simple risk studies, there may be incentive to compute an overall goodness rating. For demonstration purposes, Table 7.2 computes a sample goodness rating by assuming the criteria are equally weighted. As a result, Options 1 and 2 offer a low goodness rating and are based on strong knowledge strength. Option 3 offers the highest goodness rating, but is computed based on information with a medium knowledge strength. Option 4 offers a mid-range goodness rating, but is based on a weak knowledge strength. Finally, Option 5 offers a mid-range goodness rating that based on a medium knowledge strength. At this stage, there may be a need to consider several varying perspectives within this goodness rating model. For demonstration purposes, we will assume a single perspective goodness evaluation for investments.

Step 5: Managerial review and judgment; decision-making. As highlighted above, the method provides decision support; it does not prescribe the decision. Therefore, a sensitivity analysis can be helpful for informing decision-makers. When qualitative judgements are made to assess decision alternatives, sensitivity analysis may include posing the following questions:

- Are the highest goodness decision alternatives feasible and practical?
- Are the study conclusions logical?
- Is there agreement about the assigned goodness judgement?
- How can a particular alternative be revised to better fit the decision criteria?
- Should any of the mutually exclusive alternatives be combined?

- Are the studied criteria appropriate? Should they be revised? Should any be added or removed?
- Is another iteration of this process necessary?
- Is there need for additional data or information?
- Should this process be repeated in business sub-units?

In this case study, a 1-point increase in the z_{ij} (the relative impact of investment i on criterion j) results in a 0.5-point increase in the overall goodness rating. For example, if the ratings z_{ij} for Option 4 and Option 5 were increased by one point for either criterion, they would share the highest goodness rating across all options. This type of increase is not feasible for Option 4 (risk acceptance) due to the inability to revise this option. There may be opportunity to raise the goodness rating for Option 5 by refining the option. One refinement may include increased environmental data collection, such that the z_{52} rating can be increased. Conversely, there may be opportunity to refine Option 3 to allow for a higher goodness rating. The current rating $z_{31}=2$ can be increased by improving the ability of this option to create a long-term financial incentive. This option could be refined to combine public outreach with community training and education programs, thereby improving local economic conditions and availability of skilled labor.

Summary of results: The case study provided an approach for understanding the relationship between decision-making and the alignment with organizational values within the energy sector. The topic is becoming increasingly relevant as these organizations continue to complement financial information with aspects of safety, sustainability, community impact, etc.

This process is intended to provide decision-support, while not prescribing any specific outcome or decision. The methods are customizable, allowing analysts to adapt the process for the specific needs of an application. For example, when applied to more complex problems, it is important to consider reiteration of the process using the refined alternatives, criteria and other relevant information. For the case example, reiteration may involve excluding Options 1 and 2 from the study due to poor performance. This would allow Steps 3–5 to be repeated using three remaining options, thereby simplifying the process for decision-makers. Alternatively, the analyst may use expertise gained from the process to form ideas on additional alternatives to consider. Additional studies would need to be conducted to understand whether combining particular decision alternatives is feasible and practical in a real-world setting. There may also be momentum to remove one or both of the criteria studied, clarify any existing criteria or consider additional applicable criteria. Finally, if an integrated-weighed function is used to evaluate goodness for options, decision-makers may suggest alternative weighting schemes.

8 Improving ERM practices
Practical challenges

This chapter addresses challenges and solutions for improving ERM practice, using the ERM program and the criteria for ERM maturity introduced in Sections 3.4 and 3.5 as a basis for the discussion. The chapter also discusses troubleshooting and diagnosis of common issues and challenges that exist in forming, maintaining and improving ERM practices in an organization. Section 8.1 discusses potential challenges involved with risk resources, particularly when organizations are faced with limited financial or human resources. Section 8.2 discusses challenges with maintaining and growing risk expertise that can result from insufficient training, changes in leadership or other common organizational issues. Section 8.3 discusses common issues with forming and maintaining a risk culture. Section 8.4 discusses challenges with confirming risk practices with larger organizational needs. Section 8.5 discusses methods for troubleshooting, while Section 8.6 looks into some specific managerial or policy-related issues that can be encountered in practice, identified by trouble-shooting processes.

8.1 Challenges with obtaining and coordinating risk resources

There is no rule or minimum requirement for volume of risk resources required by an organization. While risk programs are scalable, it is possible for smaller organizations with limited resources to have a risk program effectiveness that is comparable to larger organizations with a large resource base. Additionally, there is no guarantee that larger resource-heavy risk programs are actually working as intended. For example, there have been countless incidents of organizations with comprehensive risk programs that have been unable to adequately manage their risk (Freed 2017; Bernstein et al. 2014). What matters is the quality of the risk program, which includes several key features:

- Clear documentation of ERM policies
- Agreement on responsible parties for each risk management activity
- Thorough implementation of ERM process, as described in this book

A high-quality program does not necessarily require resources associated with dedicated personnel or business units. In fact, there can be some downsides of having a single person or department manage an entire organization's risk management processes. First, this type of system may lack transparency or sufficient oversight. Second, dedicated business units may exhibit a "herd mentality", requiring them to follow processes and procedures that may not be adequately compatible with the roles and functions of other business units. Finally, this type of system might encourage other business units to not accept risk management responsibility, and instead assume all risk is managed by the dedicated personnel or business units. While a dedicated risk manager or organizational unit can also have benefits, they should be complemented by risk management roles (or partial roles) across all organizational units.

Also, consider the taxonomy described in Table 3.1. The most important elements of an advanced risk program can be achieved with minimal risk resources. For example, documented risk guidelines and policies, a clear detailed risk strategy and a system for regular benchmarking and reporting can possibly require time and discussion during the start-up, but then require fewer resources once the program is established. However, there is some danger in assuming "the job is done" once the risk program has been implemented. Once the risk program is implemented, there is reliance on the entire organization and the developed risk culture to ensure that the program is being properly implemented and not forgotten. Therefore, to maintain an advanced risk program with minimal (or many) resources, there does need to be consistency in risk-centeredness and clear processes in place for benchmarking, reporting and monitoring.

8.2 Challenges with maintaining and growing risk expertise

Risk expertise is vital to the success of an organizational risk program. The loss of risk expertise can happen for several reasons:

- If there are major changes to the organizational structure. While these programs should adapt to changes (leadership, strategic, legal, economic, etc.), any change should be carefully evaluated, with clear understanding of how any changes may impact ERM processes. It may be necessary to reiterate the ERM process following major organizational structure changes.
- If organizations improperly follow their risk program guidelines. Often, this can be due to unintentional reasons, such as "putting out fires" related to regular operations, loss or scarcity of employee resources, or loss of institutional knowledge on risk program processes. Conversely, there may be intentional reasons, such as new organizational leaders not valuing (or disagreeing with) current risk guidelines or choosing to no longer pursue the risk program once the procedures are outdated. All of these issues signal a much larger operational problem.

- Loss of risk expertise essentially implies that the organization cannot follow through with ERM activities. Any time an organization cannot follow its own documented policies and processes, there is need for a larger organization-wide overview of causes and interventions. If leadership is unwilling to support either the implementation or maintenance of a risk program, it should be made clear that the organization is explicitly choosing to accept (and not properly mitigate) all risks identified in previous iterations of the ERM process.

The failure to grow risk expertise can happen for several reasons:

- If there is a lack of resources necessary to update risk program documentation and implementation. There is need for regular review of ERM, especially as external conditions (laws, economies, market conditions, etc.), personnel, strategic visions and risk appetites change in the organization. At the very least, organizations should maintain and continue to implement their established risk program, even if resources are not available for risk program growth. However, caution is necessary. A risk program that is not catered to specific organizational needs may undermine the larger pursuit of risk management.
- If there is a lack of political will for growing risk expertise. Organizations have many competing needs within their overall strategies. If other initiatives are of higher priority, a risk program may not require a growth of expertise. But, as indicated in the previous bullet, organizations should maintain and continue to implement their established risk program.
- If the risk program is working adequately for the organizational needs. If stakeholders are content with the risk program performance, and if the organization has already achieved an advanced maturity level, then the organization may choose not to grow expertise. In this case, there is still need for frequent review of risk policies.

8.3 Challenges with maintaining and growing a risk culture

Establishing, maintaining and growing a risk culture is a significant challenge for an organization. Unlike the issues with resources and expertise described above, a risk culture can be highly influenced by the organizational leadership. The organization can control the strength of a risk culture and how to incentivize adherence to the risk culture.

An organization can choose to develop a strong risk culture that is in alignment with the organizational purpose and function. As defined by Deloitte (2013), a strong risk culture requires a commonality of purpose, universal adoption and application, continuous improvement, and timely, transparent and honest communication. These qualities can be improved if there is motivation to listen to employee rationalization of a poor risk culture (if this exists), include all stakeholders in continuous improvement exercises, and regularly communicate the agreed-upon expectations and performance with stakeholders.

Even with risk training and benchmarking procedures, there can be incentive for stakeholders to fail to follow risk guidelines. For example, there may be incentives for workers to wear incorrect personal protective equipment (PPE) for certain jobs, particularly when the PPE interferes with the effectiveness or ease of the task. Additionally, there may be incentives for workers to take shortcuts for tasks, particularly when they are not being properly monitored, as was the case of the 2010 BP oil spill (Mufson and Kornblut 2010). Thus, it is important for organizations to understand what type of behavior they are actually incentivizing. Is it acceptable for workers to be slower in performing a task if they instead perform it in compliance with risk policies? At a strategic level, is it acceptable to pursue investments with lower short-term performance if they instead more adequately follow documented risk guidelines?

If the documented and established risk policies are not practical or accepted by the organizational stakeholders, there are three options. First, organizations can adapt the risk policies to the needs and concerns of the various stakeholders. This would require careful review of current risk policy compliance. In some cases, stakeholders may not feel comfortable sharing evidence of noncompliance, so it is important to ensure stakeholders are not penalized for contributing their input. Once the stakeholder input is converted to actionable initiatives, it is important to also seek stakeholder input on feasibility and practicality of those initiatives. Second, organizations can include aspects of risk culture within the performance evaluation process. This can include rewarding proper compliance with risk policies. Conversely, this can include *not* rewarding high performance that results from noncompliance with risk policies. For example, an organization may value a worker's speed in completing a task. However, rewarding speed may incentivize a worker to take shortcuts that can negatively impact safety and security. Third, an organization can include risk culture expectations within the hiring process. This may involve asking applicants to share their values on risk and support of a risk culture; asking for discussion of risk compliance in previous job positions; or conducting other types of behavioral interviews that seek to find evidence of past risk process compliance.

8.4 Challenges with applying appropriate risk practices, that aligns with organizations needs

With the rapid availability of information, it can be relatively simple to gather sample risk guideline documentation from web resources. However, there can be dangers of accepting these types of policies that may have been created for significantly different organizations, applications and settings. The effectiveness of a risk program can be undermined by adopting policies that simply do not complement the overall strategies, needs and mission of an organization.

It can be said that any failure to successfully implement a risk problem can possibly be due to failure to thoughtfully develop the program in the first place. Risk policies and practices cannot be developed overnight. Instead, development of a risk program should be an iterative and transparent process, as described in Chapter 3.

It is also important to treat program implementation as an iterative and continuously improving process. The implementation requires full oversight and continuous monitoring, to ensure the implementation is meeting the expectations placed in the documentation. There may be need to involve a professional consulting firm that has experience with common organizational challenges.

Given these challenges, there may be incentive for organizations to experiment with risk program guidelines, such that the program and implementation are tested for some fixed length of time, prior to full company-wide adoption. This would allow for regular review and intervention (if necessary), allowing the organization to consciously decide whether the risk process aligns with organizational needs.

8.5 Methods for troubleshooting common issues in ERM and ERM programs

This section describes methods for troubleshooting issues that may exist within ERM and within ERM programs in particular. As described in the learn manufacturing literature, whenever a problem is detected, there is need to separate the problem as described by stakeholders (the perceived problem) and the "causes" of the problem. The latter part often involves data analysis and modeling of relevant phenomena and processes. Common methods used for this purpose include:

- Statistical process control using control charts to monitor processes over time. These charts usually measure some performance indicator on the y-axis, while time is represented on the x-axis. These charts often include some upper and lower control limits, such that if these limits are exceeded, the process is deemed to be not in control – suggesting that there is some problem with the process (Shewhart and Deming 1986).
- Decision-making or group model building. For example, the fishbone diagram, flow charts, Pareto charts used to identify causes and explanatory factors are commonly used in practical applications, as described in Goetsch and Davis (1997).
- Analytic models, such as neural networks, built on representations of interconnected elements which process information and learn by their response to external input. These models are able to detect patterns, anomalies or trends.
- Fault tree analysis. This method involves building a tree-like logic diagram to represent possible coincidence of events that can cause some top-level failure to occur. The diagram uses "and" and "or" logic gates to represent

the relationship among the various events, which can then be used for probabilistic analysis. See ASQ (2019a) and textbooks on reliability analysis.

- FMEA. This method first involves identifying various failure modes (defects or failures) that could possibly occur. Second, effects analysis involves identifying the consequences of those failure modes. Then, failures can be prioritized based on potential frequency, consequences, and detection. See ASQ (2019b).

As described by McFillen et al. (2013), the diagnostic process in an engineering setting typically consists of the following steps: "collection of data, development of causal inference(s), formation of hypotheses, testing of hypotheses and confirmation of the diagnosis". In line with general problem-solving processes, there is a feedback loop from the hypothesis testing back to the data collection. A cause-effect relationship model is developed allowing for causal inferences and the formation and testing of hypotheses.

In addition, we will point to methods used for organizational diagnosis, see for example Harrison (2005) and McFillen et al. (2013). The methods used are well-documented in the social science literature and include ways of collecting data such as observations, interviews, questionnaires, workshops and discussions, as well as related analysis instruments (in particular statistical inference) and research design.

The diagnosis process for organizations can preferably be conducted in line with practices from the medical field (McFillen et al. 2013). This reference outlines a diagnosis process for organizations which is supported by four spheres of knowledge: symptoms, systems, standards and solutions. As medical professionals must "know their patients' symptoms, understand the functioning and interdependencies of human systems, know the established standards that define what it means to be healthy, and possess knowledge of a wide variety of medical solutions, similar understandings are required of organizational diagnosticians" (McFillen et al. 2013). Refer to McFillen et al. (2013) for further details on these knowledge spheres in an organizational context.

Once a problem has been identified and a diagnosis (cause analysis) has been conducted, there are several types of interventions possible as described by Harrison (2005). First, there are interventions that can be used to address skills, attitudes and values of human resources. Second, there are interventions that can involve behavior in the organization, such as decision-making, communication and conflict resolutions. Third, interventions could involve changes to the organizational structure, such as by changing rewards/incentives, job descriptions and work procedures. Finally, there are interventions that can change organizational goals, strategies and cultures, such as by influential corporate cultures.

8.6 Addressing key issues resulting from the troubleshooting process

Applying the troubleshooting approaches and methods referred to in the previous section, insights are gained on challenges and problems related to the development, implementation and improvement of the ERM and ERM programs. There are several common issues encountered in ERM processes, as discussed in Kerstin et al. (2014), for example:

- Organizational agreement on risk definitions and the importance of ERM, as addressed in the ERM maturity in Section 3.5
- Defining suitable risk metrics and characterizations, as described in the discussion of the extended risk matrix in Section 2.2
- Uncertainty and modeling challenges to adequately reflect all aspects of risk, as addressed in the discussion of surprises and the unforeseen in Chapter 5

While challenges of the above type are described within various sections of this book, there is a need to look closer into specific issues that arise even when the highest level of ERM maturity has been achieved. The topics discussed in the sections below explore more specific managerial or policy-related issues that can be encountered in private and public sector settings, such as organizational resistance to risk management activities, lack of expertise and other practical issues.

8.6.1 Explicit or implicit resistance to risk management activities

Analysts and ERM managers may encounter resistance to risk management activities that are supported by a well-functioning ERM process. This type of resistance may be due to policies in place in other facets of the organization, or bureaucracies that are common in large private organizations and also the public sector. This discussion will focus on two types of resistance: explicit and implicit.

Explicit resistance involves resistance that is clearly stated and understood by the involved stakeholders. There are several causes that could arise, for example:

- The ERM process neglected to consider some specific constraint
- There is disagreement among stakeholders that was not identified during the ERM process
- Internal politics or organizational behavior problems are causing some stakeholders to resist any changes

The first step in encountering this type of resistance is to identify the cause of the resistance and begin open communication with the relevant stakeholders. It is important for the ERM team to recognize that, despite due diligence, they may not have a full understanding of every facet of the organization. They should take the opportunity to learn more and seek an alternative solution that has acceptance from stakeholders. Without stakeholder acceptance, it is possible that the involved stakeholders will not take the ERM process seriously. If there are issues of stakeholder disagreement or internal politics, the ERM team should seek support from higher managerial levels. An ERM process that does not have executive support will be deemed weak and ineffective in the long-term.

For example, suppose an ERM study found that the organization's cyber infrastructure is out of date and is highly vulnerable to various cyber-exploits. Then, suppose the information technology leaders of the organization disagree and are unwilling to support the updating of technologies. In this case, there first appears to be a missing link: one can ask if the information technology leaders were sufficiently included in the ERM process. Second, one can ask if all costs were considered when deciding to implement this particular risk activity. For example, a cost-benefit analysis may have included costs associated with purchasing updated technologies, but may have neglected to consider costs associated with retraining staff and handling unexpected problems. Finally, one can ask if this technology upgrade is really needed – including a neutral third-party expert in an additional iteration of ERM process may be necessary.

Implicit resistance involves resistance that is not clearly stated, but instead assumed due to the ERM program's inability to implement particular risk management activities. First, it is important to have an open and transparent relationship with the involved stakeholders in order for those stakeholders to feel comfortable sharing their concerns. It may be necessary to seek feedback, possibly through anonymous surveys, focus groups or testing. It is equally important to listen to the feedback and consider how to adapt the risk management activities to the expressed concerns. It may be necessary to reiterate the ERM process with increased presence of the highest impacted stakeholders. If risk management activities are not being properly implemented due to the resistance, the ERM program will be ineffective.

For example, suppose an ERM study found that the organization's cyber-infrastructure needed significant upgrades, such as introducing two-factor authentication for entry into some software applications. Then, suppose there is hesitance to the introduction of two-factor authentication for valid reasons, such as the resulting slowdown of workflows, lack of resources, lack of expertise, etc. As a result, employees take shortcuts to circumvent the new risk policy, such as by neglecting to log out of frequently used software applications. The act of the shortcut then has serious repercussions for overall system security. First, it is important for the ERM team to be made aware of this situation – recognizing that open and transparent communication with stakeholders is necessary for any risk management activities. Additionally, it would have been preferable for the ERM team to foresee this issue prior to implementation of this new two-factor authentication policy. The ERM team may approach this issue by quantifying the impact of this new authentication policy on workflows. If the workflow slowdown is deemed unacceptable, there is need to explore other risk management options. If the workflow slowdown is deemed acceptable, then there is a managerial responsibility to ensure that the authentication policy is being properly implemented.

Another type of implicit resistance involves bureaucracies existing within an organization. There may be many levels of permissions that need to be obtained prior to implementing some type of risk-related activity. In some cases, bureaucracies may be necessary, especially in organizations requiring major oversight, such as those associated with strict accounting or safety standards. In other cases, bureaucracies may not be necessary and contribute to unnecessary delays in any type of implementation. Of course, it would be rare for an organization to allow ERM processes to overrule these types of bureaucracies. Instead, it may provide value for the ERM process to include these bureaucracies within the scope of the ERM process. Such efforts can treat these bureaucracies as a potential risk, calling for a thorough analysis of how they impact operations in general (which include ERM implementation).

8.6.2 Lack of expertise to carry out ERM

An organization that is developing a new ERM program may find itself seeking evidence related to very complex mechanisms. For example, the ERM process may require thorough knowledge of rapidly changing and complex topics like cybersecurity, biological mechanisms, human behavior, etc. This type of knowledge may not exist or not be housed within the organization. To properly assess risk, the ERM team needs access to expert knowledge. Essentially, this issue falls in the domain of relying on the "modeler's decision". In any simulation or complex modeling of a system, the analyst must decide what are the most relevant inputs, outputs and mechanics that govern the system. Different analysts may and often will offer widely varying schemes for modeling a particular system, and there is not a "correct" model.

Lack of expertise may be due to not having resources available with the necessary knowledge, or due to the system being too complex to be properly understood. We refer to the discussions in Chapters 2, 3 and 5 related to unknown knowns, unknown unknowns and black swans. The proper assessment of strength of knowledge is a key issue here. It is important to recognize that a strength of knowledge assessment refers to the knowledge of the analyst – if there is insufficient knowledge strength, it is essential to classify this situation as low-strength of knowledge.

In this regard, it is important to recognize the value of the extended risk matrix and how the matrix should be used. This matrix is not designed to offer risk numbers. Instead, it should be used as a decision-making tool that allows the analyst to understand the relative importance and priorities among the various risk events. If a particular risk event involves a low strength of knowledge assessment, that information should be included in the relative prioritization of the risk when planning for risk management activities.

It is also important to recognize the value of transparency in the ERM process. The analyst is responsible for fully disclosing assumptions made – particularly in cases where expert knowledge is not available. While it is important to have a well-functioning risk program, it is equally important for the analyst to act with integrity and fully disclose deficiencies in the analysis. This builds credibility and invites others in the organization to trust the process and also the implementation.

8.6.3 Risk management activities interfere with normal operations

It is common for organizations to struggle with internalizing the importance of risk management activities, leading to challenges in achieving the balance between performance/efficiencies and managing risk, as discussed in Chapter 6.

As with any organizational endeavor, there is need for humility in the work that is completed. The ERM process should have a symbiotic relationship with the rest of the organization – it should not cause surprising or unnecessary disruptions to normal operations. If a risk management action does not align with the multi-stakeholder needs and operations, it is important for stakeholders to communicate these issues with the analysts. The most undesirable outcome would involve stakeholders not properly implementing risk management actions and not reporting. Lack of transparency can cause the analyst to be unaware of the improper implementation of risk management activities. If it is found that risk management actions are not feasible or practical, the analysts should reiterate the ERM process and practice due diligence in ensuring that all impacted stakeholders are confident that the risk management actions are achievable.

8.6.4 Organizational anarchy – agreed upon risk management activities are not being implemented

During the implementation or monitoring of risk management activities, it may be found that agreed-upon risk management activities are not being properly implemented. It is well documented in the process management literature: The process should always align with agreed-upon policies. Otherwise, an out of control process can be a major liability for an organization. If one policy is not followed, that is a strong signal that others are not being followed. Thus, this type of situation is a signal of a much larger issue – the inability to follow policy. Obviously, this type of finding can essentially impact the accuracy of the entire ERM process, as it would then be unclear if any ERM-related policies, beliefs and assumptions are actually reflective of the organization.

The next appropriate step would be to coordinate with executives and explore somewhat difficult questions, such as:

- What organizational procedures (including ERM) are being followed according to policy?
- What organizational procedures are not being followed? Why?
- Is there executive support to fix the situation?

- Is it practical and feasible for executive or managerial action to fix the situation?
- What is the timeline to fix the situation and how does that timeline fit into ERM implementation plans?

If executives are, in fact, aware of this issue and are unable to control or manage through this, then the ERM process is deemed ineffective. Without executive backing, there really is no significant recourse.

8.6.5 Multiple responsibility parties for risk management activities

Often, a risk management activity may involve multiple responsible parties. For example, implementation of new cybersecurity protocols may involve coordination between multiple departments. An information technology department may be responsible for providing and maintaining technological resources. Additionally, an operations department may be responsible for proper use of the new technologies. With multiple responsible parties, it may be challenging to coordinate implementation of risk management activities and also identify responsible parties if the risk management activities are not being properly implemented.

This should be a consideration of the analyst when implementing ERM. For each risk management activity that is implemented, the policy should clearly state the responsible parties for each component of the activity. Additionally, stakeholder outreach should ensure that various responsible parties agree with the assigned responsibilities.

There may be cases in which there is no clear responsible party for various business functions. This is a higher-level managerial concern. Until a full organizational structure is known and agreed upon by the various organizational units, a risk program should not be implemented.

9 Revisiting key case study issues

This chapter returns to the case studies presented in Chapter 1. The discussion focuses on how to use methods and principles from this book to address the key issues presented.

9.1 The GM ignition switch scandal

This section returns to the GM ignition switch case study example presented in Section 1.1. While the discussion in Section 1.1 referred to facts directly related to GM, the discussion in this chapter refers to general risk issues that relate to any company in a similar position. Therefore, the discussion of this section should be interpreted as a generalized discussion of key issues, while not speculating specifically about a single corporation (GM).

9.1.1 Overview of key issues in the GM ignition switch scandal

The GM ignition switch scandal poses a very current and relevant issue faced by organizations: How can an organization balance both safety and profit? In Section 1.1 we considered the following questions:

- What risks and uncertainties were relevant to the various stakeholders?
- How can and should a company in a similar position measure and describe performance, risk and uncertainties?
- How should the risks have been handled? What risk strategies and policies are relevant to a company in a similar position? Which should be adopted?

At the foundation of performance measurement for a publicly traded company is financial performance. Metrics, such as net income, earnings per share, price to earnings ratio and return on equity are typical metrics shared on a company's earnings report. Lawsuits and fines may have some impact on a company's financial performance. Of course, this would depend on the magnitude of costs, including settlements and penalties. In some cases, the publicity from lawsuits may impact shareholder value either positively or negatively. For example, losing a lawsuit may signal a negative impact on financial metrics. Conversely, winning a lawsuit might be a symbol of the company's strength, which could ultimately improve shareholder value.

It can be argued that investments in non-financial metrics, such as safety and sustainability, can have measurable financial benefits, in the avoidance of lawsuits, image with shareholders, customer demand, etc. In recent years, there has been increasing interest in high-performance specialized mutual funds, with examples given in WSJ (2016). Focus areas of these funds include issues such as human rights, ethical practices and sustainability. With the influx of more socially conscious investors, support from these types of funds could be beneficial for companies. Thus, following policies of ethics, human rights, sustainability, etc. could have significant benefits.

Examples of non-financial goals may include metrics such as:

- Sustainability: Absolute greenhouse gas emissions, absolute potable water use, percentage of solid waste that is diverted from a landfill, energy consumptions and CO_2 emissions
- Health and safety: Work-related injuries, fatalities, lost-time accidents, total recordable incident rate per 1,000 workers, hazardous waste releases, product safety and product recalls

Specifically, to the case study topic, non-financial performance indicators may include vehicle safety scores as measured by third-party testing agencies, deployment of safety technologies, number of noncompliance recalls, vehicle testing processes and safety engineering innovations.

There were also several key uncertainties that directly relate to this case study. At the time of the decisions involving the ignition switch scandal, there were very significant concerns over the company's viability under challenging economic conditions. This can result in emphasis on following short-term variation metrics reflecting financial viability of the company, or fuel price fluctuations leading to rapid changes in demand. It could then be easy to lose focus on the remaining relevant long-term uncertainties, including: customer reputation due to product quality, customer reputation due to taxpayer assistance and product performance.

9.1.2 How should risk be characterized for these stakeholders?

We structure this section using three key stakeholders: the corporation under similar conditions, consumers and regulators.

The corporation

According to the recommendations provided in this book (see Chapter 2) risk and enterprise risk is understood as (C,U), where C is the consequences of the activity considered and U is related uncertainties, or (A,C,U), where A is an event (or events) and C is the effects given A. In the following, we will use the latter conceptualization to highlight the events A. With hindsight, we can point to A as the event that GM produced a defect ignition switch (A_1) or as the event that GM made the decision to continue using the switch knowing that it was defective (A_2). The effects C given these events can be expressed through "a number of fatalities" (C_1), "a number of injuries" (C_2), "costs due to penalties and lawsuits" (C_3) and "losses due to reputational damage (reduction of shareholder value and customer demand)" (C_4).

Now let us make a thought-construction going back in time before the occurrence of these events. The issue is how to characterize the risks. Following the recommendation in Chapter 2, risk is to be characterized by the (A',C',Q,K), where A' is some specified events, C' is some specified consequences (given A'), Q is a measure or description of uncertainty and K is the knowledge supporting Q. We can think about the risk assessment and management being conducted in the development phase of the switch, aiming at identifying all types of faults in the system and rectify these. However, our focus here is the stage where GM has actually detected the fault. The issue is either making a decision to continue using the switch (A') or not. The related risk assessment is basically about analyzing the effects of making such a decision or, alternatively, trying to fix the problem.

Consider first the former decision (A'). Two main types of scenarios can quickly be identified: 1) the faulty switch is causing severe problems for GM (large penalties and lawsuits, reputational damage), and 2) the faulty switch is not causing severe problems for GM. A refinement of these scenarios could also be used with more specific categories, but for the sake of the discussion in this section we concentrate on scenario 1) occurring or not. We refer to scenario 1) as S.

The next issue to discuss is how likely or probable the occurrence of S is given the knowledge, K, available, i.e. $P(S|K)$. The assessment is conducted by the key managers of the company together with relevant technical experts, guided by risk analyst experts. Let us assume that it is concluded that $P(S|K) \leq 0.10$. However, the knowledge supporting this probability assignment is considered rather weak. There are little relevant data that can support the conclusion, and there is also considerable disagreement in the assessment group. Suppose some experts pointed to a rather poor understanding of the problems and their potential effects. The probability of 0.10 was based on the assumption that some type of mitigation behavior was already proposed and implemented: Drivers were instructed to remove unessential items from their key chains due to ignition switch issues. The assumption is referred to as D.

The risk assessment covers in particular a scrutiny test of the knowledge K to identify potential surprises. Could there be some unknown knowns or events on a lower level of detail ignored due to judged negligible probabilities? Essentially, the assumption D was based on an assessment of human behavior, suggesting that drivers would in-turn follow instructions regarding the removal of unessential items on the key chain. However, drivers may not have appropriately followed instructions for several reasons:

- Drivers may not have received the instructions.
- Drivers may not have perceived the seriousness of the instructions.
- The instructions in the communication differ significantly from any other vehicle, thereby not following intuitive behavior.

- Instructions violated several product safety recommendations, such as considering how consumers are likely to use the product under real-world conditions, ensuring instructions are available every time the product is used, communicating the consequences of consumer's actions and conducting usability testing to determine whether customers can properly follow instructions (Smith et al. 2003).

To characterize risk, we conduct an extended risk matrix analysis, consisting of the following elements (refer to Section 2.2.4):

- Events A' with consequences exceeding some specified levels
- Probabilities of these events
- Judgments of the strength of knowledge, SoK, supporting these probabilities

The extended risk matrix shown in Figure 9.1 shows four events:

- *Reputation*: Reputation loss resulting from public knowledge that the company did not address the ignition switch issue, despite the low cost of addressing the issue
- *Penalties*: Legal penalties associated with recall processes, accounting procedures, and safety issues related to the ignition switch issue. For example, GM faced a fine through the US Securities and Exchange Commission (SEC 2017) due to accounting control failures.

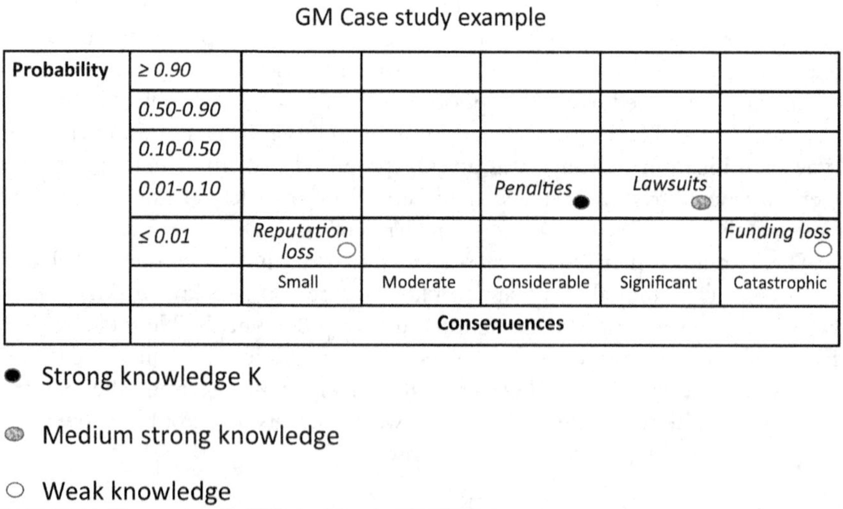

GM Case study example

Probability	≥ 0.90					
	0.50-0.90					
	0.10-0.50					
	0.01-0.10			Penalties ●	Lawsuits ◍	
	≤ 0.01	Reputation loss ○				Funding loss ○
		Small	Moderate	Considerable	Significant	Catastrophic
	Consequences					

● Strong knowledge K

◍ Medium strong knowledge

○ Weak knowledge

Figure 9.1 Example of extended risk matrix applied to GM case study

- *Lawsuits*: Lawsuits related to deaths and injuries that can be attributed to the ignition switch issue
- *Funding Loss*: Loss of bailout funding through the Troubled Asset Relief Program associated with poor economic conditions

Using the approach suggested by Aven and Flage (2018), see Section 2.2.4, *Penalties* and *Lawsuits* would be considered very high risk events, with their relatively large impacts, high probabilities and strong supporting knowledge. The natural implications could have been no continuing production of the defective ignition switch.

The event of Funding Loss would be deemed as high risk, with its relatively small probability and weak background knowledge. The event of Reputation loss is initially classified as moderate high risk, as the consequences are considered rather small, but, as these judgments are based on weak knowledge, further analysis is conducted. There is potential for higher consequences than anticipated.

A special assumption deviation risk analysis was conducted to scrutinize key assumptions, as discussed in Section 2.2.3. The idea is to consider errors in these beliefs (deviations of the assumptions made), the implications for the quantities studied in the probabilistic analysis and associated uncertainties. The uncertainties are judged by a direct argument or by using probability with related strength of knowledge judgments. All judgments here are of a qualitative form. As an illustration, consider the assumption D defined above, that drivers to a large degree followed the instructions of removing unessential items from their key chains due to ignition switch issues. As discussed above, there are many potential scenarios that could happen which lead to deviations from this assumption, the result being that the faulty switch is causing severe problems for the corporation, i.e. the event S occurs. The likelihood for considerable deviations from D is judged to be rather high – with rather strong knowledge support – given the arguments as summarized above. It is concluded that there is a considerable assumption deviation risk related to D. The preliminary judgment about the reputation risk is updated, the consequence category is increased, and the risk is judged as high risk.

For the decision, trying to fix the problem and discontinue using the switch, cost figures are derived. There are some uncertainties related to how long it would take to rectify the problems, but an order of magnitude of cost could rather quickly be estimated.

Based on this analysis, the corporation makes some conclusions concerning the risk. Making a decision to continue to use the switch would imply a very high risk, as there is potential for extreme negative consequences and the uncertainties are considerable. The probabilities for severe consequences for the corporation are judged to be relatively low, but the knowledge supporting the probability judgment is weak.

Making the decision to try to fix the problem and discontinue using the switch is considered to imply huge costs and could result in bankruptcy for the company.

Consumers

For the consumers, there is risk related to this faulty switch. It could lead to loss of lives or injuries. With limited knowledge about the specific issue, and relying on producers and regulators requirements, consumers will assume that such problems do not exist. Hence the risk is considered negligible.

Regulators

For the regulators, the risk judgments would be as for the consumers if not additional knowledge is available. However, such knowledge can be obtained by requesting information from the companies, and by doing inspections and audits. If insight about the faulty switch were available, risk assessment could be conducted as above for the corporation.

9.1.3 How should risk be managed?

We continue the thought-construction in the previous section, but now the focus is the ERM of GM, given that the fault has been detected. Risk has been assessed and characterized. Next, it needs to be evaluated and a decision made.

From a pure economic point of view the situation faced is difficult as both decision alternatives lead to high risk and potential severe negative consequences. As discussed in Chapter 3, various concerns and principles need to be balanced. If the decision considered is to continue using the switch, a cost-benefit type of analysis could be conducted, reflecting potential losses in the future. Such an analysis would be sensitive to the probability numbers used for specific categories of losses at future time periods. The uncertainties in future costs would be considerable and the analysis would provide rather arbitrary figures for expected values used. Nonetheless, such an analysis could provide useful insights if properly applied. The CBA (Cost Benefit Analysis) could, for example, show strong robustness in conclusions concerning the expected NPV by making a particular decision for different types of assumptions.

However, in a case like this with large uncertainties about the consequences of the decision, the information value from any expected value-based tool, such as a CBA, is limited. The issue is to large extent about how much weight is to be given to the cautionary principle to avoid severe losses as a result of future penalties, lawsuits and damaged reputation. There is, of course, also ethical aspects involved here, as continuing with the switch would result in humans being killed or injured. There exists no formula for finding the proper weight. The weight also has to be seen in relation to what the alternative decision is: take the costs now. These costs are huge and could have serious implications for the company and its survivability. The risk assessment has pointed to a large risk if the switch is continued to be used, and, together with the ethical aspects, the company will conclude that the decision to make is to fix the switch problem and take the costs now. If the company would continue to use its switch, it would be extremely vulnerable with respect to any type of event that could reveal the company's knowledge about the faulty switch and consecutive lack of corrective actions, and it would lose credibility as a prudent, trustworthy car producer.

As a reflection, think of a situation where a fault is discovered, but the implications are not so severe as in this particular case and the discovery likelihood of the fault is judged extremely low by the experts. Then it is obvious that the company could be tempted to take the risk if the economic factors are focused; it has a high risk appetite in the sense that it is willing to take on risk projects to pursue values (refer to Chapter 3.) Again, ethical considerations could change the decision. Also, reflections on the risk magnitude could lead to such a conclusion. The low-judged probabilities for discovery of the problems could be based on an assumption that the information would not be intentionally or unintentionally revealed, but history has shown that secrets are difficult to keep over some time when the issue is violation of accepted moral standards.

Also, as a reflection, we consider ethical standards and culture issues involved. Many organizations pride themselves on ethics and culture, often demonstrated in vision statements or strategic plans. While a company may choose to take a risk solely based on economic factors, neglecting cultural/ethical standards, as a one-time decision, the implications for ethics and culture can be much longer-lasting. A one-time lapse in ethical/cultural standards may serve as acceptance of future lapses, at both a corporate and employee level. Any deterioration of workforce standards has serious implications on structure and order within a workforce.

The ethical/cultural concerns also point to several consumer-related concerns, as discussed by Hermansson and Hansson (2007). Because many drivers were not fully aware of their own risk exposure, their risk exposure was decided by the corporation. Essentially, drivers may not have voluntarily taken a risk associated with driving vehicles with ignition switch issues. Additionally, many risk-exposed drivers did not have access to all relevant information about the risk associated with driving, nor were they included in the decision process. Finally, it is clear that the decision-maker benefitted from the drivers' risk exposure.

9.1.4 Concluding remarks

Continuing to use the faulty switch represented a minor short-term cost savings. Recall that a fix would cost less than one dollar per vehicle and $400,000 in tooling costs (Lienert and Thompson 2014). In times of severe competition and economic uncertainty, there is also an added benefit of avoiding any issues of public perception following a major vehicle recall. Of course, this type of benefit may only *delay* the onset of downsides described in the next paragraph.

While there were major benefits to continuing to use the faulty switch in the short-term, the long-term downsides were severe. The most severe downsides involved the safety of customers who were not aware of the faulty switch. The decision to continue using the faulty switch also resulted in degraded public valuation of product quality, lawsuits, penalties and some loss in shareholder value (while shareholder value continued to fluctuate).

This faulty ignition switch issue highlights a common decision-making dilemma in organizations: How should short-term gains be weighed against long-term losses? This is a strategic question that should reflect the values of the organization. It is possible that decision-makers, when tasked with preserving the viability of the corporation itself, are incentivized to prioritize preserving the image of the company and possibly preserving the possibility of a financial bailout by avoiding a major vehicle recall. Under similar circumstances, it is unclear whether decision-makers, shareholders and other stakeholders would act differently if the outcome was known.

Considering the notion of the "triple bottom line", recognizing that organizations should value both financial and non-financial performance aspects of the organization, it is clear that consumer safety should be a major factor in the risk assessment and management decision-making process.

It is also fair to recognize that vehicle manufacturers who prioritize safety and are able to communicate a focus on safety to customers can benefit greatly in the long-term through high quality perception and customer loyalty.

This case, as well as the two discussed in the coming sections, also points to the general concerns raised in Chapter 4. The risk management easily becomes too influenced by detailed KPIs and PRM (Project Risk Management) issues, instead of overall enterprise performance and risk. Short-term goals are prioritized, which could have devastating effects on longer-term profits and value generation of the enterprise. A successful risk management requires that enterprise risk is highlighted, i.e. risk where the consequences are related to the principal objectives or overall performance judged important for the organization. If the enterprise culture and management are dominated by TRM (Task Risk Management) and PRM, it is less likely that the critical and necessary questions will be asked.

9.2 The Volkswagen emission case

This section returns to the Volkswagen emissions case study example presented in Section 1.2. While the discussion in Section 1.2 referred to issues directly related to Volkswagen, the discussion in this chapter refers to general risk issues that relate to any company in a similar position. Therefore, the discussion of this section should be interpreted as a generalized discussion of key issues, while not speculating specifically about a single corporation (Volkswagen).

The discussion of the Volkswagen case study highlights several similarities to the preceding GM case study, as both companies are global automotive manufacturers and are publicly traded companies. The similarities allow for the discussion of this section to instead reflect on a different aspect of ERM: managing risk in an era of rapidly changing expectations for corporations. Aspects of sustainability and environmental protection are not as heavily regulated as aspects of safety, but environmental responsibilities are becoming increasingly regulated and valued by customers, as discussed below.

9.2.1 Overview of key issues the Volkswagen emission case

This case represents a common issue in organizations: How can an organization appropriately balance the pursuit of performance-related goals while in the presence of major risk sources. In Section 1.2, we considered the following questions:

- What risks and uncertainties were relevant to the various stakeholders, in particular the corporation?
- How can and should performance, risk and uncertainties be characterized in a situation like this?
- How should the risk have been handled? What risk strategies and policies would have been relevant to a company in a similar position? Which should be adopted?

Like the GM example in Section 9.1, a company in a similar position would likely value commonly-used financial metrics. There may be interest in also considering sustainability-related non-financial metrics that relate directly to the vehicle usage, which may include: fuel economy, emissions of pollutants, CO_2 emissions, use of technologies to aid in reduced emissions and improve fuel economy, use of alternative fuels, life-cycle energy use, life-cycle emissions and use of electric vehicle technologies. Additional customer-reputation related metrics may include: inventory turn rate, customer loyalty, used-vehicle value, average length of vehicle ownership and customer reviews.

The first key uncertainty relating to this case study involves understanding whether emissions irregularities would be detected. This type of issue will become more relevant as mechanical features of products become automated, with increasingly complex technologies and algorithms. Thus, the detection of defeat devices may become more difficult in the future. With use of artificial intelligence in these types of system features, it may even become increasingly difficult to prove any criminal intent if defeat devices are detected. These issues may in fact create additional incentives for producers to install these types of defeat devices. The second key uncertainty related to this case study involves how customers would react to knowledge of the defeat devices. While this knowledge could negatively impact customer loyalty, it is also possible that collective customer "memories" are short. In other words, customers may not forgive this type of corporate behavior, but they may forget when making purchasing decisions.

9.2.2 How should risk be characterized for these stakeholders?

We leave it as an exercise for the reader to structure the risk characterization for stakeholders, as was done for the GM case study in the previous section. The discussion here will instead focus on the main differences between the Volkswagen and GM case studies.

We focus attention of risk assessment and management to the development and implementation of the defeat device, considering whether to implement the defeat device. We can then conduct a risk assessment to understand the effects of making this decision. When considering $P(S|K)$ and how likely or probable the occurrence of S (the defeat device is detected, leading to penalties, lawsuits, reputational damage and greenhouse gas emissions) is given the knowledge available K, any assigned probability would be based on the assumption that vehicles would only undergo required emissions testing, and no additional third-party testing would occur. This type of assumption may be based on an assessment of regulatory requirements for vehicle emissions testing. However, third-party testing can and does occur, as demonstrated in the case of Volkswagen, as the third-party tests were sponsored by a regional clean air agency. The likelihood for deviations from the assumption is judged to be high, as third-party testing of vehicles is becoming increasingly common.

9.2.3 How should risk be managed?

We now focus on ERM of the corporation given that the defeat device has been implemented. From an economic point of view, it is clear that major financial gains can be achieved from installing the defeat device. With an image of clean emissions, the corporation can achieve drastic growth and brand reputation. Any cost-benefit analysis reflecting potential losses involves significant uncertainties in future sales, as knowledge of the defeat device could potentially diminish vehicle value and brand loyalty.

If the corporation continued use of the defeat device, any related evidence of guilt could have tarnished the corporation's credibility. However, if the likelihood of evidence of guilt is thought to be low by the experts, there could be financial incentive for the company to take the risk. When also considering ethical and other non-financial aspects of the issue, there may be a strong incentive to not the take the risk. As with the GM case study, a one-time lapse in ethical/cultural standards may signal to employees that these standards are not upheld as strongly as financial standards, therefore deteriorating any structure and order within a workforce.

9.2.4 Concluding remarks

Choosing to implement a defeat device could potentially have contributed to major performance-related successes, including financial gains, customer image, brand loyalty, brand reputation and sustainability-related reputation. The downsides of using the defeat device may not have been perceived as being severe, given the unforeseen third-party testing and relatively low cost of fines and penalties associated with using the defeat device. In fact, the downsides may have appeared innocuous enough to incentivize other manufacturers to also use defeat devices (Contag et al. 2017).

While there were short-term benefits to using the defeat device, the most severe downsides involved both the environmental impact and also the breach of trust with customers and shareholders. The decision to use the defeat device also resulted in degraded public valuation of product quality, lawsuits, penalties and a short-term loss in shareholder value.

The use of a defeat device explores questions surrounding how organizations should balance performance-related goals while in the presence of major risk sources. Again, similarly to the GM case study, this brings to question strategic issues surrounding staying true to a company's overall mission (both financial and non-financial). When considering the "triple bottom line", environmental impact should be weighed heavily in the risk assessment and management decision-making process. In fact, the presence of "green" technologies and processes can be a very positive factor in vehicle purchasing decisions.

9.3 Risk in information technology – Equifax data breach

This case represents a serious issue that is faced by any organization that can be impacted by cybersecurity issues within their information technology functions: How should an organization characterize risk in the presence of varying levels of knowledge, potential surprises and black swans? In Section 1.3 we considered the following questions:

- What risks and uncertainties were relevant to the various stakeholders, in particular Equifax?
- What ERM processes/procedures could avoid this type of event?

The discussion below is intended to be generalized to apply to any organization in a similar position. The intent is not to speculate specifically about Equifax.

9.3.1 What risks and uncertainties were relevant to the various stakeholders?

In the case of the Equifax data breach, the system vulnerability was known to the company, government agencies, attackers and the general public.

Additionally, Equifax had procedures in place to patch the known vulnerabilities, but breakdowns in those procedures led to the system being unpatched for several months. The situation was made more serious due to delay in informing the public about the data breach. The discussion below focuses on the aspect of uncertainty related to major assumptions being made about the organization when forming risk policies.

As discussed in Chapter 5 of this book, we interpret a black swan as a surprising extreme event relative to one's knowledge/beliefs. We consider unknown unknowns (neither we nor others have knowledge), unknown knowns (we do not have the knowledge but others do), and events that are judged to have a negligible probability of occurrence and thus are not believed to occur.

Any organization in a similar position could perform an assessment of the strength of knowledge supporting the risk assessment, by addressing issues like (refer to Section 2.2.3 and Appendix B.7):

- The reasonability of the assumptions made
- The amount and relevancy of data/information
- The degree of agreement among experts
- The degree to which the phenomena involved are understood
- The degree to which the knowledge K has been thoroughly examined (for example, with respect to unknown knowns; i.e. others have the knowledge, but not the analysis group)

For the fourth point, following Askeland et al. (2017), a key point is to address the capacity and the intention of potential risk sources.

When considering risk associated with a data breach event, there are obviously many uncertainties involving the identity and motives of potential attackers and the potential attack mechanisms. However, the most relevant issue here is the assumptions made about the organization's ability to implement documented policies. For example, it is common for organizations to have system patching policies, such as patching within 30 days for critical patches and within 90 days for non-critical patches. Having this type of policy in place could lead to system managers assessing the assumption of timely patched vulnerabilities to be reasonable, suggesting a rather low probability of the vulnerability to be a serious problem for the company. However, this type of assumption neglects to recognize the likelihood of human error or a breakdown in documented policies. Additionally, this assumption neglects to recognize that a system attacker could potentially exploit the vulnerability within an allotted 30-day patching period.

By evaluating the strength of knowledge, and in particular the item concerning assumptions, the strength of knowledge is judged as rather high and the risk related to a cyber-attack to be serious.

9.3.2 *What ERM processes/procedures could avoid this type of event?*

As discussed in Chapter 5, there are different strategies that can be used to manage the organization's vulnerabilities. First, there is designing processes that are tolerant to disruptions and can reduce consequences of failure. To be immune to failures could involve investment in more secure information technology systems or an increase in resources for managing system risk. Second, there is the option to develop a system which is able to rapidly detect and respond to system attacks. Both strategies require adequate ERM maturity, as described in Section 3.5. The key maturity characteristics are described below.

First, consider ERM maturity characteristic *C.2 Regular assessment and accountability at all levels of the organization, to ensure risk policies are properly implemented.* This characteristic would require consistency in implementation of risk policies, and also proper actions when risk policies are not being properly implemented. In this case study, it is unclear whether patching behavior was regularly assessed, but it is clear that monitoring of this behavior could have avoided this risk event. This also involves a cultural shift to avoid complacency and inattention, allowing managers to constantly test and correct any counterproductive risk behaviors.

Second, consider ERM maturity characteristic *P.3 Knowledge-dependent prioritization of risk informed by formal tools.* This characteristic may be easily overlooked as assumptions related to patching behaviors could have logically been assumed to lead to a low failure probability as discussed in Section 9.3.1. However, it is also important to test and research these assumptions, and this is exactly what the strength of knowledge approach aims at achieving.

Third, consider ERM maturity characteristic *C.4 Implementation of open, transparent and timely risk communication procedures.* In this case study, the organization did not report the data breach in a timely manner. While it is important for organizations to fully understand the magnitude of the event prior to making the event public, delays in informing the impacted stakeholders could potentially have exacerbated any data breach related consequences.

Finally, it is also important to reflect on the aspect of resilience, as mentioned in ERM maturity characteristic *R.4 Clear and detailed risk strategies (risk-informed strategies, cautionary/precautionary/robustness/resilience strategies, and discursive strategies).* In this case study, additional confusion was caused by the system recovery process. For example, the breached data was not encrypted (House of Representatives 2017), there were issues with the data breach information website, and delays in communication with stakeholders. A strong ERM strategy recognizes that all risk events may not be avoidable, but solid contingency plans must be in place prior to the risk event.

9.3.3 Concluding remarks

This case is notably different from the GM and Volkswagen case studies in several ways. First, this incident would be considered an intentional attack on the system, though the organization did not intentionally allow this situation to happen. Thus, this situation could be interpreted as an accident (not intentional) if the organization had documented procedures that were designed to avoid this type of event. Second, the breach was not immediately discovered – it was ongoing for months. Therefore, it was not a one-time occurrence or decision, but rather an ongoing and undetected issue. Third, public behavior or reactions are less relevant because users do not "opt-in" to having their information owned by this type of organization. Finally, it is difficult or near impossible to accurately measure the consequence of a data breach, since stolen identity information could have been accessed from other sources, while also the implications of a data breach can occur over years and even decades.

As it is common for organizations to have policies dictating how quickly vulnerabilities are patched, it is important to also ask why breakdowns in this policy occur. There could be many reasons, such as:

- Insufficient resources to manage patching for vulnerabilities, especially when surges occur or during low-resource periods (weekends, holidays, concurrent issues with natural disasters, etc.)
- Difficultly in prioritizing patching. In other words, recognizing which patches are of most urgent need
- Inability to understand the implications of any patch on broader information technology. For example, patching one vulnerability could potentially impact the functionality or security of a related technology.

This case study involves a common issue faced by organizations: They do not fully understand the risk landscape, as there are so many uncertainties involved with technologies and attack mechanisms. This type of situation can leave organizations feeling anxious about their inability to control or manage risk related to cyber-incidents. While the use of key ERM principles could help to avoid this type of event, it is equally important to invest in resilience, recognizing that all possible events cannot always be fully avoided.

References

Ackoff, R. (1970) A concept of corporate planning. *Long Range Planning*, 3(1), 2–8. AICPA. www.aicpa.org/InterestAreas/BusinessIndustryAndGovernment/Resources/ERM/DownloadableDocuments/AICPA_ERM_Research_Study_2016.pdf

Ambrose, F., & Ahern, B. (2008) "Unconventional red teaming", Anticipating Rare Events: Can Acts of Terror, Use of Weapons of Mass Destruction or Other High Profile Acts Be Anticipated? Available at: https://info.publicintelligence.net/DoD-AnticipatingRareEvents.pdf

Armstrong, M. (2017) *Reinventing Performance Management*. London: Kogan Page Publishers.

Årstad, I., & Aven, T. (2017) Managing major accident risk: Concerns about complacency and complexity in practice. *Safety Science*, 91, 114–121.

Askeland, T., Flage, R., & Aven, T. (2017) Moving beyond probabilities – Strength of knowledge characterisations applied to security. *Reliability Engineering and System Safety*, 159, 196–205.

ASQ (2019a) *What Is a Fault Tree Analysis?* July 8, 2019. http://asq.org/quality-progress/2002/03/problem-solving/what-is-a-fault-tree-analysis.html

ASQ (2019b) *What is FMEA? Failure Mode & Effects Analysis | ASQ*, July 8, 2019. https://asq.org/quality-resources/fmea

Aven, E., & Aven, T. (2015) On the need for rethinking current practice which highlights goal achievement risk in an enterprise context. *Risk Analysis*, 35(9), 1706–1716.

Aven, T. (2010) On the need for restricting the probabilistic analysis in risk assessments to variability. *Risk Analysis*, 30, 354–360. With discussion 381–384.

Aven, T. (2011) *Quantitative Risk Assessment. The Scientific Platform*. Cambridge: Cambridge University Press.

Aven, T. (2012a) The risk concept: Historical and recent development trends. *Reliability Engineering and System Safety*, 115, 136–145.

Aven, T. (2012b) *Foundations of Risk Analysis*. 2nd ed. New York: Wiley.

Aven, T. (2013a) Practical implications of the new risk perspectives. *Reliability Engineering and System Safety*, 115, 136–145.

Aven, T. (2013b) On the meaning and use of the risk appetite concept. *Risk Analysis*, 33(3), 462–468.

Aven, T. (2013c) On Blacks swans in a risk context. *Safety Science*, 57, 44–51.

Aven, T. (2014) *Risk, Surprises and Black Swans*. New York: Routledge.

Aven, T. (2015a) The concept of antifragility and its implications for the practice of risk analysis. *Risk Analysis*, 35(3), 476–483.

Aven, T. (2015b) Implications of black swans to the foundations and practice of risk assessment and management. *Reliability Engineering and System Safety*, 134, 83–91. Open Access.

Aven, T. (2015c) On the allegations that small risks are treated out of proportion to their importance. *Reliability Engineering and System Safety*, 140, 116–121. Open Access.

Aven, T. (2015d) Comments to the short communication by Jan Erik Vinnem and Stein Haugen titled "Perspectives on risk and the unforeseen". *Reliability Engineering and System Safety*, 137, 69–75.

Aven, T. (2016a) Risk assessment and risk management: Review of recent advances on their foundation. *European Journal of Operational Research*, 25, 1–13. Open Access.

Aven, T. (2016b) Ignoring scenarios in risk assessments: Understanding the issue and improving current practice. *Reliability Engineering and System Safety*, 145, 215–220.

Aven, T. (2016c) On the difference between risk as seen from the perspectives of the analysts and management. *ASME Journal Risk Uncertainty Part B*, 2(3), 031002.1–031002.7.

Aven, T. (2017a) On some foundational issues related to cost-benefit and risk. *International Journal of Business Continuity and Risk Management*, 7(3), 182–191.

Aven, T. (2017b) Improving risk characterisations in practical situations by highlighting knowledge aspects, with applications to risk matrices. *Reliability Engineering and System Safety*, 167, 42–48.

Aven, T. (2017c) How some types of risk assessments can support resilience analysis and management. *Reliability Engineering and System Safety*, 167, 536–543.

Aven, T. (2017d) Improving the foundation and practice of reliability engineering. In *Proceedings of the Institution of Mechanical Engineers, Part O: Journal of Risk and Reliability*, 231(3) 295–305.

Aven, T. (2017e) The flaws of the ISO 31000 conceptualisation of risk. *Journal of Risk and Reliability Editorial*, 231(5), 467–468.

Aven, T. (2018a) An emerging new risk analysis science: Foundations and implications. *Risk Analysis*, 38(5), 876–888.

Aven, T. (2018b) The meaning of a black swan, in V. Bier (ed.) *Risk in Extreme Environments*. New York: Routledge.

Aven, T. (2018c) Reflections on the use of conceptual research in risk analysis. *Risk Analysis*, 38(11), 2415–2423.

Aven, T. (2019a) The call for a shift from risk to resilience: What does it mean? *Risk Analysis*, 39(6), 1196–1203.

Aven, T. (2019b) The cautionary principle in risk management: Foundation and practical use. *Reliability Engineering and System Safety*, 191, 106585.

Aven, T. (2019c) How to determine the largest global and national risks: Review and discussion.

Aven, T. (2019d) The neglected pillar of science: Risk and uncertainty analysis.

Aven, T., Baraldi, P., Flage, R., & Zio, E. (2014) *Uncertainty in Risk Assessment*. Chichester: Wiley.

Aven, T., & Flage, R. (2018) Risk assessment with broad uncertainty and knowledge characterisations: An illustrating case study, in T. Aven & E. Zio (eds.) *Knowledge in Risk Assessments*. New York, NY: Wiley.

Aven, T., & Kirkeby, S. (1989) Reliability targets for oil and gas production systems, in T. Aven (ed.) *Reliability Achievement*. London: Elsevier, 1989.

Aven, T., & Kristensen, V. (2019) How the distinction between general knowledge and specific knowledge can improve the foundation and practice of risk assessment and risk-informed decision-making. *Reliability Engineering and System Safety*, 191, 106553.

Aven, T., & Krohn, B.S. (2014) A new perspective on how to understand, assess and manage risk and the unforeseen. *Reliability Engineering and System Safety*, 121, 1–10.

Aven, T., & Nøkland, T.E. (2010) On the use of uncertainty importance measures in reliability and risk analysis. *Reliability Engineering and System Safety*, 95, 127–133.

Aven, T., & Reniers, G. (2013) How to define and interpret a probability in a risk and safety setting. Discussion paper, with general introduction by Associate Editor, Genserik Reniers. *Safety Science*, 51, 223–231.

Aven, T., & Renn, O. (2009) On risk defined as an event where the outcome is uncertain. *Journal Risk Research*, 12, 1–11.

Aven, T., & Renn, O. (2010) *Risk Management and Risk Governance*. New York: Springer Verlag.

Aven, T., & Renn, O. (2018) Improving government policy on risk: Eight key principles. *Reliability Engineering and System Safety*, 176, 230–241.

Aven, T., & Renn, O. (2019) Some foundational issues related to risk governance and different types of risks. *Journal of Risk Research*. https://doi.org/10.1080/13669877.2019.1569099

Aven, T., Renn, O., & Rosa, E. (2011) On the ontological status of the concept of risk. *Safety Science*, 49, 1074–1079.

Aven, T., & Thekdi, S. (2018) The importance of resilience-based strategies in risk analysis, and vice versa, in B.D. Trump, M.-V. Florin & I. Linkov (eds.) *IRGC Resource Guide on Resilience* (Vol. 2, pp. 33–38). Domains of Resilience for Complex Interconnected Systems. Lausanne, CH: EPFL International Risk Governance Center. Available at irgc.epfl.ch and irgc.org.

Aven, T., & Vinnem, J.E. (2007) *Risk Management*. Berlin: Springer Verlag.

Aven, T., & Ylönen, M. (2019) The strong power of standards in the safety and risk fields: A threat to proper developments of these fields? *Reliability Engineering and System Safety*, 189, 279–286.

Bang, P., & Thuestad, O. (2014) Government-enforced self-regulation: The Norwegian case, in P. Lindøe, M. Baram & O. Renn (eds.) *Risk Governance of Offshore Oil and Gas Operations*. Cambridge, USA: Cambridge University Press.

Bazerman, M.H., & Watkins, M. (2008) *Predictable Surprises: The Disasters You Should Have Seen Coming, and How to Prevent Them*. Boston: Harvard Business Review Press.

Bea, R., Mitroff, I., Farber, D., Foster, H., & Roberts, K.H. (2009) A new approach to risk: The implications of E3. *Risk Management*, 11(1), 30–43.

Beck, U. (1992) *Risk Society: Towards a New Modernity*. London: Sage.

Bedford, T., & Cooke, R. (2001) *Probabilistic Risk Analysis*, Cambridge: Cambridge University Press.

Bergman, B. (2009) Conceptualistic pragmatism: a framework for Bayesian analysis? *IIE Transactions*, 41, 86–93.

Bergström, J., Van Winsen, R., & Henriqson, E. (2015) On the rationale of resilience in the domain of safety: A literature review. *Reliability Engineering and System Safety*, 141, 131–141.

Bernardo, J., & Smith, A. (1994) *Bayesian Theory*. New York: Wiley.

Bernstein et al. (2014) www.reuters.com/article/us-takata-airbags/exclusive-takata-engineers-struggled-to-maintain-air-bag-quality-documents-reveal-idUSKCN0I701B20141018

Bierly, P.E., & Spender, J.-C. (1995). Culture and high reliability organizations: The case of the nuclear submarine. *Journal of Management*, 21, 639–656.

Bjerga, T., & Aven, T. (2016) Some perspectives on risk management – a security case study from the oil and gas industry. *Journal of Risk and Reliability*, 230(5) 512–520.

Bloem, J., Van Doorn, M., Duivestein, S., Excoffier, D., Maas, R., & Van Ommeren, E. (2014) *The Fourth Industrial Revolution*. Sogeti VINT. https://www.fr.sogeti.com/globalassets/global/downloads/reports/vint-research-3-the-fourth-industrial-revolution

Boin, A., & Renaud, C. (2013) Orchestrating joint sensemaking across government levels: Challenges and requirements for crisis leadership. *Journal of Leadership Studies*, 7(3), 41–46.

Boin, A., & Schulman, P. (2008) Assessing NASA's safety culture: The limits and possibilities of high reliability theory. *Public Administration Review*, 68(6), 1050–1062.

Borgonovo, E., & Plischke, E. (2015) Sensitivity analysis: A review of recent advances. *European Journal of Operational Research*, 248, 869–887.

Brown, P.C., Roediger, H.L., & McDaniel, M.A. (2014) *Make It Stick*. Cambridge, MA: Harvard University Press.

Brugnach, M., Dewulf, A.R.P.J., Pahl-Wostl, C., & Taillieu, T. (2008) Toward a relational concept of uncertainty: About knowing too little, knowing too differently, and accepting not to know. *Ecology and Society*, 13(2), 30.

CEFIC (2005) CEFIC Paper on Substitution and Authorization under REACH, 1–3.

Center, C.A.F.E.E. (2014) *In-Use Emissions Testing of Light-Duty Diesel Vehicles in the United States*. https://theicct.org/sites/default/files/publications/WVU_LDDV_in-use_ICCT_Report_Final_may2014.pdf

Chermack, T.J. (2011) *Scenario Planning in Organizations*. San Francisco: BK Publishers.

Clemons, E.K. (1995) Using scenario analysis to manage the strategic risks of reengineering. *Sloan Management Review*, 36(4), 61.

Carnap, R. (1922) *Der logische Aufbau der Welt*. Berlin.

Carnap, R. (1929) *Abriss der Logistik*. Wien.

Carroll, J., Sterman, J., & Marcus, A. (1998). *Playing the maintenance game: How mental models drive organizational decisions*. Debating rationality: Nonrational elements of organizational decision making, 99–121.

Contag, M., Li, G., Pawlowski, A., Domke, F., Levchenko, K., Holz, T., & Savage, S. (2017). How They Did It: An Analysis of Emission Defeat Devices in Modern Automobiles. 2017 *IEEE Symposium on Security and Privacy (SP)*, 231–250. https://doi.org/10.1109/SP.2017.66

Cooke, R.M. (2004) The anatomy of the squizzel: The role of operational definitions in representing uncertainty. *Reliability Engineering and System Safety*, 85, 313–319.

Copeland, T.E., & Weston, J.F. (1988) *Finance Theory and Corporate Policy*. 3rd ed. New York: Addison-Wesley Publishing Company.

COSO. (2004) *Enterprise Risk Management – Integrated Framework Executive Summary*. Retrieved from https://www.coso.org/Documents/COSO-ERM-Executive-Summary.pdf

Covello, V.T., & Mumpower, J. (1985). Risk analysis and risk management: an historical perspective. *Risk Analysis*, 5(2), 103–120.

Cowell, R.G., Dawid, A.P., Lauritzen, S.L., & Spiegelhalter, D.J. (1999) *Probabilistic Networks and Expert Systems*. New York: Springer.

Cox, L.A.T. (2012) Confronting deep uncertainties in risk analysis. *Risk Analysis*, 32, 1607–1629.

Cox, T.L. (2008) What's wrong with risk matrices? *Risk Analysis: An International Journal*, 28(2), 497–512.

Dekker, S. (2012) *Drift into Failure*. Burlington, USA: Ashgate Publishing. Kindle Edition.

Deloitte. (2013). *Risk Culture: Three Stages of Continuous Improvement*. Retrieved October 30, 2019, from https://deloitte.wsj.com/riskandcompliance/2013/05/21/risk-culture-three-stages-of-continuous-improvement/

Deming, W.E. (2000) *The New Economics*. 2nd ed. Cambridge, MA: MIT CAES.

Department of Justice (2015) *Manhattan U.S. Attorney Announces Criminal Charges Against General Motors and Deferred Prosecution Agreement with $900 Million Forfeiture*. www.justice.gov/usao-sdny/pr/manhattan-us-attorney-announces-criminal-charges-against-general-motors-and-deferred. Published September 17, 2015. Accessed July 10, 2019.

DHS (2019) *Cybersecurity: Department of Homeland Security*. www.dhs.gov/cisa/cybersecurity. Accessed July 10, 2019.

Dillon, R.L., & Tinsley, C.H. (2008) How near-misses influence decision making under risk: A missed opportunity for learning. *Management Science*, 54(8), 1425–1440.

Drucker, P. (2012). *The practice of management*. London: Routledge.

Dubois, D. (2010) Representation, propagation and decision issues in risk analysis under incomplete probabilistic information. *Risk Analysis*, 30, 361–368.

Edwards, W., Miles, R.F., & von Winterfeltdt, D. (2007) *Advances in Decision Analysis*. From Foundations to Applications, Cambridge: Cambridge University Press.

EPA (2019a) Volkswagen clean air act civil settlement. *US EPA*. www.epa.gov/enforcement/volkswagen-clean-air-act-civil-settlement. Accessed July 10, 2019.

EPA (2019b) Summary of the clean air act. *US EPA*. www.epa.gov/laws-regulations/summary-clean-air-act. Accessed July 10, 2019.

EU (2019) *Review of the EU air policy – Environment – European commission*. http://ec.europa.eu/environment/air/quality/index.htm. Accessed July 10, 2019.

Ferson, S., & Ginzburg, L.R. (1996) Different methods are needed to propagate ignorance and variability. *Reliability Engineering and System Safety*, 54, 133–144.

Festinger, L. (1957) *A Theory of Cognitive Dissonance*. Stanford: Stanford University Press.

FHWA. (2019). *FHWA – Center for Innovative Finance Support-Fact Sheets*. Retrieved October 30, 2019, from https://www.fhwa.dot.gov/ipd/fact_sheets/p3_toolkit_02_riskvaluation-andallocation.aspx

Flage, R., Aven, T. (2009) Expressing and communicating uncertainty in relation to quantitative risk analysis (QRA). *Reliability and Risk Analysis: Theory and Applications*, 2(13), 9–18.

Flage, R., Aven, T., Baraldi, P., & Zio, E. (2014) Concerns, challenges and directions of development for the issue of representing uncertainty in risk assessment. *Risk Analysis*, 34(7), 1196–1207.

Francis, R., & Bekera, B. (2014) A metric and frameworks for resilience analysis of engineered and infrastructure systems. *Reliability Engineering & System Safety*, 121, 90–103.

Franklin, J. (2001) Resurrecting logical probability. *Erkenntnis*, 55(2), 277–305.

Freed (2017) Wells Fargo fires 4 executives amid probe into account scandal. *Reuters*. www.reuters.com/article/wells-fargo-accounts-idUSL1N1G61DF. Published February 21, 2017. Accessed July 10, 2019.

Freeman, R. E. (1999). Divergent stakeholder theory. *Academy of Management Review*, 24(2), 233–236.

Funtowicz, S.O., & Ravetz, J.R. (1990). *Uncertainty and Quality in Science for Policy*. Dordrecht: Kluwer Academic Publishers.

Funtowicz, S.O., & Ravetz, J.R. (1993) Science for the post-normal age. *Futures*, 25, 735–755.

GM (2005) *GM Service Bulletin*. www.cbc.ca/news2/pdf/2005%20GM%20Service%20Bulletin.pdf. Accessed July 10, 2019.

Goetsch, D.L., & Davis, S.B. (1997) *Introduction to Total Quality*. Englewood Cliffs, NJ: Prentice Hall.

Haimes, Y.Y. (2015) *Risk Modeling, Assessment, and Management*. 4th ed. New York: Wiley.

Hajek, A. (2001) Probability, logic and probability logic, in ed. L. Goble (ed.), *The Blackwell Companion to Logic* (362–384). Oxford: Blackwell.

Hanley, N., & Spash, C.L. (1993) *Cost-benefit Analysis and the Environment*. Cheltenham, England: Edward Elgar Publishing Ltd.

Harrison, M.I. (2005) *Diagnosing Organizations: Methods, Models, and Processes*. Thousand Oaks, CA: SAGE.

Henning, P. (2017) Hack will lead to little, if any, punishment for Equifax. *The New York Times*. www.nytimes.com/2017/09/20/business/equifax-hack-penalties.html. Published September 20, 2017. Accessed July 10, 2019.

Hermansson, H., & Hansson, S.O. (2007) A three-party model tool for ethical risk analysis. *Risk Management*, 9(3), 129–144.

Hollnagel, E. (2019) "*Resilience Engineering*". Accessed October 27, 2019 http://erikholl-nagel.com/ideas/resilience-engineering.html

Hollnagel, E., Woods, D., & Leveson, N. (2006) *Resilience Engineering: Concepts and Precepts*. Aldershot, UK: CRC Press.

Hong, L., & Page, S.E. (2004) Groups of diverse problem solvers can outperform groups of high-ability problem solvers. *Proceedings of the National Academy of Sciences*, 101(46), 16385–16389.

Hopkins, A. (2000) A culture of denial: Sociological similarities between the Moura and Gretley mine disasters. *Journal of Occupational Health and Safety – Australia and New Zealand*, 16(1), 29–36.

Hopkins, A. (2012) *Disastrous Decisions: The Human and Organisational Causes of the Gulf of Mexico Blowout*. Sydney, Australia: CCH Australia.

Hopkins, A. (2014) Issues in safety science. *Safety Science*, 67, 6–14.

Hosseini, S., Barker, K., & Ramirez-Marquez, J.E. (2016) A review of definitions and measures of system resilience. *Reliability Engineering & System Safety*, 145, 47–61.

House Committee on Energy and Commerce (2015) *Volkswagen's Emissions Cheating Allegations: Initial Questions*. https://docs.house.gov/meetings/IF/IF02/20151008/104046/HHRG-114-IF02-Transcript-20151008.pdf. Published October 8, 2015. Accessed July 10, 2019.

House of Representatives (2017) *Oversight of the Equifax Data Breach: Answers for Consumers*. https://docs.house.gov/meetings/IF/IF17/20171003/106455/HHRG-115-IF17-Transcript-20171003.pdf. Published October 3, 2017. Accessed July 10, 2019.

Howard, D., & Dai, D. (2014) Public perceptions of self-driving cars: The case of Berkeley, California, in *Transportation Research Board 93rd Annual Meeting* (No. 14–4502).

IFRC. (2018). *Types of Disasters*. Retrieved from https://www.ifrc.org/en/what-we-do/disaster-management/about-disasters/definition-of-hazard/

IPCC (2014) *Climate Change 2014 Synthesis Report Summary for Policymakers*. www.ipcc.ch/pdf/assessment-report/ar5/syr/AR5_SYR_FINAL_SPM.pdf. Accessed May 25, 2019.

IRGC (International Risk Governance Council) (2005) Risk Governance: Towards an Integrative Approach, White Paper No. 1, O. Renn with an Annex by P. Graham. Geneva: IRGC.

ISO (2016) 17776. Petroleum and Natural Gas Industries – Offshore Production Installations – Major Accident Hazard Management During the Design of New Installations.

ISO (2018) *Risk Management Guidelines*. ISO/FDIS 31000:2017(E).

ITU (2017) www.itu.int/dms_pub/itu-d/opb/str/D-STR-GCI.01-2017-PDF-E.pdf. Published 2017. Accessed July 10, 2019.

Jennings, M., & Trautman, L.J. (2016) Ethical culture and legal liability: The GM switch crisis and lessons in governance. *Journal of Science & Technology Law.*, 22, 187.

Jensen, A., & Aven, T. (2018) A new definition of complexity in a risk analysis setting. *Reliability Engineering and System Safety*, 171, 169–173.

Joshi, N.N., & Lambert, J.H. (2011) Diversification of engineering infrastructure investments for emergent and unknown non-systematic risks. *Journal of Risk Research*, 14(4), 1466–4461.

Kahneman, D., & Klein, G. (2009) Conditions for intuitive expertise: A failure to disagree. *American Psychologist*, 64, 515–526.

Kaplan, S., & Garrick, B.J. (1981) On the quantitative definition of risk. *Risk Analysis*, 1, 11–27.

Kaplan, S., Visnepolschi, S., Zlotin, B., & Zusman, A. (1999) *New Tools for Failure and Risk Analysis: Anticipatory Failure Determination (AFD) and the Theory of Scenario Structuring.* Southfield, MI: Ideation International Inc.

Karvetski, C.W., & Lambert, J.H. (2012) Evaluating deep uncertainties in strategic priority-setting with an application to facility energy investments. *Systems Engineering*, 15(4), 483–493.

Kerstin, D., Simone, O., & Nicole, Z. (2014) Challenges in implementing enterprise risk management. *ACRN Journal of Finance and Risk Perspectives*, 3(3), 1–14.

Keynes, J. (1921) *Treatise on Probability.* London. Lindley, D.V. (1985) *Making Decisions.* 2nd ed. London: Wiley.

Khorsandi, J., & Aven, T. (2019) *From Uncertainties to Black Swans: Three levels of Risk Management Drawing on Lessons from High Reliability Theory.*

Kloprogge, P., van der Sluijs, J.P., & Petersen, A.C. (2005) *A Method for the Analysis of Assumptions in Assessments.* Bilthoven, The Netherlands: Netherlands Environmental Assessment Agency (MNP).

Kloprogge, P., van der Sluijs, J.P., & Petersen, A.C. (2011) A method for the analysis of assumptions in model-based environmental assessments. *Environmental Modelling and Software*, 26, 289–301.

La Porte, T.M. (2006) Organizational strategies for complex system resilience, reliability, and adaptation. *Seeds of Disaster, Roots of Response: How Private Action Can Reduce Public Vulnerability*, 135153.

Laes, E., Meskens, G., & van der Sluijs, J.P. (2011) On the contribution of external cost calculations to energy system governance: The case of a potential large-scale nuclear accident. *Energy Policy*, 39, 5664–5673.

Lambert, J.H., Karvetski, C.W., Spencer, D.K., Sotirin, B.J., Liberi, D.M., Zaghloul, H.H., Koogler, J.B., Hunter, S.L., Goran, W.D., Ditmer, R.D., & Linkov, I. (2012) Prioritizing infrastructure investments in Afghanistan with multiagency stakeholders and deep uncertainty of emergent conditions. *ASCE Journal of Infrastructure Systems*, 18(2), 155–166.

LaPorte, T.R., & Consolini, P.M. (1991) Working in practice but not in theory: Theoretical challenges of" high-reliability organizations. *Journal of Public Administration Research and Theory: J-PART*, 19–48.

Lawrence (2017) *GM Settles Deadly Ignition Switch Cases for $120 Million.* www.usatoday.com/story/money/cars/2017/10/20/gm-settles-deadly-ignition-switch-cases-120-million/777831001/. Published October 20, 2017. Accessed July 11, 2019.

Le Coze, J-C. (2013) Outlines of a sensitising model for industrial safety assessment. *Safety Science*, 51, 187–201.

Lewis, C.I. (1929) *Mind and the World Order: Outline of a Theory of Knowledge.* New York, NY: Dover Publications.

Lienert, J., & Thompson, A.C. (2004) GM avoided defective switch redesign in 2005 to save a dollar each. *Reuters.* www.reuters.com/article/us-gm-recall-delphi-idUSBREA 3105R20140402. Published April 2, 2014. Accessed July 10, 2019.

Lindley, D.V. (1970) *Introduction to Probability and Statistics from a Bayesian Viewpoint.* Cambridge: Cambridge University Press.

Lindley, D.V. (2000) The philosophy of statistics. *The Statistician*, 49, 293–337.

Lindley, D.V. (2006) *Understanding Uncertainty.* Hoboken, NJ: Wiley.

Lindley, D.V. (2008) *The Black Swan: The impact of the highly improbable.* Reviews. Significance, p. 42. March 2008.

Lindøe, P., & Engen, O.A. (2013) Offshore safety regimes – A contested terrain, in M. Nordquist, J.N. More, A. Chircop & R. Long (eds.) *The Regulation of Continental Shelf Development: Rethinking International Standards.* Leiden, The Netherlands: Martinus Nijhoff Publishers.

Linkov, I., Satterstrom, F., Kiker, G., Batchelor, C., Bridges, T. and Ferguson, E. (2006) From comparative risk assessment to multi-criteria decision analysis and adaptive management: Recent developments and applications. *Environment International*, 32, 1072–1093.

Löfstedt, R. (2014) The substitution principle in chemical regulation: a constructive critique, *Journal of Risk Research*, 17(5), 543–564.

Markowitz, H. (2014) Mean –Variance approximations to expected utility. *European Journal of Operational Research*, 234(2), 346–355.

Masys, A.J. (2012) Black swans to grey swans: Revealing the uncertainty. *Disaster Prevention and Management*, 21(3) 320–335.

McElroy, R., Brown-Davis, D., & DeCorla-Souza, P. (2012). *Public-Private Partnerships: MAP-21 Changes*. Retrieved from https://www.fhwa.dot.gov/map21/docs/11sep_p3.pdf

McFillen, J.M., Deborah, A., O'Neil, William, K., Balzer & Glenn, H.V. (2013) Organizational diagnosis: An evidence-based approach. *Journal of Change Management*, 13(2), 223–246.

Meyer, T., & Reniers, G. (2013) *Engineering Risk Management*. Berlin: De Gruyter Graduate.

Miller, K.D., & Waller, H.G. (2003) Scenarios, real options and integrated risk management. *Long Range Planning*, 36(1), 93–107.

Moeller, R. R. (2011) *COSO enterprise risk management: establishing effective governance, risk, and compliance processes (Vol. 560)*. New York: John Wiley & Sons.

Mufson, S., & Kornblut, A. (2010, June). *Lawmakers accuse BP of "shortcuts."* Retrieved from http://www.washingtonpost.com/wp-dyn/content/article/2010/06/14/AR2010061 403580.html

Myers (1995) Myers L. GM forced to recall Cadillacs with emission "Defeat Device." *AP NEWS*. https://apnews.com/4b030c7601a14dcc8208fcc1d1bd30cc. Published December 1, 1995. Accessed July 11, 2019.

NC (2011) National Commission on the BP Deepwater Horizon Oil Spill and Offshore Drilling. Deepwater: The Gulf Oil Disaster and the Future of Offshore Drilling. Report to the President 11.01.11.

NHTSA (2014) Recalls. *NHTSA*. www.nhtsa.gov/recalls. Published February 10, 2014. Accessed July 11, 2019.

NHTSA (2015) *NHTSA's Path Forward*. www.nhtsa.gov/staticfiles/communications/pdf/nhtsa-path-forward.pdf. Published 2015. Accessed July 10, 2019.

NIST (2013) Cybersecurity framework. *NIST*. www.nist.gov/cyberframework. Published November 12, 2013. Accessed July 10, 2019.

NOG (2019) Black swans. *Norwegian Oil and Gas Association*. www.norskoljeoggass.no/en/operations/storulykkerisiko/black-swans – an-enhanced – perspective-on-risk/. Accessed May 25, 2019.

North, W. (2010) Probability Theory and Consistent Reasoning, Commentary. *Risk Analysis*, 30(3), 377–380.

O'Brien, M. (2000) *Making Better Environmental Decisions*. Cambridge: The MIT Press.

Park, J., Seager, T.P., & Rao, P.S.C. (2011) Lessons in risk versus resilience based design and management. *Integrated Environmental Assessment and Management*, 7(3), 396–399.

Park, J., Seager, T.P., Rao, P.S.C., Convertino, M., & Linkov, I. (2013) Integrating risk and resilience approaches to catastrophe management in engineering systems. *Risk Analysis*, 33(3), 356–367.

Parnell, G.S., Terry Bresnick, M.B.A., Tani, S.N., & Johnson, E.R. (2013) *Handbook of Decision Analysis* (Vol. 6). Hoboken, NJ: John Wiley & Sons.

Pasman, H.J., Rogers, W.J., & Mannan, M.S. (2017) Risk assessment: What is it worth? Shall we just do away with it, or can it do a better job? *Safety Science*, 99(B), 140–155.

Paté-Cornell, E. (1999) Conditional uncertainty analysis and implications for decision making: The case of WIPP. *Risk Analysis*, 19, 995–1003.

Paté-Cornell, M.E. (1996) Uncertainties in risk analysis: Six levels of treatment. *Reliability Engineering & System Safety*, 54(2–3), 95–111.

Paté-Cornell, M.E. (2012) On "Black Swans" and "Perfect Storms": Risk analysis and management when statistics are not enough. *Risk Analysis*, 32(11), 1823–1833.

Phimister, J.R., Oktem, U., Kleindorfer, P.R., & Kunreuther, H. (2003) Near-miss incident management in the chemical process industry. *Risk Analysis*, 23(3), 445–459.

Pidgeon, N., & O'Leary, M. (2000) Man-made disasters: Why technology and organizations (sometimes) fail. *Safety Science*, 34(1), 15–30.

Postma, T.J., & Liebl, F. (2005) How to improve scenario analysis as a strategic managrement tool? *Technological Forecasting and Social Change*, 72(2), 161–173.

PWC (2018) *21st CEO Survey - The Anxious Optimist in the Corner Office*. www.pwc.com/gx/en/ceo-survey/2018/pwc-ceo-survey-report-2018.pdf. Accessed December 1, 2018.

Rasmussen, J. (1997) Risk management in a dynamic society: A modelling problem. *Safety Science*, 27(2/3), 183–213.

Read, R.T.C. (2015) GM's ignition switch findings: 124 deaths, 275 injuries. *Washington Post*. www.washingtonpost.com/cars/gms-ignition-switch-findings-124-deaths-275-injuries/2015/08/25/2ad3a7d4-4b44-11e5-80c2-106ea7fb80d4_story.html. Published August 25, 2015. Accessed July 10, 2019.

Reason, J.T. (1997) *Managing the Risks of Organizational Accidents* (Vol. 6). Aldershot: Ashgate.

Renn, O. (2008) *Risk Governance. Coping with Uncertainty in a Complex World*. London: Earthscan.

Righi, W.A., Saurin, T.A., & Wachs, P. (2015) A systematic literature review of resilience engineering: Research areas and a research agenda proposal. *Reliability Engineering and System Safety*, 141, 142–152.

Roberts, K.H. (1990) Some characteristics of one type of high reliability organization. *Organization Science*, 1(2), 160–176.

Roberts, K.H., Bea, R., & Bartles, D.L. (2001) Must accidents happen? Lessons from high-reliability organizations. *The Academy of Management Executive*, 15(3), 70–78.

Roberts, K.H., & Rousseau, D.M. (1989) Research in nearly failure-free, high-reliability organizations: Having the bubble. *Engineering Management, IEEE Transactions on*, 36(2), 132–139.

Rochlin, G.I. (1993) Defining "high reliability" organizations in practice: A taxonomic prologue. New challenges to understanding organizations, in K.H. Roberts (ed.) *New Challenges to Understanding Organizations* (pp. 11–32). New York: Palgrave Macmillan.

Rochlin, G.I. (2001) Networks and the subversion of choice: An institutionalist manifesto. *Journal of Urban Technology*, 8(3), 6596.

Rochlin, G.I., La Porte, T.R., & Roberts, K.H. (1987) The self-designing high-reliability organization: Aircraft carrier flight operations at sea. *Naval War College Review*, 40(4), 76–90.

Rosness, R., & Forseth, U. (2014) Boxing and dancing: Tripartite collaboration as an integral part of a regulatory regime, in P. Lindøe, M. Baram & O. Renn (eds.) *Risk Governance of Offshore Oil and Gas Operations*. Cambridge, MA: Cambridge University Press.

Schulman, P.R. (1993) The negotiated order of organizational reliability. *Administration & Society*, 25(3), 353–372.

Schulman, P.R., & Roe, E. (2007) Designing infrastructures: Dilemmas of design and the reliability of critical infrastructures. *Journal of Contingencies and Crisis Management*, 15(1), 42–49.

Schulman, P.R., Roe, E., Eeten, M.V., & Bruijne, M.D. (2004) High reliability and the management of critical infrastructures. *Journal of Contingencies and Crisis Management*, 12(1), 14–28.

SEC (2017) *General Motors Charged with Accounting Control Failures*. www.sec.gov/news/pressrelease/2017-19.html. Published January 18, 2017. Accessed July 10, 2019.

Senge, P. (1990) *The Fifth Discipline: The Art and Practice of the Learning Organization*. New York, NY: Doubleday.

SEP (2019) *Stanford Encyclopedia Philosophy*. Interpretations of probability. http://plato.stanford.edu/entries/probability-interpret/

Shepardson (2015) www.reuters.com/article/us-gm-recall-compensation/gm-fund-approves-594-5-million-in-ignition-claims-idUSKBN0TT0DE20151210

Shewhart, W.A., & Deming, W.E. (1986) Statistical method from the viewpoint of quality control. Dover, NY: Courier Corporation.

Singpurwalla, N. (2006) *Reliability and Risk. A Bayesian Perspective*. NY: Wiley.

Sitkin, S.B. (1992) Learning through failure: The strategy of small losses, in B.M. Staw & L.L. Cummings (eds.) *Research in Organizational Behavior* (Vol. 14, pp. 231–266). Greenwich, CT: JAI Press.

Skogdalen, J.E., & Vinnem, J.E. (2012) Quantitative risk analysis of oil and gas drilling, using Deepwater horizon as case study. *Reliability Engineering & System Safety*, 100, 58–66.

Slaper, T.F., & Hall, T.J. (2011) The triple bottom line: What is it and how does it work. *Indiana Business Review*, 86(1), 4–8.

Smith Testimony (2017) *Prepared Testimony of Richard F. Smith before the U.S. House Committee on Energy and Commerce*. https://docs.house.gov/meetings/IF/IF17/20171003/106455/HHRG-115-IF17-Wstate-SmithR-20171003.pdf. Published October 3, 2017. Accessed July 10, 2019.

Smith, L. C., Smith, M., & Ashcroft, P. (2011). Analysis of environmental and economic damages from British Petroleum's Deepwater Horizon oil spill. *Albany Law Review*, 74(1), 563–585.

Smith, T.P., Singer, J.P., Balliro, G.M., & Lerner, N.D. (2003) *Developing Consumer Product Instructions*. Washington, DC: US Consumer Product Safety Commission.

SRA (2015a) *Glossary Society for Risk Analysis*. www.sra.org/resources. Accessed January 7, 2019.

SRA (2015b) Foundations of risk analysis. *Discussion Note*. http://sra.org/sites/default/files/pdf/FoundationsMay7-2015-sent-x.pdf. Accessed January 7, 2019.

SRA (2017a) *Core Subjects of Risk Analysis*. www.sra.org/resources. Accessed January 7, 2019.

SRA (2017b) *Risk Analysis: Fundamental Principles*. www.sra.org/resources. Accessed January 7, 2019.

Staff (2014) Delphi CEO says the bad ignition switch was GM's responsibility. *Reuters*. www.reuters.com/article/us-gm-recall-delphi-idUSKBN0FM1OS20140717. Published July 17, 2014. Accessed July 10, 2019.

Staff (2018) Daimler threatened with recall of over 600,000 diesel models: Spiegel. *Reuters*. www.reuters.com/article/us-daimler-emissions-idUSKCN1IQ18S. Published May 25, 2018. Accessed July 10, 2019.

Stempel (2017) GM settles hundreds of ignition switch lawsuits. *Reuters*. www.reuters.com/article/us-gm-recall-settlement-idUSKBN19E25A. Published June 23, 2017. Accessed July 10, 2019.

t' Hardt, P. (2013) After Fukushima: Reflections on risk and institutional learning in an era of mega-crises. *Public Administration*, 91(1), 101–113.

Taleb, N.N. (2007) *The Black Swan: The Impact of the Highly Improbable*. London: Penguin.

Taleb, N.N. (2012) *Anti Fragile*. London: Penguin.

Tamuz, M. (1994) Developing organizational safety information systems for monitoring potential dangers, in G.E. Apostolakis & T.S. Win (eds.) *Proceedings of PSAM II, 2* (pp. 7–12). Los Angeles: University of California.

Thekdi, S.A., & Aven, T. (2016) An enhanced data-analytic framework for integrating risk management and performance management. *Reliability Engineering & System Safety*, 156, 277–287.

Thekdi, S.A., & Aven, T. (2016) A methodology to evaluate risk for supporting decisions involving alignment with organizational values. *Reliability Engineering & System Safety*, 172, 84–93.

Thekdi, S.A., & Aven, T. (2019) An integrated perspective for balancing performance and risk. *Reliability Engineering & System Safety*, 190, 106525.

Thekdi, S.A., & Lambert, J. H. (2012). Decision analysis and risk models for land development affecting infrastructure systems. *Risk Analysis: An International Journal*, 32(7), 1253–1269.

Turner, B.A. (1976) The organizational and interorganizational development of disasters. *Administrative Science Quarterly*, 378–397.

Turner, B.A., & Pidgeon, N. (1997) *Man-made Disasters.* 2nd ed. London: Butterworth-Heinemann.

Tversky, A., & Kahneman, D. (1981) The framing of decisions and the psychology of choice. *Science*, 211(4481), 453–458.

US Department of Transportation (2016) *Benefit-Cost Analysis (BCA) Resource Guide (November 2016).* www.transportation.gov/sites/dot.gov/files/docs/BCA%20Resource%20Guide%20-%20November%202016_0.pdf. Accessed July 10, 2019.

US Department of Transportation (2019) *Motor Vehicle Safety.* www.nhtsa.gov/staticfiles/laws_regs/pdf/MVS01092008.pdf. Accessed July 10, 2019.

US DOT. (2014). *Model Public-Private Partnerships Core Toll Concessions Contract Guide.* Retrieved from https://www.fhwa.dot.gov/ipd/pdfs/p3/model_p3_core_toll_concessions.pdf

Valukas, A.R. (2014) Report to board of directors of general motors company regarding ignition switch recalls. *Jenner & Block, Tech. Rep.* https://www.nytimes.com/interactive/2014/06/05/business/06gm-report-doc.html

van der Sluijs, J., Craye, M., Funtowicz, S., Kloprogge, P., Ravetz, J., & Risbey, J. (2005a) Combining quantitative and qualitative measures of uncertainty in model-based environmental assessment. *Risk Analysis*, 25(2), 481–492.

van der Sluijs, J., Craye, M., Funtowicz, S., Kloprogge, P., Ravetz, J., & Risbey, J. (2005b) Experiences with the NUSAP system for multidimensional uncertainty assessment in model based foresight studies. *Water Science and Technology*, 52(6), 133–144.

Van Lambalgen, M. (1990). The axiomatisation of randomness. *Journal of Symbolic Logic*, 55(3), 1143–1167.

Venkatraman, N., & Ramanujam, V. (1986) Measurement of business performance in strategy research: A comparison of approaches. *Academy of Management Review*, 11(4), 801–814.

Vogus, T. J., Rothman, N. B., Sutcliffe, K. M., & Weick, K. E. (2014). The affective foundations of high!reliability organizing. *Journal of Organizational Behavior*, 35(4), 592–596.

Volkswagen (2018) *FAQ.* www.volkswagen.com.mt/content/vw_pkw/importers/mt/en/eu5-diesel-engines/faq.html. Accessed December 1, 2018.

Wagenaar, W.A., & Groeneweg, J. (1987) Accidents at sea: Multiple causes and impossible consequences. *International Journal of Man-Machine Studies*, 27(5), 587–598.

Walley, P. (1991) *Statistical Reasoning with Imprecise Probabilities.* NY: Chapman and Hall.

Ward, B. (2006) Wernher von Braun: Lessons taught . . . And learned. *Ask Magazine*, 27–31.

Weick, K.E., & Sutcliffe, K.M. (2007) *Managing the Unexpected: Resilient Performance in an Age of Uncertainty.* Jossey Bass, CA: San Francisco.

Weick, K. E., & Sutcliffe, K. M. (2011) *Managing the unexpected: Resilient performance in an age of uncertainty* (Vol. 8): New York: John Wiley & Sons.

Weick, K.E., Sutcliffe, K.M., & Obstfeld, D. (1999) Organizing for high reliability: Processes of collective mindfulness. *Research in Organizational Behavior*, 2, 13–81.

Weick, K. E., Sutcliffe, K. M., & Obstfeld, D. (2008). Organizing for high reliability: Processes of collective mindfulness. *Crisis Management*, 3(1), 81–123.

Westrum, R. (1993) Cultures with requisite imagination, in *Verification and Validation of Complex Systems: Human Factors Issues* (pp. 401–416). New York: Springer Berlin Heidelberg.

Westrum, R. (2008). Resilience and Restlessness, in Remaining Sensitive to the Possibility of Failure, edited by E. Hollnagel, C. P. Nemeth, and S. Dekker, 1–2. Aldershot: Ashgate.

WSJ (2016) *Special Report: The Top Sustainable Mutual Funds*. http://online.wsj.com/public/resources/documents/TopSustainableMutualFunds.pdf. Published in 2016. Accessed July 10, 2019.

Zio, E. (2018) The future of risk assessment. *Reliability Engineering and System Safety*, 177, 176–190.

Appendices

Appendix A
Terminology

This appendix summarizes some risk analysis and management terminology used in the book. The definitions are in line with the SRA (2015a) glossary. See this reference for additional information.

The listing is divided into three categories:

I   **Terminology on basic concepts**
II   **Terminology on related concepts, methods, procedures**
III **Terminology on risk management actions**

In the second category the "cautionary principle" is included, and in the third category the concept "managerial review and judgment", though they are not defined in the SRA glossary. "Enterprise risk" is also not defined in the SRA glossary.

I Terminology on basic concepts

Ambiguity

The condition of admitting more than one meaning/interpretation.

Complex/complexity

- A system is complex if it is not possible to establish an accurate prediction model of the system based on knowing the specific functions and states of its individual components.
- Complexity: A causal chain with many intervening variables and feedback loops that do not allow the understanding or prediction of the system's behavior on the basis of each component's behavior.

Enterprise risk

Risk of an enterprise where the consequences is related to the principal objectives or overall performance judged important for the organization.

Event, consequences

Event:

- the occurrence or change of a particular set of circumstances, such as a system failure, an earthquake, an explosion or an outbreak of a pandemic
- a specified change of the states of the world/affairs

Consequences: The effects of the activity with respect to the values defined (such as human life and health, environment and economic assets), covering the totality of states, events, barriers and outcomes. The consequences are often seen in relation to some reference values (planned values, objectives, etc.), and the focus is often on negative, undesirable consequences.

Exposure

Exposure of something:

- being subject to a risk source/agent (for example, exposure of asbestos)

Harm, damage, adverse consequences, impacts, severity

Harm: Physical or psychological injury or damage
Damage: Loss of something desirable
Adverse consequences: Unfavorable consequences
Impacts: The effects that the consequences have on specified values (such as human life and health, environment and economic assets)
Severity: The magnitude of the damage, harm, etc.

Hazard

A risk source where the potential consequences relate to harm. Hazards could, for example, be associated with energy (e.g. explosion, fire), material (toxic or eco-toxic), biota (pathogens) and information (panic communication).

Knowledge

Two types of knowledge:

Know-how (skill) and know-that of propositional knowledge (justified beliefs). Knowledge is gained through, for example, scientific methodology and peer-review, experience and testing.

Model

A model of an object (e.g. activity, system) is a simplified representation of the object

A probability model is a special type of model, based on frequentist probabilities (often referred to as "chances" in a Bayesian context).

Opportunity

An element (action, sub-activity, component, system, event, etc.) which alone or in combination with other elements has the potential to give rise to some specified desirable consequences.

Probability

Either a knowledge-based (subjective) measure of uncertainty of an event conditional on the background knowledge, or a frequentist probability (chance). If a knowledge-based probability is equal to 0.10, it means that the uncertainty (degree of belief) is the same as randomly drawing a specific ball out of an urn. A frequentist probability (chance) is the fraction of events A occurring when the situation under consideration can be repeated over and over again infinitely.

Resilience

Overall qualitative definitions

Resilience is the ability of the system to sustain or restore its basic functionality following a risk source or an event (even unknown).

Resilience metrics/descriptions (examples)

- Probability that the system is able to sustain operation when exposed to some types of risk sources or events (which can be more or less accurately defined)

A resilient system is a system for which the resilience is judged to be high (this is a value judgment).

Risk

See Chapter 2. In its most general form:

Risk is the two-dimensional combination of the consequences C of the activity (with respect to something that humans value) and associated uncertainties about C.

Risk description is a qualitative and/or quantitative picture of the risk; i.e., a structured statement of risk usually containing the elements: risk sources, causes, events, consequences and uncertainty representations/measurements. Formally we write:

Risk description = (C',Q,K), where C' is the specified consequences of the activity considered, Q the measure of uncertainty used, and K the background knowledge that C' and Q are based on.

Risk source or risk agent

Element (action, sub-activity, component, system, event, etc.) which alone or in combination with other elements has the potential to give rise to some specified consequences (typically undesirable consequences).

Robustness

The antonym of vulnerability.

Safe, safety

Safe: Without unacceptable risk.
Safety:

- Interpreted in the same way as safe (for example when saying that safety is achieved)
- The antonym of risk (the safety level is linked to the risk level; a high safety means a low risk and vice versa)

Sometimes limited to risk related to non-intentional events (including accidents and continuous exposures).

Security, secure

Secure: Without unacceptable risk when restricting the concept of risk to intentional acts by intelligent actors.
Security:

- Interpreted in the same way as secure (for example, when saying that security is achieved)
- The antonym of risk when restricting the concept of risk to intentional acts by intelligent actors (the security level is linked to the risk level; a high security level means a low risk and vice versa)

Threat

Risk source, commonly used in relation to security applications (but also in relation to other applications, for example the threat of an earthquake).

Threat in relation to an attack: A stated or inferred intention to initiate an attack with the intention to inflict harm, fear, pain or misery.

Uncertainty

Overall qualitative definitions

- For a person or a group of persons, not knowing the true value of a quantity or the future consequences of an activity
- Imperfect or incomplete information/knowledge about a hypothesis, a quantity or the occurrence of an event

Uncertainty metrics/descriptions (examples)

- A subjective probability
- The pair (Q,K), where Q is a measure of uncertainty and K the background knowledge that supports Q

Epistemic uncertainty: as above for the overall qualitative definition of uncertainty and uncertainty metrics/descriptions (examples).

Aleatory (stochastic) uncertainty: variation of quantities in a population of units (commonly represented/described by a probability model).

Vulnerability

Overall qualitative definitions

- The degree a system is affected by a risk source or agent
- The degree a system is able to withstand specific loads
- Risk conditional on the occurrence of a risk source/agent

Vulnerability metrics/descriptions (examples)

As for risk, but conditional on the risk source or event (load):

- Expected loss given a failure of a single component or multiple components
- Expected number of fatalities given the occurrence of a specific event
- Expected system loss under conditions of stress
- The probability that the system capacity is not able to withstand a specific load (the capacity is less than the load)
- A probability distribution for the loss given the occurrence of a risk source
- $(C', Q, K \mid risk\ source)$ (i.e. a risk description given the occurrence of a risk source, see Section 2.2)

As for risk, the suitability of these metrics/descriptions depends on the situation.

A vulnerable system is a system for which the vulnerability is judged to be high.

II Terminology on related concepts, methods, procedures

Cautionary principle

An ethical principle expressing that if the consequences of an activity could be serious and subject to uncertainties, then cautionary measures should be taken, or the activity should not be carried out.

Model uncertainty

Uncertainty about the model error, i.e. about the difference between the model output and the true value being modelled.

Precautionary principle

An ethical principle expressing that if the consequences of an activity could be serious and subject to scientific uncertainties, then precautionary measures should be taken, or the activity should not be carried out.

Risk analysis

Systematic process to comprehend the nature of risk and to express the risk, with the available knowledge (A.1).

Risk analysis is often also understood in a broader way; in particular in the SRA community: risk analysis is defined to include risk assessment, risk characterization, risk communication, risk management and policy relating to risk, in the context of risks of concern to individuals, to public and private sector organizations, and to society at a local, regional, national or global level.

Risk appetite

Amount and type of risk an organization is willing to take on in pursuit of values or interests.

Risk assessment

Systematic process to comprehend the nature of risk, as well as express and evaluate risk, with the available knowledge.

Risk aversion

Disliking or avoiding risk.

Technical definition: Risk aversion means that the decision-maker's certainty equivalent is less than the expected value, where the certainty equivalent is the amount of payoff (e.g. money or utility) that the decision-maker has to receive to be indifferent between the payoff and the actual "gamble".

Risk characterization, risk description

A qualitative and/or quantitative picture of the risk; i.e., a structured statement of risk usually containing the elements: risk sources, causes, events, consequences, uncertainty representations/measurements (for example probability distributions for different categories of consequences – casualties, environmental damage, economic loss, etc.) and the knowledge that the judgments are based on.

Risk communication

Exchange or sharing of risk-related data, information and knowledge between and among different target groups (such as regulators, stakeholders, consumers, media and general public).

Risk evaluation

Process of comparing the result of risk analysis (see Risk analysis (A.1)) against risk (and often benefit) criteria to determine the significance and acceptability of the risk.

Risk framing (pre-assessment)

The initial assessment of a risk problem, clarifying issues and defining the scope of subsequent work.

Risk governance

Risk governance is the application of governance principles to the identification, assessment, management and communication of risk. Governance refers to the actions, processes, traditions and institutions by which authority is exercised and decisions are taken and implemented.

Risk governance includes the totality of actors, rules, conventions, processes and mechanisms concerned with how relevant risk information is collected, analyzed and communicated, as well as how management decisions are taken.

Risk management

Activities to handle risk such as prevention, mitigation, adaptation or sharing.

It often includes trade-offs between costs and benefits of risk reduction and choice of a level of tolerable risk.

Risk perception

A person's subjective judgement or appraisal of risk.

III Terminology on risk management actions

Managerial review and judgment

Process of summarizing, interpreting and deliberating over the results of risk assessments and other assessments, as well as of other relevant issues (not covered by the assessments), in order to make a decision.

Risk acceptance

An attitude expressing that the risk is judged acceptable by a particular individual or group.

Risk policy

A plan for action of how to manage risk.

Risk prevention

Process of actions to avoid a risk source or to intercept the risk source pathway to the realization of damage with the effect that none of the targets are affected by the risk source.

Risk reduction

Process of actions to reduce risk.

Risk regulation

Governmental interventions aimed at the protection and management of values subject to risk.

Risk sharing or pooling

Form of risk treatment involving the agreed distribution of risk with other parties.

Risk tolerance

An attitude expressing that the risk is judged tolerable.

Risk trade-offs (risk-risk trade-offs)

The phenomenon that intervention aimed at reducing one risk can increase other risks or shift risk to another population or target.

Risk transfer

Sharing with another party the benefit of gain, or burden of loss, from the risk. Passing a risk to another party.

Risk treatment

Process of actions to modify risk.

Stakeholder involvement (in risk governance)

The process by which organizations or groups of people who may be affected by a risk-related decision can influence the decisions or its implementation.

Appendix B

Basic probability theory

This appendix provides some fundamental definitions and theories related to probability and expected values, based on Aven (2012b, 2019d) and Aven and Reniers (2013).

B.1 Classical probabilities

The classical interpretation, which dates back to de Laplace (1812), applies only in situations with a finite number of outcomes which are equally likely to occur. According to the classical interpretation, the probability of A is equal to the ratio between the number of outcomes resulting in A and the total number of outcomes, i.e.:

$P(A)$ = Number of outcomes resulting in A/Total number of outcomes.

As an example, consider the tossing of a die. Here P(the die shows 1) = 1/6 since there are six possible outcomes which are equally likely to appear, and only one that gives the outcome "1".

The requirement of each outcome to be equally likely is critical for the understanding of this interpretation. It has been subject to much discussion in the literature. A common perspective is that this requirement is met if there is no evidence that favors some outcomes over others (this is the so-called "principle of indifference"). So, classical probabilities are appropriate when the evidence, if there is any, is symmetrically balanced (Hajek 2001), as we may have when throwing a die or playing a card game.

This interpretation is, however, not applicable in most real-life situations beyond random gambling and sampling, as we do not have a finite number of outcomes which are equally likely to occur. While the discussion about the indifference principle is interesting from a theoretical point of view, it is not so relevant in the context of the analysis here, where we search for a concept of probability that can be used in a wide class of applications.

B.2 Frequentist probabilities

A frequentist probability of an event A, denoted $P_f(A)$, is defined as the fraction of times the event A occurs if the situation considered were repeated (hypothetically) an infinite number of times. Thus, if an experiment is performed n times and the event A occurs n_A times, the $P_f(A)$ is equal to the limit of n_A/n as n goes to infinity (tacitly assuming that the limit exists), i.e. the probability of the event A is the limit of the fraction of the number of times event A occurs when the number of experiments increases to infinity.

A frequentist probability, $p = P_f(A)$, is thus a mind-constructed quantity. It is a model concept, founded on the law of large numbers, stating that frequencies n_A/n converge to a limit under certain conditions. Unfortunately, these conditions themselves appeal to probability – we have to assume that the probability of the event A exists, and is the same in all experiments, and that the experiments are independent. To solve this circularity problem, different approaches have been suggested, see Bedford and Cooke (2001, p. 23) and van Lambalgen (1990). A common approach is to simply assume the existence of the probability, $P_f(A)$, and then apply the law of large numbers to give $P_f(A)$ the limiting frequentist interpretation. Starting from Kolmogorov's axiomatization (the standard axioms for probability: non-negativity, normalization, finite and countable additivity) and conditional probability (see e.g. Bedford and Cooke 2001, p. 40), and presuming the existence of probability, we derive the well-established theory, which is presented in most textbooks on probability, where the law of large numbers constitutes a key theorem providing the interpretation of the probability concept. For applied probabilists, this perspective seems to be the prevailing one.

One idea for justifying the existence of the probability is the so-called propensity interpretation. It holds that probability should primarily be thought of as a physical characteristic. The probability is just a propensity of a repeatable experimental set-up which produces outcomes with limiting relative frequency $P_f(A)$ (SEP 2009). Suppose we have a coin; its physical characteristics (weight, center of mass, etc.) are such that, when throwing the coin over and over again, the head fraction will be p.

The literature on probability shows that the existence of a propensity is controversial. However, from a conceptual point of view, the idea of a propensity should not be more difficult to grasp than the infinite repetition of experiments. The point being made is that if you accept the framework of the frequentist probability, i.e. that an infinite sequence of similar situations can be generated, you should also accept the propensity thesis, as it basically states that such a framework exists. Hence, for the situations of gambling and fractions in huge populations of similar items, the frequentist probability should make sense as a model concept. If you throw a die over and over again it is obvious that the properties of the die will change, so the idea of "similar experiments" is questionable. However, for all practical means we can carry out (in theory) a huge number of trials, say 100,000, without any physical changes in the experimental set-up, and that is what is required for the concept to be meaningful. The same is the case if we consider a population of, say, 100,000 human beings belonging to a specific category, such as women in the age range 40–50 in a specific country.

Given this, it is not surprising that the frequentist probabilities are so commonly adopted in practice. A theoretical concept is introduced, often in the context of a probability model, for example the normal or Poisson distributions, and statistical analysis is carried out to estimate (and study the properties of the estimators of) the frequentist probabilities (more generally the parameters of the probability models) using well-established statistical theory. However, the type of situations that are captured by this framework is limited. As noted by Singpurwalla (2006, p. 17), the concept of frequentist probabilities "is applicable to only those situations for which we can conceive of a repeatable experiment". This excludes many situations and events. Think of the rise of the sea level over the next 20 years, the guilt or innocence of an accused individual or the occurrence or not of a disease in a specific person with a specific history.

What does it mean that the situations considered are "similar"? The conditions under which the repeatable experiments are to be performed cannot be identical, as in that case we would get exactly the same outcome and the ratio n_A/n would be either 1 or 0. What type of variation from one experiment to another is allowed? This is often difficult to specify and makes it hard to extend frequentist probabilities to also include real-life situations. Think, for example, of the frequentist probability that a person V will get a specific disease. What should then be the population of similar persons? If we include all people in the same age group, we get a large population, but many of the people in this population may not be very "similar" to person V. We may reduce the population to increase the similarity, but not too much as that would make the population very small and hence inadequate for defining the frequentist probability. The issue raised here can be seen as a special case of the "reference class" problem (Hajek 2001).

We face this type of dilemma in many types of modeling. A balance has to be made between different concerns. We cannot be too person-specific if we are to be able to accurately estimate the parameters of the model.

Let us consider the operation of an offshore oil and gas installation. Here we may contemplate introducing, for example, a frequentist probability that an accident with more than 100 fatalities occurs in the next year. What the infinite population of similar situations (platforms) is to reflect to define this probability is not at all clear, as discussed in Section 2.2.1; see also Aven (2012b, p. 37). Does "similar" mean the same type of constructions and equipment, the same operational procedures, the same type of personnel positions, the same type of training programs, the same organizational philosophy, the same influence of exogenous factors, etc.? "Yes" would be the answer as long as we speak about similarities on a "macro level". But, as discussed above, something must be different, because otherwise we would get exactly the same output result for each situation (platform), either the occurrence of an accident with at least 100 fatalities or no such event. There must be some variation on a "micro level" to produce the variation on the macro level. So, we should allow for variations in equipment quality, human behavior, etc. The question is, however, to what extent and how we should allow for such variation. For example, in human behavior, do we specify the safety culture or the standard of the private lives of the personnel, or are these factors to be regarded as those creating the variations from one situation to another, i.e. the stochastic (aleatory) uncertainty, using common terminology within risk analysis (see Section 3.1)? We see that we will have a hard time specifying what the framework conditions (i.e. the conditions that are fixed) should be for the situations in the population and what could be varying.

As seen from this example, it is not obvious how to make a proper definition of the population, and hence define and understand the meaning of the frequentist probability. Clearly such a situation could also have serious implications for the estimation of the probabilities: trying to estimate a concept that is vaguely defined and understood would easily lead to arbitrariness in the assessment.

When frequentist probabilities are taken as the basis for the assessment, the analysts need to report estimates of these underlying frequentist probabilities, as well as uncertainties about the estimates. An example is presented in Aven and Reniers (2013), where the issue is discussed in a practical risk and safety context.

Probability models

A probability model is a set of frequentist probabilities. The models are used to show variation (Lindley 2000). These models allow for sophisticated probabilistic and statistical analysis. There is broad acknowledgment of the usefulness of such models for these purposes. However, a probability model is a model and needs justification. In many cases, it cannot be meaningfully defined and interpreted. Models are often simply assumed to exist in applications, and no discussion about validity is performed.

To illustrate the problem raised, consider the important task of analyzing rare events with extreme consequences. To this end, a probabilistic framework is often used, founded on the use of probability models. Reference is made to concepts like heavy and fat distribution tails. However, we seldom see that this framework is justified or questioned; is it in fact suitable for studying extreme event phenomena?

A probability model is established based on reasoning, as for the binomial or Poisson distributions, or by estimations based on observations. Both approaches introduce uncertainties, as explained in the following.

If the probability model is based on reasoning, there will be a set of assumptions on which the modeling is founded. For example, in the homogenous Poisson case, the probability of an event occurring in a small interval $(t, t+h)$ is approximately equal to λh, for a fixed number λ, independent of the history up to t. Verifying such assumptions is, however, generally difficult, as there may be little relevant data that can be used to check them, in particular in the case of rare events. Estimations and model validation using observations are applicable when huge data sets are available, but not when studying extreme events. The consequence is that the analysis simply needs to presume the existence of the model and the results interpreted as conditional on these assumptions. Thus, care has to be shown in making conclusions based on the analysis, as the assumptions could cover or conceal important aspects of uncertainties and risks.

To introduce a probability model, it needs to serve a purpose. The common argument used is that it allows for statistical inference, to apply the strong machineries of statistics and Bayesian analysis, updating our knowledge when new information becomes available (Lindley 2000). For situations where variation is the key phenomenon of interest, such models surely have a role to play, but, in cases of extreme events, variation is not really the interesting concept as there is no natural family of situations to which these events belong. Take major nuclear accidents. For the industry, historical data are informative on what has happened and how frequently. But will the development and use of a probability model to represent the variation in the occurrences of such accidents lead to new and important insights? To provide an answer to this question, let us review the potential purposes for developing such a model:

a)   To predict the occurrence of coming events
b)   To show trends
c)   To present "true" risk levels
d)   To facilitate continuous updating of information about the risk levels

Clearly, the use of such models does not allow for accurate prediction of occurrences, as the data are so few and the future is not necessarily reflected well by these data. Hence a) is not valid. We have to make the same conclusion when it comes to b) for the same reasons: meaningful trends cannot be established when the data basis is weak. According to some risk perspectives, risk as a concept is closely linked to the existence of probability models (see e.g. Aven 2011). Consider the risk quantity defined by the frequentist probability that a major nuclear accident occurs in a country in the next year. As discussed above, giving this probability an interpretation is challenging, as it requires the definition of an infinite population of similar situations to the one studied. Anyway, it is unknown and needs to be estimated. With a weak data base, this estimate could deviate strongly from the "true" risk. Hence, c) is also problematic. Probability modeling is an essential pillar for using Bayesian analysis to systematically update the knowledge when new information becomes available. However, the modeling needs to be justified for the results to be useful. As discussed above, the problem is that it is often difficult to establish in a meaningful way an infinite population of similar situations or units. There is always a need to formulate a hypothesis, as knowledge generation is built on theory (Lewis 1929; Bergman 2009; Deming 2000, p. 102), but, in cases of rare events, broader frameworks than high-level probabilistic modeling are required. Judgements of risk for such events cannot be based on macro statistical data and analysis. More in-depth analysis of risk sources, threats, barriers, consequences is needed; in other words, more in-depth risk assessments.

B.3 Logical probabilities

This type of probability was first proposed by Keynes (1921) and later taken up by Carnap (1922, 1929). The idea is that probability expresses an objective logical relation between propositions, a kind of "partial entailment". There is a number in the interval [0,1], denoted $P(h \mid e)$, which measures the objective degree of logical support that evidence e gives to the hypothesis h (Franklin 2001). As stated by Franklin (2001), this view on probability has an intuitive initial attractiveness, in representing a level of agreement found when scientists, juries, actuaries and so on evaluate hypotheses in the light of evidence. However, the notion of partial entailment has never received a satisfactory interpretation as argued by, for example, Cowell et al. (1999), Cooke (2004) and Aven (2015c). Using logical probabilities, it is not clear how we should interpret a number, say, 0.2 compared to 0.3. Hence this type of probability is not suitable for applications.

B.4 "Subjective" (knowledge–based, judgmental) probabilities

In this book, we use subjective probabilities which refers to an urn standard for comparison (Lindley 1970; Kaplan and Garrick 1981; Lindley 2006; Aven and Reniers 2013). According to this definition, a subjective probability is understood in relation to an uncertainty standard, typically an urn: if a person assigns a probability of, say, 0.1 for an event A, he or she compares his/her uncertainty (degree of belief) of A occurring with drawing a specific ball from an urn containing 10 balls. The uncertainty is the same. From this standard, we can deduce a set of rules, for example the additive rule (Lindley 2000, p. 296): "Suppose that, of the N balls in the urn, R are red, B are blue, and the remainder are white. Then the uncertainty that is associated with the withdrawal of a colored ball is $(R+B)/N = R/N + B/N$, the sum of the probabilities/uncertainties associated with red, and with blue, balls. The same result we will obtain for any two exclusive events whose probabilities/uncertainties are respectively R/N and B/N and we have an addition rule for your probabilities/uncertainties of exclusive events." Similarly, we can establish other common rules for probability, for example the multiplicative rule; see Lindley (2000, p. 298).

These rules are commonly referred to as axioms in textbooks on probability, but these rules are not axioms here, as they are deductions from the more basic assumptions linked to the uncertainty standard; see Lindley (2000, p. 299).

For applied probabilists, whether the probability rules are deduced or considered as axioms may not be so important. The main point is that these rules apply, and hence Lindley's uncertainty standard provides an easily understandable way of defining and interpreting subjective probability. The rules of probability reduce to the rules governing proportions, which are easy to communicate.

A subjective probability (regardless of interpretation) is not an objective probability, as it expresses the assigner's judgement (a degree of belief) related to the occurrence of the event of interest. The fact that a classical probability setting is used (the urn model) as a reference system to explain what subjective probabilities mean does not make the subjective probability in any way objective. It still expresses the subjective judgements of the assigner. As an example, consider the event A defined as "the sea level will increase by one meter during the coming 30 years", and say that an analyst assigns a subjective probability of event A equal to 0.1. Following the Lindley interpretation, the meaning of this statement is that the analyst's uncertainty/degree of belief that the event A will occur is the same as for the event B defined as "drawing one particular ball out of an urn that consists of 10 balls" (under standard experimental conditions). Although there is a comparison with a classical probability, the subjective probability of A is not objective. The classical probability introduced here is not a classical probability of the event A, but a constructed event B introduced to explain what the probability of A means.

In contrast, to adopt a classical probability of the event A, we have to define a finite number of outcomes which are equally likely to occur, and the probability of A is equal to the ratio between the number of outcomes resulting in A and the total number of outcomes. However, defining such outcomes is obviously problematic in this case – we cannot meaningfully construct similar 30-year periods, and we have to conclude that the classical probability has no proper interpretation for this event. We also have to reach the same for frequentist probabilities; an infinite population of similar 30-year periods cannot be meaningfully defined. Nonetheless, the analyst may assign subjective probabilities and, to explain what these mean, the urn model is a suitable tool.

There is no reference here to an underlying correct or true value. The assigned probabilities express the judgements of the assessors. However, the probabilities are based on background knowledge (covering assumptions, models and data), and this could be more or less strong. This raises the question about the information value given by the subjective probabilities produced. The probability numbers must be viewed together with the background knowledge on which the probabilities are based. This issue has motivated the research on alternative approaches, including imprecise probabilities, as discussed in the following section.

B.5 Imprecise (interval) probabilities

We all deal with imprecise (interval) probabilities in practice. If the assessor assigns a probability $P(A) = 0.3$, one may interpret this probability as having an imprecision interval $[0.26, 0.34]$ (as a number in this interval is equal to 0.3 when displaying one digit only).

Following the uncertainty standard interpretation, this means that the assigner states that his/her assigned degree of belief is greater than the urn chance of 0.26 (the degree of belief of drawing one red ball out of an urn containing 100 balls where 26 are red) and less than the urn chance of 0.34.

Alternatively, the probability is compared to a situation with 100 balls of which 26–34 balls are red, but the exact number is not specified.

Lindley (2000) argues that the interval approach leads to a more complicated system, and the complication seems unnecessary. He has not yet met a situation in which the probability approach appears to be inadequate and where the inadequacy can be fixed by employing upper and lower values. The simpler is to be preferred over the complicated, he concludes. Furthermore, he argues that the use of interval probabilities confuses the concept of interpretation with the practice of measurement procedures (Lindley 2006). To use the words of Bernardo and Smith (1994, p. 32), the idea of a formal incorporation of imprecision into the axiom system represents "an unnecessary confusion of the *prescriptive* and the *descriptive*":

> We formulate the theory on the prescriptive assumption that we aspire to exact measurement (. . .), whilst acknowledging that, in practice, we have to make do with the best level of precision currently available (or devote some resources to improving our measuring instruments!).
>
> (Bernardo and Smith 1994, p. 32)

However, other researchers and analysts have a more positive view on the need for such intervals; see discussions in, for example, Aven et al. (2014), Walley (1991), Ferson and Ginzburg (1996) and Dubois (2010). See also Section 2.2.2. In this book we use both precise and imprecise probabilities; refer to recommendations in Section 2.2.3.

B.6 Some remarks

To apply a probabilistic analysis in practice, an interpretation is required. You have to explain what the probability means. For example, is your probability to be understood as a judgement made by the analyst team based on their background knowledge, or is the probability trying to represent in a more "objective" way the data and knowledge available? The interpretation could strongly affect the decision-making process.

Many interpretations of a probability exist, but only a few are meaningful in practice. Above, it is argued that there is only one way of looking at probability that is universally applicable, provided we require a separation between uncertainty assessments and value judgements — the subjective probabilities interpreted with reference to an uncertainty standard (for example an urn). There exist many other ways of interpreting a subjective probability (refer to Aven and Reniers 2013), but they are all rejected as they are based on an unfortunate mix of uncertainty assessment and value judgements; see discussion in Aven and Reniers (2013).

Many applied probabilists find the term "subjective probability" difficult to use in practice – it gives the impression that the probability and the associated assessment are non-scientific and arbitrary; it is often replaced by terms such as "judgmental probability" and "knowledge-based probability" (Singpurwalla 2006; North 2010; Aven 2010b).

In a communication process, frequencies can also be used to explain the meaning of a subjective probability, provided it makes sense to talk about situations similar to the one studied. If the subjective probability assignment is 0.3, the analyst predicts that the event considered will occur three times out of ten. Note that this way of speaking does not imply that a frequentist probability needs to be defined – the frequency referred to is just introduced to give a feel for what the assignment of 0.3 expresses.

Frequentist probabilities (chances) $P_f(A)$ may be constructed in cases of repeatability. These probabilities are to be seen as parameters of a probability model. When a frequentist probability can be justified, we may conveniently also accept the concept of a propensity, that the probability exists per se, the probability is just a propensity of a repeatable experimental set-up which produces outcomes with limiting relative frequency $P_f(A)$.

Classical probabilities only exist in some special cases of gambling and sampling. Consequently, their applicability is very limited. Logical probabilities cannot be justified. Imprecise probabilities can be meaningfully defined using an uncertainty standard, but their applicability can be questioned in some cases. The approach may complicate the assessments, and if the aim of the analysis is to report the analyst's judgement, exact probabilities should be assigned. However, if we seek to obtain a more "inter-subjective" knowledge description of the unknown quantities studied, the use of imprecise probabilities could be an appropriate tool, as discussed above.

The overall conclusion is that, in a risk analysis and safety setting, a probability should in general be interpreted as a subjective probability with reference to an uncertainty standard such as an urn. In addition, we may use frequentist probabilities (chances) and classical probabilities when these can be justified. Imprecise probabilities can also be used in cases where it is difficult to assign specific numbers, interpreted in line with the reference to an uncertainty standard. In addition, considerations of the knowledge supporting the probabilities are required, as discussed in Section 2.2.

B.7 Expected values – why it is in general is a poor risk metric

If you throw a die, the outcome result will be either 1, 2, 3, 4, 5 or 6. Before you make the throw the outcome is unknown – it is *random* to use the terminology of statisticians. You are not able to specify the outcome, but you are able to express how probable it is that the outcome is 1, 2, 3, 4, 5 or 6. Since the number of possible outcomes is 6 and they are equally probable – the die is fair, the probability that the outcome turns out to be, say, 3 is 1/6. This is simple probability theory. Now suppose that you throw this die 600 times. What would then be the average outcome? If you do this experiment, you will obtain an average about 3.5. We can also deduce this number by some simple arguments: About 100 throws would give an outcome equal to 1, and this gives a total sum of outcomes equal to 100. Also, about 100 throws would give an outcome equal to 2, and this would give a sum equal to 2 times 100, and so on. The average outcome would thus be

$$(1 \times 100 + 2 \times 100 + 3 \times 100 + 4 \times 100 + 5 \times 100 + 6 \times 100)/600 = 3.5 \tag{B.1}$$

In probability theory, this number is referred to as the expected value. It is obtained by multiplying each possible outcome with the associated probability and summing over all possible outcomes. In our example this gives

$$1 \times 1/6 + 2 \times 1/6 + 3 \times 1/6 + 4 \times 1/6 + 5 \times 1/6 + 6 \times 1/6 = 3.5 \tag{B.2}$$

We see that formula (B.2) is just a reformulation of (B.1) obtained by dividing 100 by 600 in each sum term of (B.1). Thus, the expected value can be interpreted as the average value of the outcome of the experiment if the experiment is repeated over and over again. Statisticians would refer to the law of large numbers, which says that the average value converges to the expected value when the number of experiments goes to infinity.

More generally, the expected value, $E[X]$, of an unknown quantity X is the center of gravity of the probability distribution of X. If this probability distribution is a frequentist probability distribution, as in the above die example, we can interpret the expected value as the average value when considering a large population of units coming from this distribution. In the case of subjective probability distributions, this type of frequency interpretation is not valid.

The expected value is attractive, as it is based on one number – or potentially a few numbers if the metric is split into different consequence attributes (loss of lives, environmental damage, etc.). However, given that the aim is to describe risk, the metric has some strong limitations (Haimes 2015; Paté-Cornell 1999; Aven 2012a):

i)   It does not show the potential for extreme consequences or outcomes
ii) It does not show the uncertainties of the estimates of $E[C]$ (in case of frequentist probability settings)
iii) It does not show the strength of the knowledge on which the $E[C]$ is based (in case of knowledge-based probability settings)

The first point represents a serious weakness of this metric and is used as an argument for rejecting the metric as a single characterization of risk. Think about two situations, both having a potential for two outcomes only. In the former situation, these two outcomes are 0 and 1, and the corresponding probabilities are 0.9 and 0.1, respectively. In the latter situation, the potential outcomes are 0 and 100, and the probabilities are 0.999 and 0.001, respectively.

The expected values are 0.1 in both situations. They are, however, completely different, as, in the latter one, there is a potential for an extreme outcome, which could require a completely different risk management response than that for the former situation. If risk is defined as the expected consequences, these situations would, however, be seen as similar: the risks are of the same magnitude.

A portfolio type of argument can be used to justify the use of expected values in some cases. For example, an insurance company, with a number of activities or projects covered, is mainly interested in the average value and not the individual ones. By the law of large numbers, we know that under certain conditions, the average value converges with probability one to the expected value of each random variable. However, for this argument to be valid the number of projects must be large and there must be some stability to justify the existence of frequentist probabilities. With the potential for extreme and surprising observations, the approximation of replacing the average with the expected value could be rather poor – the uncertainties in the estimates would be large.

The question now is the extent to which we can apply the portfolio type of argumentation in practice. Think of a national or global risk assessment. In this case, we have a number of projects or activities, but, unfortunately, these cannot, in general, be seen as averaging themselves out. There are two main problems. The first is that, in such risk studies, a main focus and interest is extreme types of events, which occur relatively rarely. Secondly, the world is rapidly changing, and the stability required to think in relation to frequentist probabilities is challenged. A key aspect to consider, when looking into the future and the related risks, are concerns incorporating potential surprises and what today is not foreseen. The conclusion is that expected value computed today could be a poor predictor of the future average value, even when taking a global or national perspective.

This leads us to reflections of uncertainties. For these reflections to be meaningful, it is essential that the uncertainties are not restricted to an analysis of the uncertainties of the expected "true" frequentist consequences, $E_f[C]$. From a validity point of view, attention should be focused on the uncertainties of the observable quantities of interest, C. Uncertainty intervals for C should be derived, not only for $E_f[C]$.

In practice, E[C] characterizations are often refined by presenting the pair, P(A) and E[C|A], where A is an event (hazard, threat, opportunity) and E[C|A] is the conditional expected value, given the occurrence of A. The above discussion concerning E[C] also applies to E[C|A], although this split into these two dimensions reduces some of the issues discussed above for E[C], in particular the problem of multiplying a small probability of the event occurring with a large consequence number. However, E[C|A] is still an expected value and i) –iii) apply. Important differences in potentials for extreme outcomes are not revealed using the approach. See also discussions in Section 7.2.

B.7 Examples of methods for assessing the strength of knowledge

The knowledge K is judged as weak if one or more of the following conditions are true:

w1) The assumptions made represent strong simplifications.
w2) Data/information are/is non-existent or highly unreliable/irrelevant.
w3) There is strong disagreement among experts.
w4) The phenomena involved are poorly understood; models are non-existent or known/believed to give poor predictions.
w5) The knowledge K has not been examined (for example with respect to unknown knowns)

If, on the other hand, all (whenever they are relevant) of the following conditions are met, the knowledge is considered strong:

s1) The assumptions made are seen as very reasonable.
s2) Large amounts of reliable and relevant data/information are available.
s3) There is broad agreement among experts.
s4) The phenomena involved are well understood; the models used are known to give predictions with the required accuracy.
s5) The knowledge K has been thoroughly examined.

Cases in between are classified as medium strength of knowledge. To obtain a wider strong knowledge category, the requirement that all of the criteria s1)-s5) need to be fulfilled (whenever they are relevant) could, for example, be replaced by a criterion expressing that at least one (or two, three or four) of the criteria s1)-s5) need to be fulfilled and, at the same time, none of the criteria w1)-w5) are fulfilled.

A simplified version of these criteria can be obtained by applying the same score for strong, but assigning the medium and weak scores when a suitable number of conditions are not met, for example medium score if one or two of the conditions s1)-s5) are not met and weak score otherwise, i.e. when three, four or five of the conditions are not met.

The above system is based on Flage and Aven (2009) and Aven and Flage (2018). For an adjusted similar scheme addressing security issues, see Askeland et al. (2017). An alternative related approach is the so-called NUSAP system (Numeral, Unit, Spread, Assessment, and Pedigree) (Funtowicz and Ravetz 1990, 1993; Kloprogge et al. 2005, 2011; Laes et al. 2011; van der Sluijs et al. 2005a, 2005b).

Appendix C
Basic ERM theory

This appendix will provide an overview of basic ERM theory, as defined by COSO (Moeller 2011). When referring to risk characterizations founded on impact and likelihood, the reader should add considerations of the knowledge that supports the likelihood judgments, as argued for in Section 2.2. COSO adopts a framework consisting of several layers (Moeller 2018). The vertical layers represent the four objectives of ERM, which are *strategic, operations, reporting*, and *compliance*.

The horizontal layers represent risk components, which are *internal environment, objective setting, event identification, risk assessment, risk response, control activities, information and communication*, and *monitoring*.

The *internal environment* component consists of:

- Identifying the risk management philosophy, aimed at understanding beliefs and attitudes toward risk
- Defining the risk appetite that represents the acceptable amount of risk; eliciting the attitudes of the board of directors in response to their oversight of management actions
- Upholding integrity and ethical values that are supplemented by a strong corporate mission statement and documented codes of conduct
- Ensuring a commitment to competence, requiring knowledge and skills necessary to perform ERM-related tasks
- Creating the appropriate organizational structure with clear lines of authority, responsibility and reporting for ERM-related functions
- Clear human resource standards for hiring, training, compensating, promoting and disciplining employees

The *objective setting* component consists of identifying objectives for operations, reporting and compliance activities. Important aspects of this component include:

- Developing a mission statement to provide a formal statement of purpose that can be used for guiding the overall and functional risk strategies
- Formally defining high-level strategic objectives to achieve its mission

- Further refining the risk appetite by deciding what levels of risk it is willing to accept
- Understanding risk tolerance by deciding the acceptable level of variation around objectives

The *event identification* component consists of identifying internal and external events that would affect the ERM strategy implementation of achievement of overall enterprise objectives. While ERM practices ordinarily focus on negative consequences, these may also include events that represent opportunity. These events can be defined using practices such as event inventories based on previous risk events, eliciting concerns through facilitated workshops, surveys and using automated tools. Common types of events described in the COSO framework include:

- External economic events, such as short-term and long-term economic trends, interest rate changes and currency market shifts
- Natural hazard events, such as hurricanes, earthquakes, fires, floods, etc.
- Political events, such as election results, new legislations and policy changes
- Social factors, such as demographic changes and social movements
- Internal infrastructure events, such as changes in physical assets, processes and capacities
- Internal process-related events, such as changes in standardized procedures
- External and internal technological events, such as cyber-attacks and vulnerability patching processes

The *risk assessment* component consists of understanding the impact of risk-related events on the enterprise's achievement of objectives. COSO recommends performing this assessment using the likelihood and impact of each risk. The process consists of first assessing all identified risks, then ranking them in terms of likelihood and impact. Possible scales can be quantitative of qualitative. For example, a scale from 1–10 can be used to represent the impact and likelihood of each risk.

The *risk response* component consists of deciding how to respond to the documented risks. The options are as follows:

- Risk avoidance, the act of eliminating all exposure to the risk. This could involve selling a business unit, avoiding business activity in particular areas, or any other decisions to fully avoid the risk.
- Risk reduction, the act of reducing the likelihood or severity of consequences for a risk
- Risk sharing, the act of dividing a risk among two or more entities. The most common risk sharing practice is the use of insurance or hedging.
- Risk acceptance, or no action

The *control activities* component consists of managing policies and procedures that are needed to ensure risk responses as performed. These activities may include management reviews (senior -level and functional), physical controls (inventories, securities, etc.), performance indicators and segregation of duties to avoid any conflicts of interest. Risk control requires the following tasks:

• Understand significant risks and develop control procedures for monitoring and correcting the risks
• Design tests to determine if risk controls are working effectively
• Perform tests to determine if risk monitoring is working effectively and as expected
• Make adjustments to improve risk monitoring

The *information and communication* component consists of tools to link or support information flow among the other ERM components described above. The information flow may be documented for within-organization flows, or may include communications for suppliers, customers and other stakeholders. This can be facilitated by forming a common risk language among enterprise members and also various stakeholders.

The *monitoring* component consists of practices to ensure all components of the ERM are working effectively. Monitoring activities may include implementation of continuous reporting mechanisms for financial and operations data, reporting of risk data such as error rates, auditing of risk activities and regular updating of risk-information such as changes in government rules and industry trends. Auditing tasks may include process flowcharting of ERM procedures, reviewing ERM documented procedures, benchmarking risk activities, gathering input from stakeholders through surveys, and facilitating focus group sessions to review ERM practices.

The vertical layers in the third dimension represent levels of enterprise, which are *subsidiary, business unit, division*, and *entity-level.*

Appendix D
Critical thinking case studies

This appendix presents additional case studies that can be used for critical thinking assignments. The case studies present current issues in ERM and ask students to prepare an executive summary to explore these issues.

D.1 Critical thinking assignment: hypothetical energy company case

Suppose you have recently been hired as the ERM manager for a growing energy company. You have been tasked with developing the company's first ERM strategy, which includes coordinating tasks to identify, evaluate, mitigate and monitor operational and strategic risks. Your role also includes ensuring that the policies and strategies comply with relevant regulations and overall organizational objectives. You will serve as the acting supervisor for the following entities:

- Business continuity manager: This role leads contingency planning by coordinating training, communication, and testing of plans.
- Safety manager: This role leads safety and loss control functions. Tasks include planning and executing relevant risk assessments; reducing accidents, occupational illnesses and exposure to long-term health hazards through safety training; conducting inspections; coordinating first aid care; developing emergency preparedness plans; managing personal protective equipment; coordinating proper disposal of hazardous waste; complying with regulatory agencies; and conducting root cause analysis of past accidents.

This company primarily conducts activities including oil exploration, refining, distribution and power generation. Although the company has recently begun investing in renewable energy, including biofuels and wind power, these activities are in the early stages of development and are expected to be the highest-growth activities in future years.

With this wide array of activities, this company has also been involved with several risk-related issues. Five years ago, the company's operations resulted in a massive marine oil spill, causing several deaths and leaking over 1 million barrels of oil. This led to extensive damage to marine and wildlife habitats, involving a six-month clean-up of wetlands and beaches. This incident was devastating to the already struggling nearby fishing and tourism industries. Due to the company's negligence, the company faced a multi-billion dollar settlement, Clean Water Act penalties, criminal charges and other lawsuits.

You have recently met with executive managers to discuss their main risk concerns. As you expected, executives repeatedly described the need to avoid any future oil spills. You ask them to also describe other types of risks, such as those related to climate change and other uncertainties. The executives have not given these topics much thought and have asked you to organize discussions as you continue to implement ERM in the company.

We ask the reader to prepare an executive summary to address the following topics:

- Describe what risks and uncertainties are relevant for the company.
- Characterize the risks.
- Identify risks that are of highest priority.
- Identify the relevant stakeholders.
- Provide recommendations for how to address high priority risks.
- Discuss challenges you foresee in implementing ERM processes at this company.

The summary report should contain a short introduction; evidence that can be gathered from company websites, news articles and scholarly publications; and a conclusion.

D.2 Critical thinking assignment: hypothetical case for banks and financial institutions

During the last BankXYZ board of directors meeting, the board was furious about the organization and implementation of ERM practices. This is justified, given the role this company played in the recent financial crisis. The board was even more troubled by signals that a future crisis may be imminent. One prominent board member cited many uncertainties, and demanding action plans for addressing cybersecurity risk for protection of bank assets. Another board member called for understanding whether BankXYZ can adequately manage risk associated with new regulations that are being considered as a result of the recent financial crisis. During the two-hour conversation, the board listed many other issues, including terrorism, emerging trends in industry, the impact of changing technologies and many other risks. The conversation also made it clear that the board demanded transparency in ERM practices.

Suppose you have been asked to lead the development of a new ERM program. You have accepted this new role knowing that you are the first to be involved with developing overall risk governance documentation and practice for this bank. In the past, risk governance was handled by various divisions, with roles not always clearly defined or aligned among those divisions. Also, in the past, the board had little involvement in risk issues, and you will be tasked with initiating greater board involvement.

In this new role, you will be responsible for supervising a team of 10 risk analysts, with representation from each division of the company. The divisions are: retail banking, commercial banking, global banking and investment banking. These analysts will help you understand the current ERM practices in all divisions and also will identify deficiencies in those current practices. Your new analyst team has experience working with many types of risk, including credit risk, market risk, operational risk, cyber risk, etc. However, they have limited experience with thinking about risk from a strategic perspective. As part of the development of a new risk strategy, you have asked your team several questions about the following topics:

- How would you describe our risk culture?
- What is our risk strategy?
- What is our risk appetite?
- What elements of our current ERM processes can be eliminated?
- How will the larger organization react to any suggested changes?

While the team had significant experience with computational risk models, they struggled to characterize strategic aspects of your questions, such as related to risk culture. They also expressed concern about making drastic changes to the organization. For example, one analyst suggested that making additional requirements for accountability in the organization would likely be resisted.

We ask the reader to prepare an executive summary to address the following topics:

- What should be the next steps in developing the ERM foundation and practice in the company?
- What challenges do you foresee in creating new ERM processes at this bank?
- What risks and uncertainties are most relevant for this bank?
- Who are the relevant stakeholders?
- What types of risks matter the most to the relevant stakeholders? Why?

The summary report should contain a short introduction; evidence that can be gathered from company websites, news articles and scholarly publications; and a conclusion.

Index

Printed in the United States
by Baker & Taylor Publisher Services